The Soviet Economy Since Stalin

THE
SOVIET ECONOMY
SINCE STALIN

By Harry Schwartz

J. B. LIPPINCOTT COMPANY

PHILADELPHIA AND NEW YORK

To My Father and Mother

Preface

IN THE WAKE of the 1964 Tokyo Olympics, the Soviet press launched a furious onslaught against the country's most prominent sports officials and coaches who had promised an overwhelming triumph for Moscow's athletes. Typical was the complaint of the newspaper *Trud:* "Where are those 45 to 50 gold medals and 720 points they promised? The results leave much to be desired." The emphasis in these attacks was on the contrast between promises and performance, with relatively little attention paid to the fact that the Soviet Olympic team had won more medals than any other and had been second in gold medals only to the United States squad.

Since these articles appeared in the days after Nikita S. Khrushchev's removal as First Secretary of the Communist party and Premier of the Soviet Union, it was difficult for foreign observers to avoid the reflection that the Soviet press had something other than Olympic results in mind and was employing Aesopian language. Like the Soviet coaches, Khrushchev had promised far more than he had achieved. And although he was immune from public criticism while he was in power, Khrushchev could hardly avoid responsibility for his failures—and perhaps also for others' failures—once he had fallen. The veiled charges about his "harebrained scheming" and "bragging" published shortly after his removal suggested that his successors intended to make a public accounting of his incompetence, much as he had done with the dead Joseph Stalin almost a decade earlier.

The bulk of this volume was written before Khrushchev's ouster, but the record of both his economic successes and economic setbacks was clear enough in that earlier period so that virtually no change was required to take account of this historic

5

event. An effort has been made, however, to describe the key economic issues that probably helped determine the timing of Khrushchev's fall, as well as to take account of the first evidences of his successors' intentions in the area of economic policy. Malenkov and Khrushchev dominated the Kremlin in the years between Stalin's death and the latter's purge. This book attempts to give an objective description of their plans, their accomplishments, and their disappointments. The Soviet press, of course, tends to exalt a ruler without limit while he is in power, and then to denigrate him mercilessly once he is cast into political limbo.

The author wishes to express his deep thanks to the many who have helped him. Leon Herman graciously read the manuscript and made many helpful suggestions, but the errors that remain are solely the writer's responsibility. George Stevens, Stewart Richardson, and their associates of J. B. Lippincott Company made possible the writing of this volume and did much to help it in process. The author's wife, Ruth B. Schwartz, tolerated a writer in the agonies of composition and then copyread the manuscript and prepared the index. Thanks are due to the owners of copyright materials used in this volume for permission to reprint these materials. *The New York Times*, the author's employer, is in no way responsible for the opinions expressed here.

HARRY SCHWARTZ

Scarsdale, N.Y.
December 16, 1964

Contents

	Preface	5
I	Joseph Stalin Incorporated	11
II	An Over-all View	33
III	Malenkov's Victory and Defeat	55
IV	The Good Years, 1955–1958	74
V	Economic Factors in Khrushchev's Downfall	121
VI	Foreign Economic Relations	189
VII	Communism by 1980?	232
	Appendix: The Soviet Economy in 1965	243
	Notes	247
	Index	254

MAP

New Economic Regions   150–151

CHARTS

Organization of a Typical National Economic Council   90

U.S.S.R. State Production Committee for Power and
     Electrification   154

Central Agencies for Economic Management   157

List of Tables

1.	Output in Soviet Heavy Industry, 1924–1952	30
2.	Indicators of Soviet Economic Growth, 1952–1963	41
3.	Soviet Defense and Science Expenditures, 1952–1964	46
4.	Distribution of Soviet Investment by Sectors, 1955 and 1958–1962	47
5.	Output of Key Soviet Industrial Commodities, 1952, 1958, 1963, and 1964	49
6.	Soviet Grain Output, 1953–1962	51
7.	Soviet Output of Livestock Products, 1952–1963	53
8.	Soviet Industrial Development, 1952–1955	69
9.	Soviet Consumer Goods Production, 1952–1954, and 1954 Goals	70
10.	Soviet Consumer Goods Production, 1954, 1955, and 1955 goals	71
11.	Annual Percentage Increases in Production of Some Major Commodities, 1955–1958	93
12.	Production of Some Major Commodities, 1957, and 1972 Goals	95
13.	Soviet Grain Production, 1953–1958	107
14.	Indexes of Farm Prices Paid by the Soviet Government, 1954–1958	120
15.	Annual Soviet Industrial Production Growth Rates, 1954 and 1958–1964	124
16.	Output of Key Soviet Industrial Commodities, 1958, 1963, and 1964	125
17.	Indexes of Soviet Agricultural Output, 1958–1963, and 1965 Goal	130
18.	Soviet Grain Output, 1958–1962, and 1965 Goal	131
19.	Production of Key Agricultural Commodities in 1963 and 1965 Goals	133

20. Capital Invested in Unfinished Projects, 1958–1962   136
21. Distribution of Soviet Sown Area, 1961–1963   164
22. Average Prices Paid Collective Farms, 1952 and 1963,
        per 100 Kilograms of Produce   172
23. Soviet Foreign Trade Since World War II   191
24. Total Soviet Loans to Non-Communist Underdevel-
        oped Countries, 1954–1963   204
25. Soviet Trade with Other Communist-Ruled Nations,
        1955, 1959, 1962, and 1963   208
26. Soviet Credits and Grants to Eastern European Coun-
        tries, 1956–1961   209
27. Sino-Soviet Trade, 1950–1963   218
28. Soviet Output in 1960 and Goals for 1965, 1970, and
        1980   236
29. Farm Output in 1960 and 1963 and Goals for 1970 and
        1980   238

CHAPTER I

Joseph Stalin Incorporated

NIKITA S. KHRUSHCHEV, Premier of the Soviet Union and First
Secretary of its Communist party, faced his party's Central Committee in December 1963 and answered his critics. Some people,
he noted, were questioning the wisdom of his purchases of millions of tons of grain in the West that year and pointing out that
in earlier years the Soviet Union had been able to export grain
even from smaller harvests than that of 1963. But, Khrushchev
asked, had these people ever thought of the cost of those exports?
In 1947, he recalled, Stalin had exported grain even though in
some parts of the country "people had bloated stomachs or even
died from lack of food."

Premier Khrushchev's remarks showed that even more than a
decade after Joseph Stalin's death, the latter's ghost still haunted
the Soviet economy and Soviet society. No amount of exorcism—
neither rapid institutional change nor rapid production growth
nor even public denunciation of the dead tyrant—had availed to
banish the specter. In its strengths and its weaknesses, in its
achievements and its failures, the Soviet economy of the 1960's
was still clearly the child of the Stalinist economy—which T. H.
Rigby has termed Joseph Stalin Incorporated—whose creator had
died on March 5, 1953.

Joseph Stalin ruled the Soviet Union for almost three decades,
the most important formative period in that nation's history.
When he assumed power in the mid-1920's, Russia was a backward agrarian country. Its small industrial base then was far overshadowed by the vast mass of roughly 25,000,000 independent
peasant households which made up the great bulk of the popula-

tion and dominated the economy. When death finally removed his hands from the Kremlin's controls, Stalin's Russia was the second strongest industrial power on earth and the only nation besides the United States to possess substantial nuclear weapons capabilities. The socialized agriculture of 1953, almost entirely Stalin's creation, consisted of huge state and collective farms which were very different from the tiny peasant holdings that had been the norm thirty years earlier.

In the mid-1960's, more than a decade after Stalin's death, his impress is still clearly visible in many of the institutions and practices of the Soviet economy. This is hardly surprising, since the men who have directed the Soviet economy since 1953 received their basic training and absorbed their fundamental ideas about the nature of a socialist economy while Stalin dominated economic and political life. The post-Stalinist rulers of Russia have introduced many important changes into Soviet economic organization and operation since their master's death, but these reforms are for the most part within the broad framework of Stalin's conception of a centrally planned socialist economy. These continuing links to the past explain why comprehension of Soviet economic development since Stalin must be based upon an understanding of the Stalinist economy that preceded it.

The Stalinist economy did not come into being overnight. Lenin laid many basic foundations before his death in 1924. In the first years after seizing power in 1917, Lenin nationalized industry, trade, the banking system and much else, seeking to wipe out all elements of the free market and private economic activity. The damage done by these premature efforts to reach Utopia quickly combined with the destructive effects of the bloody civil war to produce widespread economic disorganization and discontent in the wake of sharp reductions in the nation's industrial and agricultural production.

In 1921, Lenin had to retreat before the fact of Russia's economic collapse and the resulting threat to his continued political power. To save the situation, he introduced the New Economic Policy (NEP). Its wide-ranging concessions to private enterprise —the legalization of private trade and private industrial production, the substitution of economic and market incentives for coercion, the effort to induce foreign capitalists to invest in Russia —made possible the nation's rapid economic recovery in the

1920's. Yet even as he retreated, Lenin was careful to keep control of what he called the "commanding heights" of the economy—the essential industries, the transportation and communication systems, the banks, and foreign trade—in the hands of the state. When Lenin died in 1924, the forces of socialist enterprise and of private enterprise within Russia jostled one another in an uneasy competitive coexistence, and the issue was in doubt.

The Stalin who came to world attention in the mid-1920's as a member of the collective leadership which first ruled post-Lenin Russia seemed to be a moderate. He opposed the bold ideas of Trotsky and others for rapid industrialization regardless of cost, and denounced those he called "superindustrializers" for endangering the alliance between the proletariat and the peasantry. He interposed no serious objections as the right wing of the post-Lenin leadership urged, successfully for a time, that the richer and more able peasants be given the right to hire workers and to accumulate capital.[1]* The image he presented publicly, that of a solid, reasonable, sensible moderate—a foe of wild-eyed radicals—did much to make possible Stalin's triumph over all his rivals, a triumph which established his one-man dictatorial rule over Soviet society in all its aspects.

By the irony of history, it was precisely the triumphant Stalin who carried out the program of Trotsky and the "superindustrializers," once he had swept them from his path. In the late 1920's and in the decade which followed he created Russia's Iron Age. He tamed the unions and made them an instrument of his will so that there was no effective opposition when he forced real wages down in the early 1930's. He drove the farmers into the collective farms, depriving them of their small farms despite their desperate resistance, which was reflected in the mass destruction of livestock and other agricultural capital. He focused all of Russia's energies upon one supreme goal: the most rapid possible industrialization in order to prepare the country for future battles against foreign enemies.

Stalin was obsessed with the necessity for preparing the Soviet Union for what he regarded as the inevitability of war. The Stalinist economy was created above all to prepare Russia as

* Superior figures refer to Notes at end of text.

rapidly as possible, and regardless of cost, to produce the arms
and other supplies needed to make that country a militarily
powerful state and to permit it to achieve victory when conflict
came. In 1931, when Russia's masses were groaning under the
heavy, seemingly unbearable burden imposed by the First Five
Year Plan, more and more Soviet voices began to urge that the
pace be slowed down, that fewer sacrifices be demanded from the
population. Stalin's answer was pitiless and clear:

> To slacken the tempo would mean falling behind. And those
> who fall behind get beaten. But we do not want to be beaten.
> No, we refuse to be beaten! One feature of the history of old
> Russia was the continual beatings she suffered for falling be-
> hind, for her backwardness. She was beaten by the Mongol
> Khans. She was beaten by the Turkish beys. She was beaten by
> the Swedish feudal lords. She was beaten by the Polish and
> Lithuanian gentry. She was beaten by the British and French
> capitalists. She was beaten by the Japanese barons. All beat her
> —for her backwardness: for military backwardness, for cultural
> backwardness, for industrial backwardness, for political back-
> wardness. She was beaten because to do so was profitable and
> could be done with impunity. . . .
>
> Do you want our socialist fatherland to be beaten and lose its
> independence? If you don't want this, you must liquidate our
> backwardness and develop a real Bolshevik tempo in building
> our socialist economy. There is no other road . . .
>
> We lag behind the advanced countries by 50–100 years. We
> must make good this distance in ten years.[2]

In the process of industrializing his country to prepare for war,
Stalin was able to extract the required sacrifices only by turning
his country into the classic totalitarian state of the first half of the
twentieth century. The Stalinist state rested on secret police terror, slave labor camps, total thought control, and the phenomenon
that later came to be called "the cult of personality," i.e., the
sycophantic adulation of his own person that made Stalin the
final authority on every subject he cared to mention in public.

The role of Western Europe and the United States in this early
industrialization of the Soviet Union cannot be overlooked even
in this brief survey. It was to these countries that Stalin turned to
buy the advanced technology he needed to make the Soviet

Union a modern industrial power. Thousands of Western engineers, chemists, architects, and other technicians came to the Soviet Union to help design, build, and, initially, operate new plants, as well as to train Soviet specialists in needed skills. Machinery worth many millions of dollars was bought in the West, particularly during the late 1920's and early 1930's. Substantial numbers of Soviet citizens went to the West during these years to study in European and American schools and factories. This massive infusion of Western technological knowledge slackened off sharply during the late 1930's, when the paranoid atmosphere induced by the great purge trials reigned over Russia. But during the early 1940's, a substantial new injection of Western technology was part of the American and British aid delivered during World War II.

The war Stalin had feared came in June 1941 when Hitler violated the 1939 Nazi-Soviet pact and sent his armies lunging into Russia. In the terrible six months that followed the initial onslaught, Soviet armies retreated to the gates of Moscow. With survival in doubt, the entire economy was put on a war footing far more comprehensive and rigorous than anything the United States knew during World War II. Insofar as possible, the industrial complex in the territories under Moscow's control was converted to military production. Manufacture of goods for all but the most essential civilian needs stopped completely. Stalin introduced a harshly differentiated ration system to distribute the available inadequate supplies of food, clothing, and fuel in rough proportion to each citizen's contribution to the struggle for national survival. Virtual military discipline was imposed upon those who remained out of the armed services. Every possible urban worker—male or female, adolescent or aged grandfather—went into the armament factories to toil sixty or more hours a week every week for the duration of the war. The farm labor force during the war consisted almost exclusively of women, old men, and children. The non-combatant Soviet population paid a terrible price in premature mortality, hunger, sickness, and cold during the war, while on the fighting fronts probably more than 10 million Soviet soldiers in the prime of life were killed or wounded in battle.

The tide turned at the battle of Stalingrad, and the resurgent Red Army began to push westward, recovering vast areas lost earlier. The territory regained—once the most fertile and most industrialized part of the country—was a devastated wasteland in 1944 and 1945, its farm lands mined, its factories and houses and transport lines largely destroyed, and millions of its remaining inhabitants the victims of malnutrition and disease. A vast task of rebuilding lay ahead, one that many in the West believed would take decades.

When the war ended, the Soviet people expected a period of respite so they could recover from the hardships and sufferings of the previous 15 years. But neither they—nor many in the West —had reckoned with Stalin, his paranoid image of the world, and his megalomaniacal dreams of world domination. Stalin saw Russia still surrounded by enemies, those who had so recently been his allies against Germany and Japan. He was also tempted by the weakness of his country's neighbors. In February 1946 Stalin gave public notice that his policy of concentrating on the creation of military strength had not changed. To a nation bone weary and tired beyond belief he announced the most ambitious program of economic expansion in its history. He justified these plans by declaring that only if the Soviet Union tripled its industrial production in 15 years "can we consider that our homeland will be guaranteed against all possible contingencies," i.e., guaranteed against invasion. In similar Aesopian but understandable language he gave notice that acquisition of nuclear weapons would have the highest priority, asserting, "I have no doubt that if we give our scientists proper assistance they will be able in the near future not only to overtake but to surpass the achievements of science beyond the boundaries of our country."[8]

The success of Stalin's postwar concentration upon the creation of modern military power is still powerfully felt now, more than a decade after his death. By the time Stalin died, the Soviet Union already possessed jet planes and atomic bombs and was only five months away from the successful explosion of its first hydrogen bomb. And much of the work responsible for the Soviet rocket and space feats of 1957 and afterward was planned, initiated, and accomplished under Stalin's direction. All this was made possible by his emphasis on rebuilding and expanding the key heavy and armament industries that contribute to military and economic power. To accomplish this, the shackles imposed upon the Soviet people in the 1930's and during World War II were largely maintained under the pressure of secret police terror. It is this coercive system for directing an entire nation's energies primarily toward war preparation that is usually termed the Stalinist economy. Let us look at this system's chief features.

First, heavy industry had prior claim on all of the nation's resources. The bulk of the country's capital investment and the cream of its manpower went into expanding Soviet steel, electric power, petroleum, machinery, and armaments output. Agriculture, housing construction, and consumer goods production had to make do with miserly allocations of capital and skilled manpower in order to make this extreme concentration on heavy industry possible. In 1949, when the first Soviet atomic bomb explosion was detected abroad, that country already was one of the world's leading producers of steel and electricity. But it produced practically no refrigerators, washing machines, or television sets, and it manufactured only 45,000 automobiles for a population of over 170,000,000 persons. In the year that the Soviet Union became the world's second nuclear power, its industry turned out less than one pair of shoes per Soviet citizen. And in the war-devastated western areas at that time, millions still lived in caves, dugouts, rickety huts, and other makeshift habitations because conventional housing was lacking.

Second, Stalin squeezed the great bulk of the capital required for Soviet industrialization out of his people by imposing what the economist calls "forced savings." He manipulated prices, wages and other key levers of the economy so as to divert vast amounts of current production from consumption to investment. The actual diversion was done through the planning system, which allocated resources primarily to heavy industry, as we have seen. Stalin extorted vast profits from agriculture by the simple process of paying the collective farms and farmers very low prices for their produce, and then reselling that produce at far higher prices in the cities. In 1936, for example, the Soviet government bought rye from collective farms in one area for 13 rubles per 100 kilograms, imposed an 80 ruble turnover tax—a general sales tax imposed on food and consumer goods—on this quantity of rye, and sold it to flour mills for 93 rubles, the cost figure from which the price of bread was calculated. In the same area collective farms received 17 rubles for 100 kilograms of wheat on which the state collected a 90 ruble turnover tax, making the total price 107 rubles.[4] These prices are in old rubles.

These extraordinarily high taxes on food and consumer goods made their retail prices very high. To compensate partially for this, Stalin followed a policy of keeping rents—for normally very cramped quarters—low, while medical care was paid for by the state. Parents had to pay, also, for much of their children's education in Stalin's last years. The result of this policy was that in cities, Soviet real wages were so low that most families could meet their minimum needs only if both husband and wife worked. In the countryside during Stalin's last years the very low incomes most peasants received from the collective farms gave them little incentive to produce. The resulting backwardness of agricultural production was reflected in the severe food difficulties with which the Stalin regime still struggled more than five years after World War II.

Third, to control the Soviet population and keep it working, Stalin relied upon a complex mixture of coercion, propaganda, and selective economic incentives. Much of the coercion was exercised by the secret police and by the ever present threat of death, or imprisonment in forced labor camps, for any who dared express political or economic discontent. The slave labor system was also a significant economic factor during much of Stalin's rule, employing millions of political prisoners and (after World War II) prisoners of war on the most varied construction, lumbering, and mining projects, particularly in Siberia, Central Asia, and beyond the Arctic Circle. The atmosphere of terror thus created pervaded all of Soviet society, affecting even Stalin's closest collaborators. Khrushchev put it this way in his secret speech of February 1956: "Stalin was a very distrustful man, sickly suspicious; we knew this from our work with him . . . The sickly suspicion created in him a general distrust even toward eminent party workers whom he had known for years."[5]

But secret police terror could not provide the positive incentives needed to build the Soviet economy. For these Stalin relied upon material and psychic levers. His propaganda constantly reminded his people of the danger of foreign attack and of the need to sacrifice so that the country could be strong. Patriotism was equated with maximum productivity. Individuals who set new production records were made into popular heroes, receiving the

kind of personal publicity that in the West is normal for outstanding athletes and television stars. One very important incentive
was the highly differentiated system of rewards that character-
ized the Stalinist economy. Stalin converted the term "egalitarian"
into an insulting epithet; the essence of socialism, he insisted, was
a system of payment reflecting differences in quality and quantity
of work, regardless of the resulting inequality of earnings. In
1931 Stalin thundered, "We must draw up wage scales that will
take into account the difference between skilled labor and un-
skilled labor, between heavy work and light work. We cannot
tolerate a situation where a rolling mill hand in a steel mill earns
no more than a sweeper."[6] The "workers' fatherland" quickly
became a land of great income inequality. By the time Stalin
died, the poorest paid millions of Soviet urbanites earned only
ten or twenty rubles a month, while at the other extreme a tiny
handful earned 1,000 rubles or even more monthly.*

Stalin was generous to those who served him faithfully and
effectively. He made available to them comfortable homes, domestic servants, automobiles, vacations in exclusive Crimean rest
areas. Even the mildly progressive Soviet income tax was arranged
so that it would not seriously weaken the incentive effect of the
differentiated earnings system; no matter how high a salary one
earned from the Stalinist state, the income tax rate did not exceed
13 per cent. The glaring contrast between the luxury and plenty
of the high placed officials, generals, scientists, writers, and similar
beneficiaries of the Stalinist economy on the one hand, and the
grinding poverty of the bulk of the population must have aroused
much envy and anger. But the secret police stood ready to detect
and to punish malcontents who expressed their views.

In the nature of things, the highest rewards and the most potent
incentives Stalin could offer were actually—and even potentially—
available only for a small fraction of the Soviet population. For
the mass of Stalin's subjects compulsion, economic and non-
economic, was the most effective spur. Stalin recognized this
during most of the last 15 years of his rule when he adopted, and
enforced, some of the world's most severe labor legislation. These

---

* Here and afterward in this volume, use is made of the new "heavy ruble"
introduced on January 1, 1961 and equal to ten rubles of the type circulating
in the preceding decade. The nominal equivalent of this "heavy ruble" is
$1.11, but this exchange rate must be used with great caution.

laws prohibited unauthorized absence from work, reporting to work late, and unauthorized changes of jobs by those who worked for the state. Prison terms, fines, and other punishments were meted out to those who broke these laws, and a system of labor books—in effect a kind of job passport for workers—was introduced to give the state maximum control over its workers and their movements. In the countryside, poverty-stricken peasants sought to improve their lot by concentrating their energies on the small garden plots Stalin had been forced to grant them in the mid-1930's. This threat to the collective farms' labor supply was met by passing laws requiring collective farmers to devote at least a minimum number of days to work in the socialized fields. What Stalin had created, in short, was a twentieth century industrial feudalism with many features reminiscent of the serfdom Russia had known a century earlier.

Stalin ruled Russia through the secret police, which controlled and watched both the mass of Soviet citizens and the elite Communist party. But to operate the economy, other institutions were needed: the planning mechanism concentrated in the *Gosplan* (State Planning Committee); the industrial administrative apparatus organized along ministerial lines and operating much of the economy on the principle of economic accountability (*khozraschet*)—that is, in a manner resembling in part Western corporate management; the trade unions that supervised the non-farm labor force; and the agricultural control system composed of the collective farms (*kolkhozy*), the machine tractor stations (MTS), and the state farms (*sovkhozy*).

The helplessness of even the highest economic planners before Stalin's caprice and suspicion was vividly demonstrated in 1949 when the head of *Gosplan*, Nikolai Voznesensky, was suddenly removed from his high post and expelled from the Communist party. Shortly afterward he was arrested and later executed in secret.[7]

In June 1963 Premier Khrushchev gave this picture of what economic planning had really been like under Stalin:

> I will mention a fact to show how plans were approved at that time. This happened shortly before Stalin's death. The Council of Ministers met to approve the annual plan and Stalin came to the meeting. Ordinarily he did not preside over the Council of Ministers. This time, however, he presided. He picked up the

folder containing the draft of the plan and said: "Here is the plan. Who is against it?" The ministers looked at each other and said nothing. "Then it is accepted," Stalin said and the meeting ended. As we left the meeting, he said, "Let's go to a movie." He arrived at the movie theatre and said, "We took them for a good ride!" Who had been taken for a ride? It was the ministers.

The plan went awry. Great miscalculations were made in it because the ministers had had no real hand in its preparation and did not agree with it. Other officials who had read it also disagreed with it. But Stalin himself did not pay much attention to questions of planning and he was not anxious for others to pay much attention to these questions.[8]

In this situation the experts of *Gosplan* could do little but improvise ways and means of realizing Stalin's objectives. They had only crude techniques at their command, and were not subject apparently to much in the way of criticism and checking from other parts of the economic administration. Professor Peter Wiles has called Stalin a Kafka with an abacus, but Khrushchev's testimony suggests Stalin had little taste for even the abacus. Hence we need not be surprised that much Soviet planning in Stalin's time was a combination of reality and fantasy. Each five year plan projected a pattern of growth both for heavy industry and for the industries serving the population's needs—light industry, agriculture, housing construction, and the like. But as each plan was implemented, it became clear that the country simply did not have all the resources needed to reach all its goals. The solution was typically simple. The goals for agriculture, for housing construction, and for consumer goods production were conveniently forgotten and all possible resources were concentrated on heavy industry and arms production, as well as on Stalin's favorite show projects of the moment, such as the Moscow subway built in the 1930's.

Economic analysis was moribund during Stalin's last years because he had little taste for it, and Soviet economists had learned that their function was simply to praise and restate their master's economic pronouncements. The sterility and confusion this introduced into Soviet planning were vividly described by Stalin himself in 1952:

Some time ago it was decided in the interests of cotton cultivation to correlate the price of cotton and grain, to determine carefully the price of grain sold to the cotton growers and to raise the price of cotton delivered to the state. Our managers and planners submitted a proposal which could only astonish the members of the Central Committee, since under this proposal the price suggested for a ton of grain was the same as that for a ton of bread and almost the same as that for a ton of cotton. The authors of the proposal had nothing sensible to say to the remarks of members of the Central Committee that the price of a ton of bread should be higher than that of a ton of grain, in view of the extra expenditures for milling and baking, and that cotton in general costs more than grain as is shown also by world prices of cotton and grain.[9]

The Soviet system of industrial administration in Stalin's last years operated through a series of industrial ministries each of which tended to become a semi-independent realm ruled on much the same principles that Stalin employed in governing Russia. The Ministry of Iron and Steel Production, for example, controlled all the steel plants of the nation, all the iron mines, and a vast network of subsidiary enterprises—from industrial research institutes and specialized educational institutions to professional and technical journals, as well as large amounts of housing for the steel industry's personnel. A typical ministry might employ several hundred thousand or even several million people, all subordinate to the minister in Moscow. He reigned as unquestioned lord over his subordinates in accordance with the Soviet principle of *edinonachalye* (one man rule). As might be expected, these ministries sought to become self-contained empires, each trying to extend its authority over as much of the Soviet economy as possible and to make itself as self-sufficient and independent of other ministries as it could. This tightly centralized control from Moscow plus the empire-building tendencies inherent in such organizations produced frequent duplication of facilities and effort, as well as friction and competition between ministries.

Under each minister, an elaborate administrative apparatus directed the enterprises in which the actual production was carried out. The director of an enterprise—which might be a factory, a mine, a group of stores, or a railroad line—also exercised one-man rule in relation to his subordinates, but he tended to be bound hand and foot by his superiors, who sought to give him as little leeway as possible for making independent decisions. For the enterprise director, as for his superiors, the basic criterion of success was his ability to fulfill his production goal. The director who reached or exceeded his production goal was rewarded with rich bonuses and could look forward to promotion; the director who fell short of his goal faced possible demotion, disgrace, and the deprivation resulting from failure to receive bonuses. In the worst periods of Stalinist terror in the 1930's, failure to fulfill the production plan raised the possibility that one might be accused of deliberate sabotage or of being an "enemy of the people" who deserved to be punished by prison sentence or worse. Under this unremitting pressure for production, the managerial bureaucracy sought to produce by every possible means. In many cases workers were required to work long hours overtime and were denied free time on Sundays and holidays when production lagged behind schedule. Managers frequently broke the law to get raw materials and components that were not available through legal channels, often employing the illegal *tolkachi* (expediters) who knew how to use bribes or connections to get supplies. This was an atmosphere in which corruption and influence (*blat*) were widespread, and a common saying was that "*blat* is higher even than Stalin." When all else proved unavailing, managers would falsify their production statistics in order to present the most attractive possible picture of their "success." Such tactics were met by intensive efforts to check and control the actual performance of industrial enterprises by a variety of inspectors and controllers. Many crooked managers were caught, but the same pressures caused others to adopt similar tactics. The pressure for production never relented.

Economic relations between Soviet enterprises were, and still are, primarily organized along the lines of what the Russians call *khozraschet*, or economic accountability. This is a system that bears a partial resemblance to the operations of private business organizations in Western economies. Put most simply, each enterprise bases its relations with others on purchase and sale for money. Each enterprise is legally an independent entity, with its own charter, working capital, and bank account. It can sue or be sued and it may enter into contractual relations. But, of course, all of these enterprises are completely owned by the Soviet state, and their economic activities are directed by the economic plan rather than by the forces of supply and demand in a market. Moreover, profit is normally a subsidiary goal of a Soviet enterprise. In the Stalin era, the emphasis was primarily upon fulfilling the production goal in physical terms, i.e., in tons of steel, kilowatt-hours of electricity, or millions of ball bearings, as the case might be. In this system, an enterprise has as basic capital a grant from the state. That Soviet calculations of cost make no allowance for interest on capital—and also normally include very inadequate depreciation and amortization charges—tends seriously to reduce the economic rationality of Soviet investment decisions.

The banking system primarily serves three functions in the organization of Soviet industry: (a) the State Bank handles virtually all financial transactions between enterprises, crediting sellers of goods and debiting purchasers; (b) the banking system provides short-term loans for working capital and it also acts as the state's agent in disbursing capital investment allocations—on which no interest is charged—to the designated enterprises; (c) most important, the banking system acts as a vast inspection and checking organization. An army of bank employes keeps sharp watch to try to assure that managers use the resources at their command economically and in accordance with the economic plan's directives.

By the end of the 1920's, Stalin had purged the labor leaders who believed that the main function of their unions was to protect their members' interests against their employer, even when that employer was the state. This purge completed, the unions became completely subservient organs of the Communist party. Their primary function was to urge workers on to greater effort and higher productivity. By the end of the Stalin era, it was taken for granted that local union officials were factually subordinate to enterprise directors, that they would never lead a strike, and that, as disciplined party members, they would never protest too vigorously—if at all—against any abuse or hardship to which their members might be subjected.

All this was rationalized on two grounds. One argument held that since the factories were socialist property, they were owned by all the people and any strike by workers would be a strike against themselves. Moreover, since there were no private owners receiving profits, Stalin's propagandists argued, gains from higher production would automatically accrue to the workers, and only by raising output could workers hope to improve their living standards. In this atmosphere unions had little to say about wage rates; they tended not to concern themselves about poor working conditions; and their powers to distribute vacation assignments in rest homes and to supervise recreational facilities at a given plant were used to reward the best workers, thus creating additional incentives for higher productivity. The Soviet labor movement under Stalin, in short, became the greatest company union the world had known to that time.

The bulk of the Soviet peasantry in the Stalin era was concentrated on the collective farms, most of which had been set up under extreme pressure from the state and the Communist party in the early 1930's. The conflict over collectivization at that time was in effect a second revolution, one in which tens of millions of Soviet farmers lost the land and independence they had gained in 1917. The peasants fought back, sometimes with arms. More often they employed sabotage, killing livestock, burning farm buildings, and refusing to work hard on the newly collectivized lands. In the course of this struggle many thousands of *kulaks*— the less impoverished and often more able peasants—were killed, sent to slave labor camps, or expelled from agriculture into non-farm occupations. Thus when the collective farm system finally emerged victorious, its triumph had been won at enormous cost in farm capital destroyed and in capable farmers lost. Even so, Stalin was able to stabilize the situation only by permitting islands of private enterprise on the sea of collectivized acres—the small garden plots allocated to peasant families so each could raise fruits, vegetables and potatoes, as well as maintain a few head of livestock, as specified by law.

Stalin wanted the collective farms because it was easier to control 250,000 such large units than 25,000,000 peasant farms. And strict control was required to assure that the state received a large fraction of each collective farm's production at very low cost. The first commandment of farm life under Stalin was that the state delivery plan had to be fulfilled before any other needs were met. To enforce this commandment, Stalin established a state monopoly of the large machinery—tractors, combine harvesters, and the like—used by the collectives. This equipment was owned and operated by the government's machine tractor stations, or MTS, which performed much of the farm work on the collectives, plowing, seeding, and harvesting the socialized fields. The MTS received a share of the crop as payment for the work done by their equipment, and political officers attached to their staffs acted as party overseers in the countryside, keeping an eye on the political reliability of the peasantry and seeking to enforce the collective farms' timely delivery of their quotas.

In this situation a constant undeclared war raged between the state and the peasantry. Stalin wanted the collective farmers to work hard and efficiently on the socialized fields, even though the earnings received from the collective farms were normally very low because of the depressed prices paid by the state. Many peasants preferred to devote their energies to their small gardens on which they raised—for sale or their own consumption—potatoes, fruits, berries, and vegetables. Many peasants also maintained a cow and a few pigs and chickens, thus producing meat, milk, and eggs that could be sold at relatively high prices in the free markets of nearby towns and cities. Where they could, peasants often stole food and feed grains from the collective farms, enlarged their garden plots illegally at the expense of the collectivized land, pastured their livestock in the *kolkhoz* fields, and worked as little and as lackadaisically as possible for the collectives. Stalin fought back by issuing decrees requiring collective farmers to work at least a minimum number of days annually on the socialized fields. Local Communist party units sought to secure good work by installing their own nominees as chairmen of collective farms in their areas. But the peasants often resented these outsiders put over them and, too, many of the chairmen lined their own pockets by stealing produce and money. In many rural areas, local officials regarded tribute from the collective farms—a pig for Christmas or a few geese for Easter—as normal perquisites of their positions.

During World War II, the collective farms were gravely weakened by the departure of men called up for military service, but the force of patriotism and the stimulus provided by the very high prices paid for food in the free market acted to keep production going. After the war, the enormous human losses of the conflict were felt particularly on the collective farms. The relatively low incomes available on the farms made work in the cities and towns more attractive both for rural youngsters coming of age and for returning war veterans. Soviet agriculture in the late 1940's was therefore still largely dependent on the labor of women, old men, and children. A decade later—after the income gap between Soviet urbanites and farmers had been narrowed— the 1959 census found that women provided 57 per cent of the collective farm labor force. That percentage had been much higher in 1949.

The collective farms were and are cooperatives, at least nominally. Members' earnings come from the income left after production expenses and taxes are paid. Members' earnings therefore may fluctuate widely from year to year, depending on how well a farm does. On state farms—which the government owns and operates—workers are hired employes receiving wages. Under Stalin, state farm workers tended to be guaranteed a more stable and more nearly adequate income than most collective farmers. State farms were also favored in the allocation of machinery and other farm production essentials. But in 1953 the state farms were of relatively minor importance in Soviet agriculture, cultivating only about 10 per cent of the country's total sown area.

In early 1964 Premier Khrushchev gave this vivid picture of the poverty of Soviet collective farmers under Stalin:

> The party has condemned the anti-collective farm price policy which was carried out during Stalin's life. At that time, the procurement prices were so low that the collectives could not even compensate for their production expenditures from the earnings of their sale of produce. The labor of the majority of the collective farmers were practically not paid for. Thus, for example, for one labor day the payment in 1952 was one kopek [one penny, HS] in Kaluga and Tula provinces, 2 kopeks in Ryazan and Lipetsk provinces, 3 kopeks in Bryansk and Pskov provinces, and 4 kopeks in Kostroma and Kursk provinces. Many collective farms for years did not pay even a single kopek for a labor day. . . .
>
> Matters were no better in the state farms. The government bought their production at such low prices that the state farms could not work profitably; as a rule they had losses. They were given subsidies to cover these so-called "planned" losses.

Shortly before his death, Stalin even proposed to dissolve the
state farms and transfer their land to the collective farms . . .
Stalin said: the state farms are unprofitable; they need subsidies; they have to be dissolved.[10]

At the end of Stalin's reign, the objective observer could see
a glaring discrepancy between conditions and results in the two
major areas of the Soviet economy. On the one hand, great strides
were being made in heavy industry and the armament production
it supported. Here growth was rapid. These advances had made
the Soviet Union one of the two major economic and military
powers of the world. On the other hand, the relatively neglected
areas of the economy—notably agriculture—showed the effects of
their low priority in their poor production performance which in
turn kept the standard of living low. Khrushchev made his first
major postwar appearance as a national figure in Moscow in early
1950 as the man who had a solution for the country's agricultural
problems. His program called for the amalgamation of the small
and medium sized collective farms into much larger aggregates.
These new "supercollectives," he claimed at the time, would be
farmed more efficiently and more productively. But though he
soon reduced the number of separate collective farms from roughly
250,000 to under 100,000, the hoped-for major increases in food
and fiber production did not take place. Here is the way Khrushchev described, in 1958, the agricultural crisis which Stalin's
successors found when they took over in 1953:

One must say directly that the agricultural situation at that
time was difficult. Although the collective and state farms had
healed the wounds brought by the war, they could not satisfy
the country's requirements. As a consequence of great deficiencies in the direction of the collective and state farms . . .
the growth of agricultural production had slowed down. It is
easy to convince oneself of this if a glance is taken at the
record of farm production during 1948 to 1953. During these
years the gross harvests and deliveries of grain essentially did
not increase. Milk production also had not grown, and the
average annual production of meat was below the level the
country had attained before the war.

There had been created a noticeable disproportion between
the development of industry and of agriculture, between the

state's actual requirements for grain and other products and the factual production. This could have held back the further expansion of socialist industry, the growth of the welfare of the workers, the movement of our country to Communism, and it could even have finally weakened the economic might of the Soviet Union and the entire socialist camp.[11]

Georgi M. Malenkov had lied to the 19th Soviet Communist party Congress in October 1952, Khrushchev charged in the same speech. Malenkov claimed then that the 1952 Soviet grain harvest had been 8,000,000,000 poods* (approximately 130,000,000 metric tons) and that the grain problem of the Soviet Union had finally been solved. Khrushchev continued:

> Malenkov conducted himself dishonorably, using data of the so-called biological yield,† although everyone knows that the "biological harvest" is far from being the same as real grain in the granaries. You can hardly bake bread from the concept of "biological yield." Bread is baked from grain which is gathered in the barns.

> The actual grain production situation was different. The collective and state farms did not harvest 8,000,000,000 poods even in 1952, which had the highest yield of that period. They gathered only 5,600,000,000 poods [about 92,000,000 metric tons, HS]. Although the collective and state farms delivered to the government even part of the seed supply, only about 2,100,000,000 poods of grain were collected by the state. This amount did not satisfy the current requirements of the government, let alone permit the creation of necessary reserves.[12]

But the Malenkov claim that Khrushchev assailed was made when the latter delivered the official report of the Central Committee to the 19th Congress of the Communist party. It must have had the approval at that time of Stalin and all the other 1952 leaders, including Khrushchev. What the latter was charging in 1958, therefore, was that the entire Soviet leadership had publicly exaggerated the Soviet grain crop of 1952 by 40 per cent, claiming abundance where actually there was often near hunger. This was surely a searing indictment of Stalinist economics.

* A pood is a unit of weight equal to about 36 pounds or 16.4 kilograms.
† The biological yield was an estimate of the harvest made as it grew in the fields, without any allowance for the large losses suffered during harvesting of the crop and its transport to barns and mills.

The record of Stalin's stewardship over the Soviet economy is more complex, however, than Khrushchev's polemical attacks would suggest. Let us attempt a more balanced evaluation.

Russia under Stalin provided a classic case of forced rapid national economic development whose lessons—both positive and negative—are of international significance. The greatest impact was upon the Soviet people, whose traditional way of life was shaken more profoundly than it had been since the end of serfdom in the 1860's. Tens of millions were transferred from agricultural to industrial and other non-farm occupations. A massive transfusion of scientific and technical knowledge from abroad was injected into Soviet society, producing a large cadre of skilled workers and a substantial technological elite of scientists, engineers, and other technicians on a scale never before known in that nation's history. Stalin expanded the range of Soviet industrial production many times, creating formidable capability in many economic areas—machinery, armaments, electronics, chemicals, atomic energy and its byproducts—that had grown only moderately or not at all before his time. And he raised the physical volume of Soviet industrial production enormously, despite the terrible setback inflicted by World War II. The data in Table 1 show the magnitude of this achievement in heavy industry, the production sector Stalin always favored with highest priority:

Table 1. OUTPUT IN SOVIET HEAVY INDUSTRY,
1924–1952

Commodity	Unit	1924	1940	1945	1952
Steel	million metric tons	1.0	18.3	12.3	34.5
Coal	million metric tons	12.7	166.0	149.3	300.9
Oil	million metric tons	6.1	31.1	19.4	47.3
Electricity	billion kilowatt-hours	1.6	48.3	43.3	119.1
Machine tools	thousands	2.0*	58.4	38.4	74.6
Tractors	thousands	.01	112.9†	7.7	116.7‡
Cement	million metric tons	.4	5.7	1.8	13.9
Sulphuric acid	million metric tons	.2*	1.6	.8	2.7

* 1928.   † 1936.   ‡ 1950.
Source: *Narodnoye Khozyaistvo SSSR v 1961 godu, passim.*

For all their limited coverage, the data in Table 1 vividly represent the economic transformation of the Soviet Union under Stalin. It was this industrial production thrust that was at the center of Russia's tremendous leap from the weakness and backwardness that existed when Lenin died to the awesome strength—from a military point of view—Moscow possessed when Stalin died. By comparison with Stalin's achievements in this field, those of Peter the Great and Count Witte seem pale indeed. The cost in human suffering and loss of freedom was immense, but no objective historian can doubt that the entry of Russia into the ranks of the major industrial and technological powers of the world will forever be inseparably linked with the name of the Georgian tyrant.

This industrial upsurge inescapably underlined the magnitude of Stalin's failure in agriculture. During his reign private peasant farms gave way to giant collectives and the horse was replaced by the tractor as the prime mover in the fields. But the key product of Soviet agriculture, grain, showed no increase even vaguely resembling the mounting curve of steel or electricity in output. In 1913, the territory now included in Soviet boundaries produced 86,000,000 metric tons; in 1940 that same area gave 95,500,-000 metric tons; in 1952 the harvest was only about 92,000,000 tons. The 1952 crop may well have been the largest grain harvest since 1940. A more representative picture is given if we consider the last five years of Stalin's rule, 1949–1953. During that period annual Soviet grain production averaged only 80,900,000 metric tons, or little more than 10 per cent above the corresponding output in 1909–1913.[13]

In the present territory of the Soviet Union, there were 58,400,000 cattle on January 1, 1916; on January 1, 1953, that same area had only 56,600,000 cattle.[14] But the Tsarist Russia with which comparison is made above had less than 160,000,000 people to feed; when he died, Stalin ruled over almost 190,000,000 people. An apologist for Stalin could point to some objective reasons for the poor agricultural performance after World War II. He could cite the great damage inflicted upon Soviet agriculture by the war, as well as by the great convulsion and capital destruction that accompanied the collectivization of the early 1930's. But having granted the importance of these factors, it still seems indisputable that Stalin's policy toward agriculture—in particular his failure to pay what farmers considered just prices and his low priority for capital allocation to agriculture—deserves much of the blame. Moreover, the decision to embark upon forced collectivization had also been Stalin's.

But beyond Stalin's specific accomplishments and failures, the central fact that faced his successors after his death was that the economic mechanism he had created was intolerably bad. Professor Gregory Grossman has summarized the deficiencies of this mechanism well:

> If we ask what in Soviet agriculture at Stalin's death caused this deplorable state of affairs, we find, to put it crudely, that nearly everything was wrong: planning, organization, management, the price system, taxation, the physical equipment and facilities, the composition of the labor force, the distribution system, and, above all, incentives.

> The other sectors of the economy had their share of woes, too, despite—and at times because of—the rapid growth of industry and related branches. To mention a few: overcentralization and overbureaucratization, especially in the form of hypertrophied industrial ministries; cumbersome and often inept planning, which paid virtually no attention to economic efficiency; technological conservatism at most levels; an elaborate incentive structure, in part ineffective and in part perversely effective; a bad price structure, though with the saving grace that it had relatively little to do with resource allocation; emphasis on quantity of output at the expense of quality; chronic shortages of industrial supplies and equipment; and so on.[15]

A vast job of rebuilding and restructuring faced Stalin's successors. Their efforts in this direction and the results of those efforts will occupy us throughout much of the rest of this volume.

CHAPTER II

An Over-all View

THE IMPROBABLE COMBINATION of Soviet Premier Nikita Khrushchev and United States intelligence chief Allen Dulles worked
together informally but effectively to raise a new specter before
Americans during the late 1950's and early 1960's. The specter was
that of growing Soviet economic power. In innumerable speeches
Premier Khrushchev boasted of the economic war he had declared against the United States, predicting that by 1970 his
country would have achieved victory by becoming wealthier and
more productive than the American citadel of capitalism. As
Director of the Central Intelligence Agency, Mr. Dulles raised his
authoritative voice to warn that the Soviet dictator's words could
not be laughed off, that the Soviet Union was moving ahead economically more rapidly than the United States, and that this
threat had to be taken seriously. As a result of these admonitions,
not a few Americans became convinced of something that would
have been unthinkable in the United States earlier: the much-
despised Soviet economic system might prove itself better than
the American if the United States did not improve its rate of
economic growth. "Growthmanship" became a popular pastime
among some American intellectuals and businessmen.

The depth of this concern became strikingly clear in early
1964. The C.I.A.—from which Mr. Dulles had retired—made public its calculations for 1962 and 1963, which showed that Soviet
economic growth had slowed down dramatically, to less than 2.5
per cent annually. It added that the gap separating American and
Soviet production levels was once again widening so that Moscow's prospects for victory in the economic competition during
the foreseeable future had dimmed substantially. A naive observer
might have thought that a wave of joy would have swept the
United States at this good news. The reality was the reverse,

however, and numerous American voices were quickly raised to criticize the C.I.A. and its new estimates. Having finally been convinced that there was such a thing as a Soviet economic threat, many Americans seemed reluctant to believe that even temporarily Moscow had received a setback and Washington was doing comparatively well.

Before World War II, while Khrushchev was still an obscure party bureaucrat, other Soviet spokesmen had boasted and dreamed of economic triumph over the United States. In 1929, for example, Soviet economists had predicted that in fifteen or twenty years their country would be far ahead of the United States. One of them, N. K. Kovalevsky, had even forecast that by 1944 Soviet consumption levels would be three times as high as those of Americans.[1]

Almost nobody in the United States appears to have paid the slightest attention to this prediction. In 1931, as noted above, Stalin called on his people to catch up with the advanced West in ten years. Stalin and Vyacheslav M. Molotov returned to this subject in 1939. Molotov declared that in ten or fifteen years the Soviet Union would probably be able to exceed the highest production levels the United States had ever achieved.[2]

The historical record gives no suggestion that any panic was provoked by this forecast in the United States, then still depression-ridden. Even after a decade of hard times, the great majority of the American people and their leaders were firmly convinced that the Soviet economy was nothing to worry about. Yet two decades later—when the United States and much of the rest of the capitalist world were enjoying some of the most prosperous times in history—Khrushchev's forecasts of Soviet economic victory were received very soberly indeed. Few people recalled that the year by which he expected to win, 1970, was long after the dates originally mentioned before World War II by the Soviet spokesmen whose similar forecasts had proven ludicrously mistaken.

Behind this sharp difference of American reactions before and after World War II was undoubtedly the great contrast in United States images of Stalin's Russia and of Khrushchev's Russia. During most of Stalin's reign, Americans thought of the Soviet Union as a hungry, miserable, and backward land ruled by secret police terror. By the early 1960's this had given way to a picture of Russia as the land of the sputniks, a world scientific leader whose achievements in space suggested to many that it could do any-thing it set its mind and resources to accomplishing.

Propaganda images are poor guides to rational understanding. If proof of this elementary fact were needed with respect to Khru-shchev's Russia, it was provided by the Soviet agricultural debacle of 1963, which forced the Kremlin to turn frantically to the West for the grain needed to feed the Soviet people. Some quarters—but not the C.I.A.—attempted to use that Moscow set-back to prove that all talk of a Soviet economic threat had always been an illusion.

Whatever the future may bring, however, it is clear that Soviet economic growth since Stalin's death has profoundly influenced the world scene. The Western concern with the Soviet economic challenge is only one aspect of that influence. In world markets, the Soviet Union has appeared increasingly since 1953 as a major purchaser of some commodities—machinery in Western Europe, for example—and as a new major seller of other commodities, notably petroleum. As Soviet economic power expanded, some of the swiftly mounting resources available to the Kremlin were diverted to the underdeveloped countries where the appearance of Soviet technicians and loan agreements opened a new area of competition with the West, particularly the United States. In the early 1960's, the rapidity and efficiency with which the Soviet Union moved in to bolster Cuba's economy frustrated Washing-ton's effort to destroy the Castro regime through economic sanctions. If nothing else, the flow of Soviet oil, food, and ma-chinery to Cuba gave Americans vivid evidence of the realities behind the proud statistics of rapid economic growth Premier Khrushchev cited at every opportunity. The sales of Soviet gold to London and Swiss banks during these years helped signifi-cantly to stabilize the Western world's monetary system, while the Soviet entrance into world grain markets as a purchaser in late 1963 had far-reaching effects. By the mid-1960's the Soviet Union was universally recognized as a major economic power, one whose strengths and weaknesses had to be carefully taken into account by other countries.

For the ordinary Soviet citizen, however, the record of the post-Stalin years has been of concern primarily in its impact upon his standard of living, his working conditions, and his opportuni-ties. In this period he has been witness to such major changes as the ending of the Stalinist slave labor system, the elimination of many of the limitations on his freedom to change jobs, the enormous expansion of housing construction and the substantially increased production of consumer durable goods such as refrigerators and television sets. But he has also been disappointed time and again by unfulfilled promises—notably Khrushchev's 1957 pledge that meat production would be dramatically and quickly lifted to United States levels—and he has suffered from the consequence of major setbacks such as the grain harvest failure that produced bread lines throughout the Soviet Union in early 1964.

Violent storms have raged through the institutional structure of Soviet economic life during this period as the Kremlin rulers have tried one expedient after another to secure more rapid progress in production. The entire administrative apparatus of Soviet industry underwent major reorganization in 1953, 1954, 1957, and again in the early 1960's. In agriculture the collective farm system was transformed in many ways and one major Stalinist feature of the Soviet countryside, the machine tractor stations, disappeared altogether. A new emphasis upon economic rationality appeared, one which gave cost accounting an unaccustomed importance in Soviet economic life and made mathematical economics—a subject virtually prohibited in Stalin's last years—a field of absorbing interest to Soviet leaders and economists alike. If all the hopes of the post-Stalinist Moscow leadership for economic progress have not been achieved, it has not been because of any lack of willingness to engage in far-reaching and radical innovation on many fronts. But on the fundamentals of the Soviet system—the primacy of state planning, the dominant role of the Communist party, the continuance of socialized farming—Premier Khrushchev and his colleagues have remained firm. Therein lies, we may suspect, one root cause of their failure to reach more impressive results than they have achieved.

The post-Stalin Soviet leaders have had to wrestle constantly with the problems of allocating their resources among many competing requirements and claimants. Time and again they have been plagued by overcommitment, by needs exceeding available means. The pinch resulting from such overcommitment forced the cancellation of the Sixth Five Year Plan in 1957. Military needs have often had first claim on Soviet resources in the atmosphere of high international tension and the resulting armaments race which has usually prevailed since Stalin's death. The

Soviet space achievements were a dividend from the intensive weapons development program since the Soviet space rockets were originally developed to power hydrogen bomb-carrying intercontinental ballistic missiles. A high rate of capital investment has been maintained as the indispensable source of the rapid rate of production growth which has been the constant Soviet objective. Funds have had to be found for a growing volume of foreign aid, both to other Communist-ruled countries and to non-Communist underdeveloped countries, which are being wooed increasingly. Finally the needs of Soviet consumers have pressed more heavily upon Moscow planners as the end of the secret police terror after Stalin's death created the need to win popular support by raising living standards. Competition for resources has been the key factor in the recurrent Soviet debate over whether to retain the Stalinist emphasis on heavy industry at the cost of consumer goods. So long as Soviet output was growing rapidly in the 1950's the problem of meeting these competing demands was eased because there was much more available to allocate each year than the year before. But as Soviet production growth slowed down after 1958 choosing among competing demands grew more difficult. Premier Khrushchev stated one aspect of the problem bluntly when he addressed the Communist party Central Committee in February 1964:

> Of course everybody would like to have more of everything necessary to meet his requirements. This is an understandable and legitimate aspiration. If one looks at how the people of Tsarist Russia lived, how people lived in the first years of Soviet rule, how they lived before the war, and how we are living now, the difference is colossal. Let us take housing for instance. In 1951 in towns and workers settlements, the total area of dwelling houses built was 24,000,000 square meters, while in 1963 it was 77,000,000. But even now one hears voices saying: "Too little," and these voices are right. There will be more, but this cannot be done at once and it cannot be done at the expense of our defense. If we accepted an unreasonable reduction of defense expenditures, if we started building more houses and forgot about defense, we would be like blind men who cannot assess the real situation correctly.[3]

This was a sober recognition of the hard choices before the Soviet government. Moreover, this admission of continued urgent demands for improved living conditions came at the height of a period during which hundreds of millions of dollars were being spent abroad to buy grain to feed the Soviet people.

Adding to the difficulties faced by Soviet leaders in deciding on allocations has been their recognition of the acute need to provide their people with greater material incentives. Shortly after Stalin's death they raised prices paid to farmers, and then introduced other price increases later. In industry during the 1950's they could not afford a general increase in wages in addition to the price cuts announced in April 1953 and April 1954. Instead, they took the less expensive step of raising minimum wages and old age pensions in the mid-1950's, trying to recoup part of the cost by reducing the highest salaries, despite the disincentive effect of the latter measure. Since 1954, at least, Soviet leaders have been plagued by fear of inflation because their economic policy has tended to increase the population's disposable income more rapidly than the volume of goods and services available for purchase. In 1960, nevertheless, Khrushchev tried to institute what amounted to a modest general wage increase for most urban workers by announcing a phased abolition of the small Soviet income tax to be drawn out over five years. Two years later, however, he had to abandon even this modest effort because of the strain on Soviet resources. Even before the "postponement" of the income tax abolition, in June 1962, Khrushchev had been forced to raise retail meat and butter prices by 30 and 25 per cent respectively, in order to get funds to increase prices paid to farmers for livestock. This produced anger, bitterness, and widespread demonstrations, notably the bloody encounters between workers and troops at Novocherkassk near Rostov.[4]

Two years later the trend toward a Soviet welfare state was resumed when Premier Khrushchev announced, and the Supreme Soviet approved, three key measures to be implemented during 1964 and 1965: an increase in the minimum wage, the introduction of a system of pensions for collective farmers, and wage increases for millions of poorly paid government employes, notably doctors, teachers, and shop clerks.[5]

Any quantitative assessment of Soviet economic change since Stalin must begin with the substantial population increase in this period. Between early 1953 and mid-1964, this population rose from about 188,000,000 to 228,000,000 people, an increase of more than 20 per cent whose absolute size was almost equal to the population of France.[6] Looking ahead, Stalin's successors had to lay plans for meeting the needs of an expected 248,000,000 population in 1970 and 280,000,000 in 1980.

The rapid growth of Soviet cities and towns absorbed almost all of these additional Soviet citizens between 1953 and 1964, reflecting the great migration from rural areas during this period. When Stalin died, only about 43 per cent of all Soviet people lived in urban communities. Eleven and a half years later that figure had grown to 53 per cent. It was only as recently as 1961 that the rural population became, for the first time, a minority in the land that had traditionally been thought of as Peasant Russia. Some 80,000,000 inhabitants lived in Soviet cities and towns in early 1953; little more than a decade later that total had almost reached the 120,000,000 mark. During all these years the rural population—107,800,000 on January 1, 1953—never went above 110,000,000. It was only 107,700,000 on January 1, 1964.

These post-Stalin years were also a time of significant geographic redistribution of population. Both for economic and for strategic reasons—the latter reinforced by the political conflict with Communist China—the Soviet regime sought to populate the relatively thinly settled lands in the Urals, Siberia, and Central Asia. The mineral and agricultural riches of Asiatic Russia and the urgency of developing them were a major theme of national policy and public pronouncements from the mid-1950's to the mid-1960's. Some important results were obtained. Kazakhstan— the site of the vast virgin lands farm program—had less than 6,000,000 inhabitants in 1939. When Stalin died it probably had less than 7,000,000 people. At the beginning of 1959 it already had 9,154,000 inhabitants, while by mid-1964 the population had risen to 11,700,000.[7]

The population increase in the great Soviet Asian industrial centers was equally spectacular. The number of inhabitants of Tashkent went from 778,000 at the beginning of 1956 to 1,051,000 eight years later. In the same period Novosibirsk leaped from 731,000 to 1,013,000 and Sverdlovsk from 707,000 to 897,000. On a percentage basis, Alma Ata, capital of Kazakhstan, did even better; its population went from 330,000 in early 1956 to 607,000 as 1964 began.[8] Behind these dry figures is the reality of a great drive by millions of pioneers who have brought vast areas under the plow, tamed great rivers, built innumerable factories, and discovered rich new mineral deposits in one of the last major frontier areas of this increasingly small and overpopulated planet. The discovery of rich diamond fields in eastern Siberia and of important new oil and natural gas deposits east of the Urals helped spur this migration.

Two other aspects of the population dynamics of the Soviet Union during this period deserve consideration here, even if only briefly. One is the slow rectification of the very uneven male-female ratio in the Soviet Union which was a result of the vast military casualties of World War II. In 1953, available estimates suggest, males made up only 43 or 44 per cent of the total Soviet population. By 1964 this figure was apparently nearing 46 per cent. By 1964, presumably the imbalance was concentrated among those over 35 because those below that age were either not yet born during World War II or were too young then to have served in the armed forces. But it is worth remembering that in the post-Stalin years discussed in this volume, a substantial majority of the adult working population of the Soviet Union consists of women. This shortage of adult males helps explain why women workers are employed in so many physically exacting tasks, as miners and members of construction gangs, for example, as well as farm laborers.

The slowing down of the rate of Soviet population growth and the decline of the Soviet birth rate in the late 1950's and the first half of the 1960's also deserves mention. During 1958, Soviet estimates indicate, the population of the country grew by about 3,900,000, but in the year ended July 1, 1964 the absolute increase is officially estimated at only 3,200,000. In 1958, the rate of natural increase of population had been 18.1 per thousand inhabitants; in 1963 it was only 14.0 per thousand. The birth rate declined from 26.6 per thousand in 1954 and 25.3 thousand in 1958 to only 22.4 per thousand in 1962 and 21.3 per thousand in 1963. Between 1958 and 1962, the annual Soviet marriage rate declined some 20 per cent (from 12.5 to 10 per thousand). Presumably these trends reflected the fact that it was in those years that the sharply reduced number of young people born during World War II were entering adult life and beginning to establish families.[9]

Turning now to the growth of production in the post-Stalin era, it should be emphasized that there is no serious dispute that this growth is real. Argument arises only over the amount by which output has risen. The pictures painted by official Soviet statistics and by the estimates of Western observers differ surprisingly little. The key Soviet data are shown in Table 2 in two forms, the first of which facilitates comparison of production in 1958 and 1963 with that in the last full Stalinist year, 1952, while the second form permits comparison of growth between 1952 and 1958 with that between 1958 and 1963.

Table 2. INDICATORS OF SOVIET ECONOMIC GROWTH, 1952–1963

Year	Gross Social Product	Gross Industrial Production	Gross Farm Production
		(Per cent of 1952)	
1952	100	100	100
1958	180	192	156
1963	250	304	150*
		(Per cent of 1958)	
1958	100	100	100
1963	139	158	96*

* Estimated.

SOURCES: Data for 1952 and 1958 from *SSSR v Tsifrakh v 1962 godu*, p. 34 and from *SSSR v Tsifrakh v 1963 godu*, p. 29. Farm data for 1963 estimated on basis of statistics in *Pravda*, January 13, 1964.

The upper portion of the table makes clear the extreme disproportion between industrial and agricultural production growth during 1952–1963. It shows a rise of 150 per cent in gross social product—that is, total material production excluding services. This resulted from a tripling of industrial output while farm production grew by only 50 per cent. The second portion of this table shows how radically Soviet output growth has slowed down since 1958. In total output, the 1952–1958 increase was 80 per cent; the 1958–1963 increase only 39 per cent. In industrial production we are faced correspondingly with an increase of 92 per cent in the earlier period and of only 58 per cent in the later period. And in agriculture the claimed 56 per cent production increase during the first six years of the post-Stalin period was followed by a 4 per cent decline at the end of the following five year period. Thus the substantial slowing down of over-all Soviet economic growth in recent years emerges from official Moscow data. These Soviet data indicate that the slowdown of economic growth continued into the first half of 1964. The 7.5 per cent increase in industrial output claimed for that period over the first six months of 1963 was the smallest such percentage gain claimed since the conversion from wartime to peacetime production was completed in the mid-1940's. Such fragmentary data as the mid-year 1964 economic report gave on agricultural output during the first six months of that year—primarily production of livestock products—suggested a decline compared with a year earlier because of the sharp reduction in livestock herds that had taken place in late 1963 following the very bad grain harvest.[10] Fragmentary data available in mid-October 1964 indicated that year's grain harvest had been good and was substantially above that of 1963.

Independent Western estimates agree in general that Soviet economic growth was relatively rapid in the early years of the post-Stalin period and that this growth has slowed down since 1958. One estimate prepared in the United States, for example, puts the average annual rate of growth of Soviet gross national product—material production plus services—at 6.8 per cent during 1950–1958 and at 4.6 per cent during 1958–1962. The year to year Soviet growth rates have also been markedly uneven. This is shown by estimates for the annual percentage increases in Soviet gross national product:

1958	1959	1960	1961	1962
9.9	3.9	5.0	6.5	2.2

For 1963, presumably, the corresponding figure was approximately the same as that of 1962. These and related data suggest that in 1963 Soviet gross national product may have been roughly 80–90 per cent more than in 1952. This is no mean achievement, but it is well below the official Soviet claim that gross social product—which excludes services—was about 150 per cent higher in 1963 than in 1952.[11]

At the time of its famous "press conference" on the Soviet economy in January 1964, the Central Intelligence Agency issued a good summary of the course of the Soviet economy since Stalin and the primary factors influencing it. That summary is given below, together with some additions by the author which are indicated by brackets:

The first years of Khrushchev's leadership were marked by a series of successes. [Industrial production—particularly heavy industrial output—grew rapidly. Major progress was achieved in developing new types of weapons, including jet bombers, increasingly powerful hydrogen bombs, and intercontinental ballistic missiles.] The expansion of planted acreage through the New Lands [virgin lands] program gave agriculture its first real lift since 1937. Economic growth was rapid—probably better than 6 per cent a year for the 1950–59 period as a whole, aided by cuts in armed forces personnel and in military spending which took place in 1956 and 1957.

While housing continued to be very tight, there were noticeable improvements in living standards, particularly in foodstuffs but also in consumer goods as compared with the late Stalin years. [A sharp increase in housing construction in the late 1950's and early 1960's improved the housing situation somewhat, but much of this increased building simply went to meeting the needs of the many new millions rapidly flooding into the cities.] After 1959, however, economic growth began to slow appreciably. The rate of expansion of fixed investment, upon which growth depends, was not maintained. With annual increases in investment cut in half, falling to between 4 and 5 per cent in 1962–63, a sharp curtailment in economic growth was inevitable. In 1962, Soviet gross national production was about $260 billion, or 47 per cent of that of the United States . . .

To a great extent Soviet economic difficulties stem from a series of programs too ambitious for available resources. With a gross national product less than half that of the United States, the Soviet leadership has invested in new plant and equipment amounts nearly as large as investment in the United States and has maintained a military-space program approaching in real cost that of the United States.

Much of the blame for recent reductions in the rate of growth falls on the sharp increase in Soviet defense spending, which between 1959 and 1963 increased by about one-third. However, the problem centers less on the total size of defense outlays than on the diversion of scarce critical resources—both manpower and materials. The military "bite" was particularly severe on the best engineering talent, on the most skilled construction specialists, and on the associated high quality materials and components. The costs of increased military efforts showed up in shortfalls in industrial investment, especially in the chemicals industry, and in the gross underfulfillment of the Soviet plan for automation and modernization of industry.

Although the slowdown in industrial output has had its effect, the serious decline in economic growth in 1962 and 1963 is largely due to the failures in agriculture.

A necessary corollary of the headlong rush to develop heavy industry was the neglect of agriculture. Starved for investment funds, agriculture was faltering badly by the time Stalin died. Khrushchev succeeded . . . in temporarily reversing the downward trends. The New Lands put more grain into Soviet stomachs, into livestock, and into foreign markets—perhaps most importantly from the standpoint of political stability, into the European Satellite countries to make up deficits in their own laggard farm output. But the returns from the vast new acreage plowed up in 1955–58 proved to be temporary. Once the original soil moisture and fertility were used up, output fell off. In 1963, a severe drought in the traditional farming areas, as well as in Kazakhstan and Siberia, resulted in a near disaster. Output on a per capita basis in 1963 was about 10 per cent below that of 1958. Total agricultural output declined some 4 per cent in 1962 and probably more than 4 per cent in 1963. The plight of Soviet agriculture is further illustrated by the composition of the Soviet diet. In total calories, the average Russian citizen is not far behind his American counterpart. But 70 per cent of the Soviet diet consists of grain and potatoes, compared to 28 per cent in the United States. Only 25 per cent of the Soviet diet consists of quality foods—livestock products, vegetables and fruits.

The impact of a short grain crop on this pattern of diet is obvious. Bread for human consumption must be curtailed.

Livestock herds must be reduced. There is plenty of recent evidence on the disappearance of flour from stores, of distress slaughtering of livestock, and of the elimination of free bread from factory cafeterias.[12]

The C.I.A. statement directs attention to some of the fundamental factors that help explain the growth of total Soviet output since 1952. Let us look at some of these factors, beginning with investment.

In comparable prices, total Soviet capital investment was 14,100,000,000 rubles in 1952, 25,800,000,000 rubles in 1957, and 40,200,000,000 rubles in 1962. Thus in the first five years of the post-Stalin period, capital investment grew by more than 80 per cent. In the next five years, however, it increased by less than 60 per cent. The slowing down in growth is even more evident if we focus upon particular year to year changes. In 1958, for example, capital investment rose by more than 16 per cent over 1957. In 1961 and 1962, on the other hand, the corresponding gains were only about 4 or 5 per cent annually, a precipitous decline from the percentage increases customary in the 1950's.[13]

As suggested in the C.I.A. statement, part of the reason for the slowdown in production and investment growth appears to be the sharp rise in defense expenditures, particularly in 1961. Because military equipment is priced relatively cheaply compared to many other goods, the real value of a ruble spent for defense is much greater than that of a ruble spent for most other purposes. As a result the changes upward and downward of the Soviet defense budget during the post-Stalin period have probably represented greater fluctuation in real resources being employed than would be true if the same monetary changes were observed in other areas of the Soviet budget. The published defense budget is generally believed to cover only part of that country's military costs. In particular the expenses of military-connected scientific research and development are probably included in the published science budget. The latter has gone up spectacularly in the period considered here. The science budget also presumably includes at least part of the cost of the very substantial space program of the Soviet Union. The available data on these two categories of the Soviet budget are shown in Table 3.

One other element deserves to be mentioned in this brief discussion of the factors behind the rapid growth of Soviet output

Table 3. SOVIET DEFENSE AND SCIENCE
EXPENDITURES, 1952–1964

Year	Defense	Science
	(billion rubles)	
1952	10.9	1.0†
1953	10.5	1.1
1954	10.0*	1.3†
1955	10.7	1.5†
1956	9.7	1.7
1957	9.1	2.1†
1958	9.4	2.4
1959	9.4	2.8
1960	9.3	3.3
1961	11.6	3.8
1962	12.7	4.3
1963	13.9*	4.9*
1964	13.3*	5.2*

* Planned.   † Estimated by interpolation.

SOURCES: *Dimensions of Soviet Economic Power*, p. 37; *Narodnoye Khozyaistvo SSSR v 1962 godu*, pp. 635, 637; *Pravda*, December 17, 1963.

in the 1950's and the slowdown of the early 1960's: changes in the labor force. Most of the increase of Soviet industrial production during this period came from higher productivity per man-hour, while productivity increased also in agriculture over this period as a whole. Between 1953 and 1962, total civilian employment rose little more than 20 per cent, from about 82,000,000 persons to about 99,400,000. In industry the growth of employment over this period was almost 50 per cent, from about 16,300,00 to almost 24,-300,000. Part of this increase was required, however, to make up for the reduction of the standard Soviet work week from 48 hours at the beginning of the period to 41 hours at the end. The Soviet agricultural labor force actually declined from about 40,900,000 workers in 1953 to about 39,500,000 in 1962.[14] The availability of large numbers of underemployed agricultural workers who could be drawn upon for non-agricultural labor needs without affecting farming's production potential was very important in the period considered here. During the late 1950's and early 1960's the availability of these rural workers for non-farm jobs softened the impact on the Soviet economy of the very small size of the age groups reaching working age—age groups consisting of youngsters born during and immediately after World War II.

The substantial gains in productivity resulted primarily from the large capital investments in industry and agriculture, much of which went for improved machinery and advanced technology. The allocation of new investment among different branches of the Soviet economy also provided annually an index of the changing priorities of the rulers of the Soviet Union. Table 4 presents some relevant data.

Table 4. DISTRIBUTION OF SOVIET INVESTMENT*
BY SECTORS, 1955 AND 1958–1962

	1955	1958	1959	1960	1961	1962
			(billion rubles)			
Housing	3.8	7.5	8.3	8.3	7.9	7.7
Agriculture	3.8	4.7	5.1	5.2	5.7	6.4
Transport and communications	1.5	2.2	2.7	3.1	3.3	3.6
Industry, total	8.2	11.2	13.0	14.3	14.9	15.8
Iron and steel	.6	.9	1.1	1.2	1.3	1.4†
Chemicals	.3	.4	.7	.9	1.1	1.2†
Fuels and power	3.0	3.9	4.0	4.2	4.4	4.6†
Construction materials and construction	.8	1.4	1.7	2.0	2.1	2.0†
Consumer goods	.9	1.5	1.8	2.0	1.8	1.8
Machine building	1.1	1.3	1.5	1.8	2.0	2.2†
Others	1.5	1.9	2.2	2.3	2.3	2.6†

* Fixed investment in new rubles at 1955 prices.
† Estimated.
SOURCE: *Annual Economic Indicators for the U.S.S.R.*, pp. 41–42.

Table 4 shows clearly the differential pattern of investment growth over this period. Housing investment reached its peak in 1960 and declined in 1961 and 1962. Agricultural investment, on the other hand, grew quickly during the early 1960's after relative stagnation in the late 1950's. Investment in the chemical industry doubled between 1958 and 1960, but then its growth slowed down drastically during the following two years. The investment allocation to consumer goods industries actually declined in 1961.

At this point we can try to evaluate the gap between total output in the United States and the Soviet Union, and the degree to which it has changed since Stalin's death. The problems of measurement here are complex, in part because of the lack of complete information on Soviet production and in part because of the very different structures of prices in the two countries. Nevertheless a consistent methodology has been used by American students of the problem and the results appear to be of an acceptable order of accuracy. A pioneer investigator in this field has been Professor Morris Bornstein of the University of Michigan. His studies indicate that the Soviet gross national product was about one-third that of the United States in 1950, about 37.8 per cent as much in 1955, and a little less than half in 1958.[15] For 1960, another American investigator found that the Soviet G.N.P. was still somewhat less than half that of the United States, and we have quoted above the C.I.A. estimate that in 1962 the ratio was 47 per cent, still slightly less than half. During the first five years of the post-Stalin period rapid progress was made by the Soviet economy toward narrowing the gap separating Soviet from American production. But since 1958, the ratio has remained roughly constant, the result in part of the slowdown in Soviet growth and in part of the improved performance of the American economy. In absolute terms, one investigator put 1962 Soviet gross national product at $256,300,000,000 as against $551,800,-000,000 for the United States.[16]

The official Soviet statistical handbooks for 1960, 1961, and 1962 estimate the gross social product of that country to have been about 60 per cent of the corresponding American figure during all three years; they do not claim any marked rise in this ratio during this period. It is important to recall that the United States concept of gross national product includes services while the Soviet concept of gross social product excludes services. Since the service industries play a far greater role in the United States than in the Soviet Union, these two different sets of ratios are really not as contradictory as they may appear at first sight. Moreover, both the Soviet and American figures agree that no sharp changes took place in the ratio of the two countries' total output during 1960–1962. In 1963, the available evidence suggests, the United States lead in total output over the Soviet Union increased somewhat, primarily because of the decline in Soviet agricultural production during that year. But the official Soviet claim is that in 1963 Soviet gross social product and national income both were "more than 60%" that of the United States.

Turning now to industry, it is fairly evident that the officially claimed tripling of Soviet industrial production between 1952 and 1963 is somewhat exaggerated. But if we take the more moderate estimates of most independent American studies of this subject, we conclude that during much of the 1950's Soviet industrial output was growing by 8 to 10 per cent annually, and that in the early 1960's that growth had dropped somewhat to perhaps 6.5 or 7 per cent. Even these more moderate rates indicate that total Soviet industrial output more than doubled between 1952 and 1963.[17]

A more concrete picture of Soviet industrial growth emerges from the data in Table 5 on increased production, in physical terms, of particular commodities:

Table 5. OUTPUT OF KEY SOVIET INDUSTRIAL COMMODITIES, 1952, 1958, 1963, AND 1964

Commodity	Unit	1952	1958	1963	1964 (estimated)
Steel	mil. metric tons	34.5	54.9	80.2	84.5
Coal	mil. metric tons	300.9	496.1	532	550
Oil	mil. metric tons	47.3	113.2	206	225
Electricity	billion kwh	119.1	235.4	412	455
Fertilizers	mil. metric tons	6.4	12.4	19.9	25
Machine tools	thousands	74.6	138.3	183	180
Tractors	thousands	98.9	219.7	325	320
Cement	mil. metric tons	13.9	33.3	61	63
Cotton cloth	bil. sq. meters	3.6	4.3	5.1	5.4
Silk cloth	mil. sq. meters	.2	.7	.8	.8
Leather shoes	million pair	237	356.4	463	475
Television sets	millions	.04	1.0	2.5	2.9

SOURCES: Data for 1952 and 1958 from official statistical handbooks, for 1963 from *Pravda*, January 24, 1964, and for 1964 estimated from statistics on output during the first half of that year given in *Pravda*, July 23, 1964.

Two points emerge prominently from these data. One is the very great increase in production of many commodities. Steel output increased almost 150 per cent over these twelve years; oil production in 1964 was almost five times as much as in 1952 and the amount of electricity generated in 1964 was almost four times as much as in 1952. These and related gains made the Soviet Union the formidable world economic power it was in the mid-1960's. Soviet steel production in 1963 was more than that of Britain, France, and West Germany combined, as well as more than 80 per cent of United States steel output. The rapid rise of oil production during these years made possible Soviet emergence as a significant factor in world petroleum markets. At the same time, however, even the small sample of Soviet production data given above shows that there were areas where industrial output lagged. Thus coal production was virtually stagnant after 1958, as was the production of silk cloth. But on the whole, these data for specific commodities—and for others which could be added—fully substantiate the general picture of Soviet industry as a rapidly growing giant throughout the post-Stalin period to date. Soviet industry was nevertheless a colossus that served primarily heavy industry and the needs of Soviet military forces, giving the Soviet consumer second priority. By the mid-1960's, no more than a modest beginning had been made toward providing consumers with television sets, refrigerators, washing machines, and other durable household goods. During the entire period 1953–1964, moreover, total Soviet production of passenger cars was little more than 1,000,000, or less than two months' average United States automobile output in 1963. All this reflects the priorities of the Soviet leadership, which values rockets, sputniks, and space ships, with their enormous military or propaganda potential, much more highly than prosaic automobiles for the vast majority of earthbound Soviet citizens.

In agriculture, production data for key items confirm the earlier picture of a much less impressive performance than that of industry. Grain production is the foundation of both Soviet agriculture and the Soviet diet, and therefore deserves the closest attention. Since weather plays such a large role in crop fluctuations, it is perhaps best to begin with averages that include years of good and poor weather both. According to official data, during 1949–1952 the average grain harvest was 82,500,000 metric tons. For the years 1953–1962, the corresponding average was 119,400,000. Looking at individual years, we find that in 1952 the grain harvest was about 92,000,000 metric tons. Production in subsequent years was officially estimated as shown in Table 6.

Table 6. SOVIET GRAIN OUTPUT, 1953–1962

Year	Million Metric Tons	Year	Million Metric Tons
1953	82.5	1958	141.2
1954	85.6	1959	125.9
1955	106.8	1960	134.4
1956	127.6	1961	138.0
1957	105.0	1962	147.5

SOURCES: *Selskoye Khozyaistvo SSSR*, p. 227; *SSSR v Tsifrakh v 1962 godu*, p. 141.

Some evidence suggests the Soviet estimate of 1963 grain output is 134,000,000 metric tons. These data have not gone completely unchallenged. An American observer has suggested that the 1958 harvest was really only about 125,000,000 metric tons, the 1956 and 1961 harvests only 115,000,000 tons, and the 1959 and 1960 harvests only 100,000,000 tons.[18] Another American observer has estimated the 1963 Soviet grain harvest at about 105,000,000 metric tons and that of 1964 as substantially higher. In 1964, key grain-growing areas enjoyed favorable weather and their increased output reflected this.

The C.I.A. statement quoted earlier implies that agency does not accept the official 1962 grain figure. But even if the suggested corrections are accepted, the fact of substantial growth in grain production is clear, at least between 1952 and 1958. The failure to make substantial gains beyond 1958 combined with the continued growth of Soviet population probably forced serious depletion in the early 1960's of existing grain stocks. As a result, the poor 1963 grain harvest compelled the Soviet government to look to the West for a billion dollars' worth of badly needed grain imports. The pressure of this increased population on the Soviet state's resources was particularly severe because of the almost complete concentration of the post-1952 population increase in the cities and towns. Urban residents are far more dependent upon the government for most of their food supply than are farm folk. This background emphasizes the importance of the volume of annual government grain procurements from farmers. In 1962 the Soviet government procured 56,600,000 metric tons of grain; in 1963 it was able to get only about 45,000,000 tons. The 1963 level of procurements was only slightly below those of 1959 and 1960 when the Soviet Union was a net grain exporter. The need to import some 12,000,000 tons of grain during the 1963–1964 crop year is partly explained by the fact that on January 1, 1964 the Soviet government was responsible for feeding almost 15,000,000 more people in cities and towns than had been there four years earlier. In October 1964 the Soviet press reported that the government had procured more grain from the 1964 harvest than had been secured from any earlier year's output.

Production of other key crops has also increased since Stalin's death, though usually more slowly than the Soviet leadership hoped. Raw cotton production amounted to 3,850,000 metric tons in 1953; ten years later it had finally been brought over the 5,000,000 ton mark after many years of stagnation at approximately 4,500,000 tons. Sugar beet production exceeded 23,000,000 tons in 1953, reached a record level of 57,700,000 metric tons in 1960, and was somewhat below that during 1961–1963. The output of sunflower seeds—a major source of vegetable oil—roughly doubled between the early 1950's and the early 1960's. Potato production, on the other hand, increased only about 20 per cent between 1953 and 1958, then remained essentially stagnant until it plunged below even the 1953 mark in 1962.

The most sought after food in the Soviet Union is meat. This is true both nutritionally and politically. Even in the mid-1960's most of the caloric content of the Soviet diet comes from bread, cereal, macaroni, and other grain foods. Any major improvement in the quality of the Soviet diet requires primarily a large increase in its meat content. The Soviet people realize this. The strength of their demand for meat has been reflected in the high prices meat sellers can command in the free peasant markets. The political sensitivity attached to meat production has been shown by Premier Khrushchev himself, notably by his decision in the spring of 1957 to promise the Soviet people that by 1960 or 1961 they would have as much meat per capita as Americans.[19]

The promise was not kept and, worse yet, in mid-1962 the price of meat had to be raised 30 per cent in an effort to equalize supply and demand and to get funds with which to pay farmers more for their meat to encourage higher production. Premier Khrushchev's speeches of June 1962 make clear his tremendous chagrin and the political impact of the blow to his prestige. Rarely has he adopted so defensive a tone as he did in this period.

These same considerations apply, though in lesser measure, to the other major livestock foods, milk and eggs. Moreover, the hides of domestic animals provide leather for shoes and other consumer products, while wool is of course an important textile raw material. These factors make the development of livestock product output in the post-Stalin era of special importance. The relevant data are shown in Table 7.

Table 7. SOVIET OUTPUT OF LIVESTOCK PRODUCTS, 1952–1963

Year	Meat	Milk	Wool	Eggs
	(million metric tons)			(billions)
1952	5.2	35.7	.22	14.4
1953	5.8	36.5	.24	16.1
1954	6.3	38.2	.23	17.2
1955	6.3	43.0	.26	18.5
1956	6.6	49.1	.26	19.5
1957	7.4	54.7	.29	22.3
1958	7.7	58.7	.32	23.0
1959	8.9	61.7	.36	25.6
1960	8.7	61.7	.36	27.4
1961	8.7	62.6	.37	29.3
1962	9.5	63.9	.37	30.1
1963	10.2	61.2	.37	28.8

SOURCES: *Selskoye Khozyaistvo SSSR*, p. 150; *SSSR v Tsifrakh v 1962 godu*, p. 150; *Pravda*, January 24, 1964.

The data make the situation, and Premier Khrushchev's difficulties of recent years, quite clear. In the case of meat, milk, and wool, production growth was moderately rapid from 1952 to

1959, but then stagnation and even retrogression set in. In the case of meat, the situation in 1963 was much worse than the production figures imply. The relatively sharp jump in 1963 output reflected accelerated slaughtering of livestock because of the feed shortages caused by the bad grain harvest that year. Between January 1, 1963 and the same date a year later, the number of Soviet pigs declined from 70,000,000 to 40,700,000; the number of cattle fell from 87,000,000 to 85,300,000, and the number of sheep from 139,700,000 to 133,600,000. The setback was not a minor one, and its impact was felt all through 1964, particularly in reduced meat output.

The agricultural production record clearly tells a much less cheerful story than Premier Khrushchev had hoped for. But it should not be forgotten that even in 1963—let alone in some of the better years earlier—food and fiber production were well above the levels of the Stalin period. Premier Khrushchev's policies— which we shall explore later—did end the low level stagnation characterizing Stalin's last years. Soviet leaders now find themselves up against a new set of retarding factors, but the retardation is being felt at a much higher output level. Premier Khrushchev, however, could not offer such a defense in public since it would have contradicted his image of the Soviet economy dashing forward rapidly, an impatiently swift steed quickly catching up with the decrepit old nag of capitalism. But the contrast in recent years between Khrushchev's bright promises of a rapidly expanding standard of living and the realities of their daily experience must make many Soviet people conclude that his agricultural policies have essentially failed. Having promised the Russian equivalent of a chicken in every pot, Premier Khrushchev must have feared the consequences of his failure to deliver. The Soviet purchase of a billion dollars' worth of Western wheat in late 1963 and early 1964 was his response to political pressure from the people, whose great expectations had been aroused earlier by his grandiose promises. Put most bluntly, Khrushchev must have feared for his own position, and perhaps even for the Soviet regime, if he had tried to force his people to subsist on the food from the inadequate domestic harvest, as Stalin did before him. In the end, of course, Khrushchev's effort to avoid the consequences of his failures ended in defeat, and he was removed from power by the political coup of mid-October 1964.

CHAPTER III

Malenkov's Victory and Defeat

ON SEPTEMBER 1, 1953, an angry editorial appeared on the first page of *Pravda*. "It has become known," the Communist party organ wrote, "that the officials of ministries, administrative offices and other agencies often arrive at work two to three hours late and finish work late at night, keeping some employes at work unnecessarily and calling them to the office outside of working hours." Nothing got done in the mornings, *Pravda* complained, because high officials didn't get to their desks until the afternoon. The Soviet government had decided, the paper announced triumphantly, to rectify the situation. Beginning that morning, all major Soviet offices would work from 9 A.M. to 6 P.M. and employes would get one hour off for lunch.

Everyone in Moscow who read this understood that the new leaders in the Kremlin had made another departure from Stalin's practices. Stalin liked to work at night. The officials who served him knew that they could get a peremptory phone call from him at midnight or later, a call asking for information or demanding immediate action on some matter. Those officials had adjusted their own working hours and those of their subordinates accordingly. Six months after their old master's death, the new leaders in the Kremlin, headed by Premier Georgi M. Malenkov, had finally decided to put themselves and the vast bureaucratic machine they headed on a more normal working routine.

By the time this change occurred, it was already clear that the new Malenkov regime, though composed of those who had been closest to Stalin in his last years, was moving swiftly to ease some of the tensions their predecessor's rule had generated. The new masters, busily extolling the virtues of "collective leadership" over one-man rule, were of course not united. Behind the scenes a bitter power struggle was going on, a conflict whose first major victim, secret police chief Lavrenti P. Beria, disappeared from public view in June 1953. Behind the scenes, too, as later became evident, the personal rivalries found expression in policy differences. But, during 1953 at least, an effective majority of the first post-Stalin Soviet leadership agreed that it was vital to ease the country's economic strains and to win popularity among the masses of Soviet consumers and farmers by concessions Stalin had refused to give.

When Stalin died, the Korean War was still on, posing the possibility that it might spread and bring the Soviet Union into nuclear conflict with the United States. The men in the Kremlin were very aware of their inferiority in military technology *vis-á-vis* the United States. They probably worried at first that Washington might take advantage of the confusion surrounding Stalin's death to unleash an attack on Russia. They were very conscious of the partial conversion to a war economy Stalin had ordered earlier in the 1950's to provide arms for the Chinese and North Koreans and also to prepare for possible Soviet involvement in the fighting. Their foreign policy soon after his death reflected clearly their understanding that, to minimize domestic dissatisfaction effectively, they would first have to make their international position more secure.

The initial moves of the new post-Stalin regime were taken primarily to assure the power of the new rulers in a situation full of political and economic tensions. One of the first steps was a major concentration of governmental power into the hands of a few people, primarily the members of the new, smaller party Presidium. With respect to the economy, this meant the consolidation of fourteen major economic ministries into four huge new ministries. More important still, the new rulers began a peace offensive toward the West, striving to create an atmosphere in which the enormous strains on the Soviet economy in early 1953 could be relaxed somewhat by cutting down production of conventional armaments and—for the second time in a decade—reconverting part of Soviet industry to civilian production. This aspect of the new rulers' policy was achieved when the Korean War truce came in mid-1953. This eased international tension and made military production, for the moment at least, a less pressing need. Heavy slashes were also made quickly in some of the grandiose projects Stalin had inaugurated around 1950; some, like the plan for the vast shelter belt of trees Stalin had announced would end drought in the country, were simply abandoned. Others, such as several of the giant hydroelectric stations Stalin had scheduled for construction on the Volga, were halted for shorter or longer periods and the labor and other resources that could be transferred from them were shifted to more immediately pressing needs. The Soviet Union was economically overextended, Stalin's successors knew, and in their first months in power they acted decisively to cut back wherever possible.

The situation in the country was too tense, however, to permit of long delays in making at least some gestures toward improved consumer welfare. On April 1, 1953, therefore, the new rulers announced a comprehensive series of price cuts on consumer goods and food—10 per cent on bread, 15 per cent on meat, 50 per cent on vegetables, sauerkraut and grapes, 14 per cent on dresses, 8 per cent on shoes, and even 10 per cent on perfumes. The official decree boasted that consumers would save over 5,000,-000,000 rubles annually from the price cuts. In June another concession was granted. The amount of compulsory state bond purchases required annually of the Soviet people was cut in half, producing a saving of roughly 1,500,000,000 rubles. This time, however, there was explicit admission of the pressures at work. Malicious rumors were afloat, the Finance Minister announced, that a new currency reform—a devaluation of the ruble —was about to take place. "These rumors have no basis and are false and harmful," he asserted, but it is hardly likely they would have been denied so formally and so publicly if they had not resulted in large scale panic buying in different parts of the country.[1] And if the Soviet leaders had had any doubt about how touchy the situation was in their domain, the East German revolt of June 1953 must have dispelled skepticism. Implicitly these disturbances raised the specter of similar troubles within the Soviet Union itself.

These first moves increased the purchasing power of the Soviet population, but they did not automatically increase the supply of goods available for sale. There can be little doubt that in the months after Stalin's death many a Soviet consumer found himself with more money to spend than he could find commodities he wanted to buy. The appearance of these shortages may have

produced the devaluation rumors. In October, Anastas I. Mikoyan—the veteran chief of the Soviet consumer economy—
openly admitted the gap between the increased purchasing power
of consumers and the supplies available for sale. "We are lowering
the prices even of goods of which we still do not have enough,"
he declared, justifying this by the assertion, "It must be said that
this arouses further demand and prods us to increase more rapidly
the production of goods in short supply."[2]

By early August 1953 the new leadership was ready to announce its over-all economic policy. The fighting in Korea was
over. The disturbances in East Germany had been crushed. And
Soviet scientists had given word of a major success: they had
perfected a hydrogen bomb and were confident they could test
it successfully. For Premier Malenkov and a majority of the
Soviet leadership, this seemed to be the time to shift the emphasis
toward consumer needs without endangering the nation's security. It was as the herald of good news in the military and
other fields that Premier Malenkov spoke before the Supreme
Soviet on August 8th. "The government considers it necessary to
report to the Supreme Soviet that the United States has no
monopoly of production of the hydrogen bomb," he told his
audience, thus supplying the implicit justification for the new
economic policy.

Premier Malenkov began by stressing the continuity of the
new policy with the old. Heavy industry is "the foundation of
foundations of our socialist economy," he said, adding, "We shall
continue in every way to develop heavy industry." But, and
here came the new element, on the basis of past progress in heavy
industry, "We have all the necessary conditions for bringing
about a sharp rise in production of consumers goods. We have
every possibility to do this and we must do it." Now, he maintained, the country was in a position to pour more capital into
consumer goods production and agriculture. He defined the new
goal in these words:

> It is our pressing task in two or three years to raise sharply the
> general availability of foodstuffs and manufactured goods, of
> meat and meat products, fish and fish products, butter, sugar,
> candy, textiles, clothing, shoes, cooking utensils and tableware,
> furniture and other cultural and household goods; to make a

substantial increase in the supply to the public of all consumers' goods.[3]

Elsewhere in his speech he spoke of "an abundance of food" to be achieved in the next two or three years. He demanded better quality in the goods offered Soviet consumers, and deplored the fact that "an acute shortage of housing is felt everywhere." He hinted that the government was tapping Soviet reserves to provide more goods for consumers and announced that "a large number of machinery plants have been converted to the production of mass consumer goods."

To emphasize the seriousness of the effort he was proposing, Malenkov spelled out drastic changes in farm policy, too. The government planned to raise prices it paid to farmers for their produce so as to provide greater incentive for higher production, he announced. The traditional state hostility to collective farmers' private gardens was to end. Taxes on farmers' incomes and quotas for compulsory deliveries of garden produce to the state were to be cut substantially. He promised a 2,000,000,000 ruble increase in the incomes of collective farms and collective farmers, increased supplies of farm machinery and farm technicians plus more capital investment. If everybody buckled down to the job on the farms, he asserted, "the task of creating an abundance of food for the people and of raw materials for consumer goods industry in the next two or three years will be successfully met."

Malenkov had gained great personal prestige by appearing publicly as the apostle of a better life soon. This lesson and the potential political dangers thus posed were not lost on Nikita Khrushchev. A month later he occupied the center of the Soviet stage as the great friend and reformer of Soviet agriculture, dominating the September 1953 Central Committee meeting on that topic. Soviet agricultural production was inadequate, he declared, in part because of the past emphasis on heavy industry and in part because inadequate material incentives had been given farmers. Low incomes on the farms had caused a flight of peasants to the cities, and production had been hurt by illegal limitations on the farmers' private gardens. The country had fewer cattle than it had had in either 1916 or 1928, he revealed. Triumphantly, he announced that important increases would be made in prices paid to farmers for meat, milk, potatoes, and vegetables. Moreover, he added, the reductions in the compulsory delivery quotas Premier

Malenkov had announced would permit farms and farmers alike to sell more food on the free markets, where prices were much higher than those paid by the government.

Only very great pressures could have produced the kind of policies Malenkov and Khrushchev enunciated in this period, for these policies were dangerous. The glittering visions of imminent abundance dangled before the Soviet people could only arouse great expectations in a nation long accustomed to deprivation. What would happen if those expectations were disappointed?

Even more startling was the open support for the private enterprise activities of Soviet farmers. The new changes made it more profitable than earlier for peasants to concentrate their energies on their private gardens, neglecting their work on the collective fields. Some persons in Moscow must have asked how this could be reconciled with socialism. Perhaps most startling for the orthodox was the emergence of Malenkov and Khrushchev as advocates of at least one type of private property, individually owned livestock. Thus Khrushchev declared in his September 1953 speech to the Central Committee:

> Only people who do not comprehend the policy of the Party or the policy of the Soviet state see any danger to the socialist system in the presence of personally owned productive livestock on a collective farmer's private plot within the limits set by the Collective Farm Statutes. We must also get rid of the prejudice that it is shameful for a worker or an employe to own livestock as private property.[4]

This aspect of the farm policy enunciated in this period represented a drastic shift to the right. But while putting more stress on incentives for farmers and giving their private property instincts wider scope, the September 1953 meeting moved also to strengthen party control over the countryside and to diminish the collective farms' independence of action. It gave both the Machine Tractor Stations and the local Communist party units greater control over the collectives. A key move to strengthen party influence in the countryside was the decision to abolish the post of Assistant Director of the MTS for Political Affairs. Instead, each MTS was assigned a secretary of the local county (*rayon*) Communist party organization and a group of party instructors. These functionaries, operating under the direct control of the first secretary of the county party organization, were intended to make sure that the party ruled the countryside through the MTS.[5] But even this strengthened party influence was not enough to counteract fully the stimulus the August–September 1953 measures had given collective farmers to work their private gardens at the expense of the socialized fields. To combat this neglect of the collective fields, the party made clear in the summer of 1954 that it wanted the amount of work done by each peasant in the socialized agriculture increased. It was bluntly "suggested" to collective farm directors that they require each male collective farmer to earn at least 300 work days annually and each female collective farmer to earn at least 200 work days annually. Compulsion was to offset the peasant's economic incentives for greater attention to his own garden plot.[6]

In this period, the Soviet press conducted a major campaign to expose and point up consumer goods shortages, poor service in stores, and other similar weaknesses of the civilian economy. The campaign's object was to convince the population that at long last the leadership knew how bad things were and really intended to improve the situation. But as the flood of decrees detailing specific plans for improving the consumer's lot became public in September and October, careful observers could see that only a relatively limited effort was actually in prospect for the next two years. In the case of textiles, for example, the Fifth Five Year Plan—adopted in October 1952—had called for 1955 sales to the public to be 70 per cent higher than in 1950. The new plan for "abundance" announced in October 1953 lifted the target only to 80 per cent above the 1950 mark. The original plan had called for hosiery sales in 1955 to be 100 per cent above the 1950 level; the new plan called for a 120 per cent rise. The revision was only little more ambitious in the case of meat products, sugar, butter, and clothing. In the basic food and clothing areas, in short, there was more promise than reality in the Malenkov program. Really major increases were projected over the original 1955 goals only for durable consumer goods. The original plan, for example, had called for 2.4 times as many sewing machines to be sold in 1955 as in 1950; the new plan set the target at 5.1 times. The original plan had predicted a doubling of radio and television sales; the new document called for 1955 sales of these items to be 4.4 times their 1950 level.[7]

Yet even this limited program was not achieved. The actual improvement in Soviet living standards in 1955 as compared with 1953 was well under what Malenkov, Khrushchev, and Mikoyan had explicitly promised, let alone what they had implied. The struggle over the policy issues involved in this failure went on during 1954 and culminated in early 1955 in Malenkov's involuntary resignation as Premier of the Soviet Union. During this struggle, Khrushchev shifted his ground considerably and emerged near the end of the Malenkov era sounding like a Stalinist advocate of complete primacy for heavy industry. What factors caused this stand, and its sharp disappointments for the Soviet people?

The first setback became known to the Soviet leadership in the late summer or early fall of 1953. It was the sharp decline of the grain crop below the 1952 level. In October 1952 Malenkov had assured the Soviet people that the country's grain problem was solved forever. A year later it was clear to the leadership that he had been wrong. The 1953 grain harvest, 82,500,000 metric tons, was almost 10,000,000 tons below the 1952 level. It was smaller even than the grain harvest Tsarist Russia had gathered in the same areas in 1913, four decades earlier. The shattering impact of this news upon the Soviet leadership is evident from the fact that they tried to hide this catastrophe from their people. They did not hesitate even to lie about the matter. The official report on 1953 economic progress declared, "Although there was unfavorable weather in a number of regions of the country, the actual grain harvest in 1953 was close to that of 1952."

In late 1962, almost a decade after the event, Premier Khrushchev finally made public the seriousness of the grain situation that had faced his country in late 1953 and early 1954. He published then the secret memorandum he had sent his Presidium colleagues on January 22, 1954 outlining the gravity of the situation and proposing the large scale plowing up and seeding of virgin and fallow lands in the Urals and Siberia. Here is the way the secret memorandum described the situation at that time:

Grain production at present still does not guarantee the requirements and does not cover all the needs of the national economy, and the state grain reserves do not permit carrying out everywhere and in sufficient quantity trade in bread products, especially the better sorts, and in groats. As a consequence of the inadequate quantity of grain, it has been necessary to limit grain exports.

The quantity of grain remaining in the collective farms of a series of provinces, territories and republics, after their fulfill-ment of their delivery obligations to the state, does not cover all the needs of the collectives' socialized economy. Particularly short is the remaining supply of feed grains, without which a sharp expansion of livestock is impossible. . . .

In 1953 grain procurements were approximately at the level of 1948, but the expenditure of grain increased more than 50 per cent.

From these data it is also evident that procurements from the 1953 harvest do not cover the necessary expenditure of grain on internal needs. This gap, and also the expenditure of grain for export, have led to the necessity of squandering grain from the government reserve in the quantity of 160,000,000 poods [over 2,500,000 metric tons] which is impermissible.

He added that because of the grain shortage, the 1954 grain ex-port plan, devoted almost entirely to helping meet the food needs of other Communist-ruled nations, had had to be set at 3,120,000 tons, though the export needs were for 4,800,000 tons.[8]

Khrushchev sought to soften the blow somewhat when he rose to speak before the Central Committee in February 1954. He re-called that he had said the previous September that the country was "self-sufficient in grain." But, he added, grain needs were constantly growing, and the people wanted to eat better bread and more meat. But finally he admitted that "the level of grain output so far has not met all the needs of the national economy," and that the collective farms were suffering a shortage of feed grains.

The solution Khrushchev offered was the beginning of what has since been called the virgin lands program. In the Volga valley and beyond it in Siberia, he declared, there were large areas that could be plowed up and profitably planted to grain. "The most modest estimates," he said, showed that 13,000,000 hectares (over 30,000,000 acres) could be planted to grain in the next two years. He envisaged creation of a system of highly mechanized factories in the field, huge state farms worked with a minimum of tractor drivers and other machinery workers.

Even if the new lands produced only a ton of grain per hectare, he argued, this would provide well over 10,000,000 tons more grain; if the yield could be raised to a ton and a half per hectare, almost 20,000,000 more tons would be available. There was no hint in these optimistic forecasts that the land he proposed to have planted was mainly in marginal areas of erratic and often inadequate rainfall. Later it became known that behind the scenes voices were raised to point out that this represented a huge gamble whose wisdom was questionable. But at the time there was no public sign of opposition. The chief difficulty Khrushchev referred to in his public statement was the small population of the virgin lands areas and the consequent difficulty in recruiting all the needed manpower. But the decision had been made to go ahead, and he announced that more than 10,000 combines and about 60,000 tractors, as well as other farm machinery, had been allocated for the new grain campaign. No word was said at this meeting about the fact that the needs for organizing and equipping the new grain factories had not been anticipated when the original Malenkov program of the summer of 1953 had been drawn up. It was implicit in Khrushchev's new proposal that compensatory cuts in capital and labor supplies would have to be made elsewhere.[9]

The suspicion that there had been a struggle in 1954 over these unexpected and additional needs for resources was confirmed four years later. An agricultural official, denouncing the "anti-party group" of defeated party leaders, including Malenkov, declared at the December 1958 Central Committee meeting:

> To what tricks did this despicable group not resort! The State Planning Commission of that time declared that there was no money, no material stocks, for cultivating the virgin lands and opposed the allocation of funds for tractors, houses, metal, beams. The supply organizations objected categorically, saying there were no resources.[10]

Khrushchev's 1954 speech initiated the most radical—and most expensive—agricultural innovation of the first post-Stalin decade. The rains came that year, and gave a good crop on the limited area of virgin and fallow land planted in 1954. Thus encouraged, Khrushchev energetically pushed the program in the years that followed. By 1956 some 36,000,000 hectares had been plowed up

—20,000,000 of them in Kazakhstan alone—and by 1962 the total area plowed up and made available for planting had reached 42,000,000 hectares, or about 100,000,000 acres. In sheer magnitude and speed, this was one of the great land opening feats of history. There is no reason to doubt the Soviet official estimates that the investment in the area exceeded $4,000,000,000. Hundreds of thousands of farm workers, with tens of thousands of machines, were sent from European Russia into the wastelands of Siberia and Kazakhstan as centrally recruited twentieth century pioneers. Often living under the most primitive conditions with inadequate protection against the extremes of heat and cold, these Soviet fighters for grain performed great feats of personal endurance as they opened up a whole new Soviet grain empire. Some came to this hard work because of the romance and the glamour with which Soviet propaganda endowed the task of plowing up the vast grassy plains. Others were tempted by the lure of what Russians call "the long ruble," a term perhaps best translated into colloquial English as "the big buck." Each year many of the previous year's arrivals left in disgust and anger, disappointed by the harsh living conditions and repelled by the difficult climate. But each year more came. In the early 1960's, Khrushchev was still pushing cultivation in these vast new land areas he had ordered opened up, but—as we shall see below—the returns from this vast effort and huge investment were far from what he had hoped for.[11]

The second factor which helped speed the demise of the Malenkov program was the alarm raised in the Kremlin by the successful United States hydrogen bomb tests in the Pacific during early 1954. The whole matter is naturally clouded in official secrecy on both sides, but an accurate chronicle would seem to be the following:

In late 1952 the thermonuclear device detonated by the United States was not a hydrogen bomb because it was too big to be transportable. Its great size and weight derived from the large refrigeration apparatus needed to keep the heavy hydrogen in the device liquid. The Soviet Union apparently exploded the first device that could be called a practical hydrogen bomb in August 1953, after its scientists had discovered how to eliminate the need for liquid hydrogen by substituting a solid substance, probably lithium deuteride, which the United States had not employed in 1952. This made the Soviet hydrogen bomb light enough to be transportable, and 1953 Soviet comments assumed that this feat gave Moscow a significant military advantage over the United States. Then in early 1954 the United States apparently duplicated and perhaps improved on the Soviet feat, thus threatening a quick end to any Soviet military advantage derived from the 1953 accomplishment. Certainly Khrushchev seemed to be preoccupied with the hydrogen bomb problem when he addressed the Czechoslovak Communist party in the summer of 1954. In a passage which *Pravda* omitted, he claimed, "We were even quicker than the capitalist camp and invented the hydrogen bomb before they had it; and we, the Party of the working class, we know the importance of this bomb."[12]

Subsequent developments suggest that Soviet military chiefs and their political allies used the American advances as reason to demand sharply increased spending on military research and development. Their goal must have been development of intercontinental ballistic missiles capable of carrying hydrogen bombs to the United States if need be. Certainly any such important development in Soviet military technology would be incompatible with either the letter or the spirit of the hopes for a welfare state that Malenkov had aroused in 1953.

Malenkov fought back, however. Speaking in March 1954, he introduced a major new note into Soviet discussions of war. A conflict fought "with modern methods of warfare means the ruin of world civilization," he declared.[13] But at that time official Soviet doctrine was still based on the Leninist and Stalinist view that war between capitalism and communism was ultimately inevitable. This doctrine provided ideological justification for the Soviet emphasis on military preparation. Malenkov's statement for the first time raised the possibility that a future world war might be mutually so destructive for all combatants that there might be no sense in continuing the arms race. This must have caused a furore behind the scenes and a few weeks later he had to retreat from this position. Nevertheless, he pressed on with his pro-consumer policy. On April 1, 1954 a new round of price cuts on foods and consumer goods was put into effect. These reductions, smaller than those announced a year earlier, testified that there was still political power behind the program to improve living standards that the Premier had enunciated in August 1953.

The debate on the relative priorities to be accorded the most expensive modern weapons as against consumer goods was not the only economic problem dividing the Soviet rulers during this period. Questions regarding the administration of Soviet industry also gave rise to controversy during 1953 and early 1954. Immediately after Stalin's death, the small group of men in the Communist party Presidium who took over power then concentrated authority in their hands and in the hands of those they trusted. One aspect of this was the merging of many key economic ministries into a few giant organizations. This overcentralization caused many difficulties, and there must have been a good deal of pressure from the next lower ranks of the economic bureaucracy for a wider diffusion of authority. It is not unlikely that this pressure was also connected with the conflict over the most urgent policy matters as well. In any case, by the end of April 1954 the concentration of economic authority ordered in March 1953 was reversed and once again a large number of relatively small economic ministries was set up. At the same time the new ministers and their highest ranking subordinates were given increased powers in an effort to introduce more flexibility and greater speed of decision-making into the bureaucratic economy. Not the least interesting aspect of this reorganization was the public emergence of what was called the Ministry of Medium Machine Building, an organization that, later developments indicated, was charged with developing and producing Soviet nuclear weapons.

While the debates and organizational changes went on among the Soviet leaders during 1954, inflationary pressures mounted throughout the land. Peasant incomes rose because of higher prices and increased production. Earnings of urban workers tended upward more rapidly in the relatively relaxed atmosphere following Stalin's death. A highly placed Soviet economist, Academician A. Ostrovityanov, estimated later that in 1954 the monetary income of the Soviet population was 25 per cent higher than it had been in 1952. But, he added, the growth of purchasing power "has proceeded far more quickly than the growth of agri-

cultural and consumers goods production."[14] Nikita Khrushchev
put the matter this way in late 1954:

> Certain people will ask: Why, despite the increase in the vol-
> ume of procurements and purchases of agricultural products,
> are needed goods not always to be found in the shops? . . . It
> is because the demand for consumers goods has increased to a
> tremendous extent and because the people now have more
> money. Prices have been reduced by billions of rubles, the real
> wages of workers and employes have risen sharply as have col-
> lective farmers' incomes. Consequently no matter how much
> we increase the output of goods, the demand of the population
> is still not being fully satisfied. In meetings with collective
> farmers throughout the country I have heard the wish ex-
> pressed a number of times that more sugar, more footwear,
> more woolen fabrics were on sale.[15]

But even as Khrushchev's speech was published, the struggle
over the Malenkov line was reaching a climax and Malenkov was
in retreat. Khrushchev's public statements were more and more
openly emphasizing the primacy of heavy industry. On January
24, 1955, Malenkov's defeat was made clear when *Pravda* printed
Dmitry Shepilov's article assailing the proponents of the pro-
consumer line and asserting definitively the need for all-out
priority for heavy industry. Shepilov aimed nominally at some
Soviet economists but his real target was the Premier. These
economists, Shepilov charged:

> . . . assert that since 1953 the Soviet Union has entered a new
> phase of economic development whose essence is supposedly a
> sharp change in the Party's economic policy. While the Party
> used to put the emphasis on developing heavy industry, now
> supposedly the main emphasis has shifted to developing light
> industry, to output of consumers goods . . . These economists
> suggest setting the same rate of growth for heavy and light in-
> dustry or even allowing light industry to grow more rapidly
> than heavy industry throughout the entire period of transition
> from socialism to communism.

> If opinions of this kind were to become general, it would
> greatly damage the entire cause of communist construction. It
> would completely confuse our cadres on basic questions of
> Party economic policy. Practically, it would mean that devel-
> opment of our heavy industry, which is the backbone of the
> socialist economy, would tend downward, leading to a decline
> in all branches of the national economy and producing a drop

rather than an increase in the working people's living standards. It would undermine the economic power of the Soviet Union and weaken its defense capacity.

The decision had been taken to put rockets and the virgin lands program ahead of consumer goods. Malenkov's resignation as Premier and Mikoyan's as Minister of Trade followed shortly, though both men remained in the Communist party Presidium.

The ferocity of the battle which had been waged was suggested by the violence of Khrushchev's language against the Malenkov faction. He did not hesitate to suggest that his opponents really represented the right wing heresies Stalin had defeated in the 1920's. Khrushchev asserted that the idea that light industry "can and should overtake all other branches of industry . . . is profoundly incorrect reasoning, alien to the spirit of Marxism-Leninism. This is nothing but slander of our party. This is a right deviationist belching, a vomiting of the anti-Leninist ideas which Rykov, Bukharin and their sort once disseminated."[16] The brief Malenkov era was over. Just how completely it would be expunged from the record became evident three years later, when a major collection of Soviet government and Communist party documents was issued. Not a single one of the 1953 decrees ordering improvements in consumer goods production, output of processed foods, and the organization of Soviet trade was mentioned. They had become, in Orwell's sense, un-decrees.[17]

At this point we may inquire as to what actually happened in the Soviet economy during the short-lived Malenkov era. Part of the answer is given by the data in Table 8 showing the annual percentages of growth of industrial production as a whole, of heavy industry, and of industries producing goods for consumers:

Table 8. SOVIET INDUSTRIAL DEVELOPMENT, 1952–1955

Year	All Industry	Heavy Industry	Consumer Goods
	(annual percentage increase)		
1952	12	12	11
1953	12	12	12
1954	13	14	13
1955	12	15	8

SOURCE: *Narodnoye Khozyaistvo SSSR v 1961 godu*, p. 171.

Table 8 makes clear that, compared with Stalin's last full year of rule, very little change occurred in the proportion between heavy and light industry production during 1953 or 1954. Both were years of rapid growth by both major branches of the Soviet industrial complex. The real change, ironically, occurred in 1955 when the abandonment of the Malenkov line raised heavy industry's growth rate slightly and cut consumer goods output's growth rate quite sharply. At the least, it is clear that Soviet heavy industry—and by inference the growth of Soviet military and economic capabilities—suffered no real damage during the Malenkov era. In 1952 the official data tell us, heavy industry accounted for 69.2 per cent of all industrial production; in 1954, the corresponding percentage was 69.5.

A more meaningful picture of the effects of Malenkov's political primacy on the Soviet consumer emerges if we look at the actual production data for 1953 and 1954, and if we compare the actual output during the latter year, as shown in Table 9, with the goals announced in October 1953.

Table 9. SOVIET CONSUMER GOODS PRODUCTION,
1952–1954, AND 1954 GOALS

Commodity	Unit	1952 Output	1953 Output	1954 Output	1954 Goal
Cotton textiles	million meters	5.0	5.3	5.6	5.5
Leather shoes	million pair	237.0	238.1	255.2	267.0
Hosiery	million pair	588.3	611.9	673.1	673.0
Sewing machines	thousands	801.0	993.2	1281	1335
Refrigerators	thousands	30.9	49.2	94.1	207
Granulated sugar	million tons	3.1	3.4	2.6	4.3
Fish	million tons	2.1	2.2	2.5	2.7

SOURCES: *Narodnoye Khozyaistvo SSSR v 1958 godu, passim; Pravda,* October 28 and 30, 1953.

The data make clear that production of consumer goods—with the conspicuous exception of sugar which reflected the poor sugar beet harvest of 1954—did rise appreciably during 1953 and 1954. Actual 1954 output exceeded that year's targets for two commodities shown in Table 9. The largest percentage gains were in durable consumer goods. But not even the Soviet leaders had claimed that the 1954 production for consumers would represent anything like abundance. However, Malenkov had promised "abundance" in two or three years time so that in 1955 Soviet consumers should really have begun to enjoy the major benefits of his program, had it been carried out. Table 10 indicates the degree to which consumers' hopes were dashed instead by the abandonment of the Malenkov program in 1955.

Table 10. SOVIET CONSUMER GOODS PRODUCTION, 1954, 1955, AND 1955 GOALS

Commodity	Unit	1954 Output	1955 Output	1955 Goal
Cotton textiles	million meters	5.6	5.9	6.3
Leather shoes	million pair	255.2	271.2	318.0
Hosiery	million pair	673.1	772.2	777.0
Sewing machines	millions	1.3	1.6	2.6
Refrigerators	thousands	94.1	151.4	330.0
Granulated sugar	million tons	2.6	3.4	4.8
Fish	million tons	2.5	2.7	3.2

SOURCES: The same as for Table 9.

These data help make clear the reasons for the bitterness of the 1954 debate within the Soviet leadership. To have tried seriously to achieve the 1955 goals would have required greatly expanded investment in the consumer goods industries with corresponding cutbacks in investment in heavy industry, armaments, and research and development on modern weapons. In addition, such an effort would have required far greater agricultural production than was actually achieved in 1954. Even the official Soviet index of farm production makes clear how very modest the initial response of Soviet agriculture was to the higher prices and other aids decided upon in 1953. Overall, the index records only a 5 per cent increase in farm production in 1954 over 1953, made up of a 3 per cent gain in crop output and an 8 per cent gain in livestock output. Because of bad weather in the Ukraine, grain production in 1954 might have been even lower than in 1953. Only the expansion of grain acreage in the virgin lands—the first small installment of Khrushchev's program—permitted 1954 grain production to be 3,000,000 tons higher than a year earlier. Neither the amount of food nor the amount of agricultural raw materials Malenkov had hoped for was produced in 1954, and this also helped doom his program.

Both the achievements and the limitations of the Malenkov era —from the consumer point of view, at least—are summarized by considering some calculations prepared by Abram Bergson. He finds that between 1952 and 1954 consumption's share of the Soviet gross national product (total output of all goods and services) rose from 44.4 per cent to 51.2 per cent. Over the same period the share of the G.N.P. taken by gross investment fell from 28.7 to 25.5 per cent, and the share taken by the defense appropriation in the Soviet budget declined from 12.7 to 10.3 per cent. These changes, accomplished in a two year period, were not negligible. As a result, in 1954 Soviet consumers received a higher share of national output than in any other year over the period 1941–1955. But in 1928 Soviet consumers had received directly 64.7 per cent of the G.N.P., and even in 1940 they had received 51.0 per cent.[18]

As for heavy industry, we have already cited some general figures showing its continued rapid growth during the Malenkov era. We may illustrate this more specifically by considering a few concrete examples. Soviet steel production increased about 7,000,000 metric tons between 1952 and 1954, roughly 20 per cent. Oil output rose almost 25 per cent in the same period. The amount of electricity generated increased over those same two years by 25 per cent. World attention may have been concentrated in these years on the drama of the effort to improve the lot of Soviet consumers. The prosaic reality was much more a further major advance in the economic and military power of the Soviet state.

In retrospect, perhaps the importance of the short-lived Malenkov era was that it made new beginnings. The Soviet people saw that their rulers had made some concessions and the issue of the standard of living had been brought into the forefront of public discussion. The debacle in Soviet agriculture had been partially admitted and the need for radical measures recognized. Perhaps most important for the long run was the fact that the absolute power of the secret police had been overthrown with Beria's purge. The use of police terror as an instrument of rule was diminishing, raising the question of what could be used to succeed it. Doors and windows were being opened in every area of the Soviet society, including the economic. As later events would prove, the new forces thus set in motion could not be reversed, and even the defeat of the first pro-consumer politician to succeed Stalin would not stem these tides. It would not be long before Khrushchev was ready to outbid Malenkov for popular favor.

CHAPTER IV

The Good Years, 1955–1958

IN RETROSPECT, the Soviet leaders may well think of 1955–1958 as the good years, the period when hopes ran high and accomplishments were not very far behind. It was a time both of rapid production growth and of great institutional change. These were the years of the first sputniks and their profound impact upon world opinion. As Nikita Khrushchev watched his country grow visibly stronger, wealthier and more influential before his eyes, everything seemed possible in this best of all possible worlds and the ebullient Soviet leader became ever more sanguine in his economic and other projections for the future. There were disappointments and setbacks, too, and a five year plan was even abandoned in mid-passage during this period. But on balance these four years made up one of the brightest chapters in Soviet economic history, a time when new national energies came to flower and seemed to promise rich fruit.

The Soviet economy grew in much more balanced fashion during these years than it had earlier. Over the four years as a whole both industry and agriculture increased their production substantially and rapidly. The official Soviet claim is that national income rose 50 per cent in these four years, while a careful Western analyst has published figures suggesting that Soviet net national product grew by roughly a third.[1] Even the lower figure is quite impressive. The official Soviet industrial production index claims a 1955–1958 rise of almost 50 per cent, with heavy industry growing about 55 per cent and consumer goods output increasing 38.5 per cent.[2] A carefully compiled Western index of Soviet civilian industrial output places the 1958 volume of such production at almost 50 per cent above the 1954 level.[3] In this period of rapidly rising Soviet nuclear and rocket strength, it seems unlikely that the military component could have altered this figure very much, if at all, on the down side. In agriculture, the official Soviet production index puts 1958 output at about 50 per cent above that of 1954.[4] A Western index of the same output puts farm production growth over the same period at only slightly below 50 per cent.[5] There is general agreement, in short, that this was a period of rapid and impressive Soviet production growth.

Major institutional change and substitution of new administrative practices for old went along with this mounting economic growth. During 1955–1958, the entire system of industrial organization was altered more radically than in decades. The Machine Tractor Stations, one of the earliest and most fundamental features of the Stalinist agricultural system, were completely wiped out. The greatly improved agricultural production picture of these years reflected the excellent weather of 1956 and 1958, but other factors also played a role, notably the large scale planting of the virgin and fallow lands to wheat and the emergence of corn as a major feed crop for Soviet livestock. The old Stalinist slave labor camps were largely wound up in these years and a new concern for human welfare began to be exhibited in the raising of pension and minimum wage levels. By the end of the 1950's, under the impress of these and other changes, Western observers were not only expressing trepidation about the threat of Soviet economic competition but wondering whether the Soviet Union was not evolving toward a kind of socialist welfare state.[6] On the day in 1953 that Stalin died there was in the West neither widespread concern about Soviet economic growth nor—outside of Communist circles—any serious belief that the Soviet Union was anything but a primitive tyranny.

The key event of this period was the 20th Congress of the Soviet Communist party in February 1956. Almost a decade afterward, the shock waves let loose at this meeting are still being felt in the Soviet Union and abroad. Many of these shocks came from Khrushchev's "secret" speech denouncing Joseph Stalin, a speech in which he implied—in some cases more than implied—that Stalin had been an economic bungler whose dictatorship had been extremely costly for the Soviet people. The ferocity of Khrushchev's attack is evident from this key section of his speech:

> The cult of [Stalin's] personality has caused the employment of faulty principles in party work and in economic activity. It brought about rude violations of internal party and Soviet

democracy, sterile administration, deviations of all sorts, covering up the shortcomings and varnishing of reality. Our nation gave birth to many flatterers and specialists in false optimism and deceit. . . .

Stalin's reluctance to consider life's realities and the fact that he was not aware of the real state of affairs in the provinces can be illustrated by his direction of agriculture.

All those who interested themselves even a little in the national situation saw the difficult situation in agriculture, but Stalin never even noted it. Did we tell Stalin about this? Yes, we told him, but he did not support us. Why? Because Stalin never traveled anywhere, did not meet city and collective farm workers; he did not know the actual situation in the provinces.

He knew the country and agriculture only from films. And these films had dressed up and beautified the existing situation in agriculture. Many films so pictured collective farm life that the tables were bending from the weight of turkeys and geese. Evidently, Stalin thought that it was actually so. . . .

If Stalin said anything, it meant that it was so—after all, he was a "genius" and a genius does not need to count. He only needs to look and can immediately tell how it should be. When he expresses his opinion, everyone has to repeat it and to admire his wisdom.[7]

The Soviet economists and economic administrators who became aware of this attack must have immediately realized that Khrushchev's speech opened the door to tremendous potential changes in the Soviet economic system. Stalin had largely fashioned that system as it existed in early 1956. If he had been as ignorant and as stupid about agriculture as Khrushchev claimed, how much wiser could he have been in other areas of the economy?

For the economists, the blow was particularly bitter. They had been accustomed for years to avoid any original ideas and to act only as sycophantic commentators on Stalin's various economic pronouncements. And they smarted too under the complaint voiced at the meeting by Anastas I. Mikoyan even before Khrushchev's secret speech. "We do not see any creative work from our economists," Mr. Mikoyan had declared. But Mikoyan's declaration had been softened by his declaration that the absence of useful economic research was explainable by the lack of economic data. His words clearly foreshadowed the end of much of traditional Soviet statistical secrecy. They were soon followed by a relative flood of statistical revelation which made it possible for the first time in a generation for rank and file Soviet citizens to discuss much of their country's economic life intelligently. The two steps, the assault on Stalin's authority and the decision to make public key statistical data, clearly opened the way for an era of fresh thinking, and even of possible major institutional innovation.

No less important was the enunciation of a series of new Soviet strategic principles in Khrushchev's public speech at the Congress. Here his aim was the modernization of Soviet policy to meet the problems of a world in which thermonuclear weapons existed. He junked the old Stalinist and Leninist assumption that world war between capitalism and communism was inevitable. Such war might come, he admitted, but it was not fatally inevitable. Communism could win the world without war, Khrushchev suggested, by defeating capitalism economically. He put the matter this way:

> When we say that the socialist system will win in the competition between the two systems—the capitalist and the socialist—this by no means signifies that its victory will be achieved through armed interference by the socialist countries in the internal affairs of capitalist nations. Our conviction of the victory of Communism derives from the fact that the socialist system of production is decisively superior to the capitalist system of production.[8]

This new line immediately introduced novel elements into Soviet policy formation. If world war was not inevitable—and Khrushchev hinted that it was probably quite unlikely—was it necessary to spend so much resources for military purposes? Would the interests of the Soviet Union and of Communism not be served better by diverting funds to more rapid expansion of the economy? And since Khrushchev argued that Soviet economic successes would capture the minds of people in the capitalist world, did that not imply that such capture would come about by improvements in the Soviet standard of living? A year earlier Khrushchev had defeated Malenkov by charging the latter was paying too much attention to Soviet consumers. Now he was obliquely introducing ideological grounds which could be used to revive Malenkov's ideas.

Other portions of the speech show clearly Khrushchev's effort to win public popularity by announcing the glad tidings of major concessions to the Soviet people. Thus he was able to announce that the minimum wages paid Soviet workers would be raised while reductions had been ordered in the "unjustifiably high wages" of the best paid. He was also able to announce that the existing 48 hour work week would be cut. The process would begin "soon," he said, with two hours taken off the Saturday work day. Later, he added, daily work hours would be reduced from eight to seven, all without any reduction in wages. The lowest pensions paid retired Soviet workers would be raised, he announced, while "unjustifiably high" pensions would be reduced. Finally came what many in his audience may have regarded as the most revolutionary proposal of all these measures: Khrushchev suggested that Soviet trade unions—long the most supine company unions in the world—begin to fight for the interests of their members. His words deserve to be recorded here:

> The quality of union work clearly lags behind life's needs . . . Our trade unions primarily lack militancy in their work. They need creative ardor, initiative, and adherence to principle in raising basic and vital questions about steps to raise labor productivity or, for example, matters of wages, housing and construction, of meeting the daily needs of workers and employes. Everyone knows that labor-management agreements are reached in the enterprises. But everywhere these contracts are not carried out, and the trade unions remain silent as though everything were in order. Generally the trade unions have stopped having disputes with the enterprise directors; peace and harmony reign supreme between them. However, though, one should not fear to spoil relations when the interests of the cause are involved. Sometimes it is even desirable to have a hard fight.[9]

There was method in what many of Khrushchev's auditors must have thought was madness. Khrushchev understood that the glaring weakness of the Soviet labor unions was that the Soviet workers did not regard them as their own organizations, but looked upon them as simply another bureaucratic device to make them work harder. If the unions could refashion their image so their members believed they really were helpful, then the unions could be more effective in achieving their historic prime function: helping raise labor productivity. Soviet unions improved somewhat thereafter, but they have never come near the militancy of a typical United States or Western European union.

Nominally the most important document emerging from this 20th Congress was the text of the new Sixth Five Year Plan designed to govern Soviet economic development during 1956–1960. This was an ambitious plan, aiming for a 60 per cent increase in national income and a 65 per cent increase in industrial output over the five year period, as well as a 30 per cent increase in real wages of workers and employes. This document need not concern us unduly here because it was officially abandoned by the Soviet regime in late 1957. We shall consider the causes of this abandonment later in this chapter.

The months that followed the 20th Congress saw a good deal accomplished to fulfill promises made or implied at that meeting. What some have called the liberation of the Soviet people from Stalinism began to take place. In popular Soviet parlance, the change was summed up in the saying: "Now our police work only the day shift." A decree of April 25, 1956 abolished the criminal responsibility and threat of imprisonment which had been held for almost fifteen years over workers leaving their jobs without permission, or failing to show up for work without an officially acceptable reason. There is reason to believe use of such criminal penalties against workers had largely or entirely ceased several years earlier, but there was at least great symbolic importance in the revocation of this obnoxious decree. Criminal responsibility was also removed from collective farmers who failed to work the required minimum number of days on the collective farm fields, from city workers who refused to be drafted for agricultural work, from hitchhikers on freight trains, from industrial executives and others who sold industrial equipment and materials illegally, and from transport workers guilty of violations of discipline. The process of releasing prisoners from slave labor camps was speeded up, and major changes were made in the whole system of prison labor. As a result, key economic and geo-graphic areas formerly worked almost entirely with prisoners had to convert to use of free laborers who had to be attracted by appropriate high wages and other benefits. Even consumers bene-fited as a decree of June 1956 gave them the right to return de-fective goods to stores.

The changes in hours, wages, and pensions promised by Khru-shchev also began to be put into effect. Thus several million workers had their earnings raised to the new monthly minima of 27 rubles in rural areas and 30 rubles in urban areas. Several million pensioners also benefited as minimum monthly pensions were raised to 22.5 rubles in rural areas and 30 rubles in towns. These minimum wages and pensions are equivalent to about $7–$8 a week. They had been much lower earlier. The maximum old age pension was lowered to 120 rubles a month. Finally on Sep-tember 1, 1956, a decree abolished all tuition charges in Soviet high schools, vocational schools, and higher educational institu-tions. Thus in a few months some of the worst or most resented features of the Stalinist system that limited ordinary Soviet citi-zens were either eliminated or eased.[10]

Welcome as these changes were, they did not, of course, sig-nify that the Soviet regime had become a welfare state or that it had fully given up its right to use coercive noneconomic measures against its citizens. Already in 1957 several Soviet republics began passing laws directed at "physically fit, adult citizens" convicted of leading an "antisocial, parasitic life," engaging in "malicious evasion of socially useful work," or living on "unearned income." The intended targets were persons who made their living pri-marily from some form of illegal private enterprise, as well as collective farm members who neglected their work on the social-ized fields and spent the bulk of their time tilling their small garden plots.[11] Punishment—usually deportation to forced labor colonies in remote areas for two to five years—could be inflicted after a "parasite" was found guilty by some local citizen group given authority in such matters. Later there was additional retro-gression, including the authorization of capital punishment for major economic crimes, such as large scale embezzlement, trade in precious metals and foreign currencies, and organization of substantial private commerce at inflated prices. In at least one major case, the death penalty was applied retroactively to defendants originally convicted before the new legislation took effect.

In spite of these measures, the greater attention to popular desires and grievances had not vanished by 1957. On the contrary, Kremlin sensitivity was probably greater than ever that year because of the lesson implicit in the Eastern European unrest late in 1956. The best proof of this was the greatly expanded housing construction program announced in mid-1957, a program aimed at easing one of the sorest afflictions of Soviet daily life. For the great mass of Soviet city dwellers in the mid-1950's, home was usually one room for an entire family. A typical four room apartment in a Soviet city would house four families in unpleasantly crowded conditions that frayed nerves, stimulated family discord and fights with neighbors, and generally cast grave doubt on all the official boasting about the great gains made by the Soviet people under the socialist system. The decree of July 31, 1957 faced directly up to the situation. It noted the rapid rise of population and the fact that the country's urban population had more than tripled in three decades, and declared, "the housing problem continues to be one of the most acute. The residents of many cities, workers' settlements and villages need good housing. Many families still live in dilapidated houses." The decree indicated the magnitude of the problem by declaring that even with a stepped-up program of construction the housing shortage could not be eliminated for ten or twelve years. As a first step it ordered an increase in housing construction, and backed that order up with a program for raising the production of construction materials and for increasing the efficiency of such construction. It also ordered that private housing construction be encouraged by loans and by more generous provision of materials.[12] More than words were involved in all this for Soviet housing construction—spurred on by the widespread introduction of standardized plans and pre-fabrication techniques—did increase sharply in the next few years, and the conditions in which an appreciable portion of the Soviet people live did improve somewhat. Western observers have often commented on the poor quality of this new construction. But to Soviet citizens the fact that millions of families are finally beginning to get their own small two room apartments and a measure of privacy seems often to outweigh dissatisfaction with the poor quality of building.

The actual data tell vividly the story of what happened to housing construction. The figures show the amount of urban housing completed annually, in millions of square meters: [13]

Year	Housing Built	Year	Housing Built
1953	30.8	1957	52.0
1954	32.6	1958	71.2
1955	33.4	1959	80.7
1956	41.0	1960	82.8

The zeal for reform and change in sensitive and important areas of Soviet life was apparent throughout the Soviet economy in this period. Let us see how this trend appeared in Soviet industry, and how it was applied to deal with the deficiencies inherited from the Stalin era and with new problems that had arisen.

As early as the summer of 1955, the new Soviet leaders had completed a comprehensive study of their industry's operations. In this study they had paid much attention to comparing Soviet practices and technology with the practices and technology prevailing abroad. The first of what later became a flood of delegations of technicians had been sent to Western countries to gather data for comparison. It seems clear that the Soviet leadership was well aware that for many years the bulk of its managerial and administrative apparatus had been cut off from information about trends in foreign industry, and had been misled by Stalinist propaganda about the "superiority" of everything Soviet and the "bourgeois degeneration" of everything in the West.

The speech Premier Nikolai A. Bulganin delivered to the Communist party Central Committee meeting of July 1955 made clear that the leadership was deeply unhappy about the state of Soviet industry. Much of the speech was a scathing indictment of that industry's technological stagnation and backwardness. Some Soviet machine tool plants, Bulganin reported, were turning out equipment with cutting speeds only a third of those in similar foreign makes. Much Soviet machinery was heavier than comparable foreign models, he declared, and Soviet trucks and automobiles were inferior in economy of fuel consumption, performance, and speed to foreign vehicles. He charged the Ministry of Machinery and Instruments with being devoted largely to the production of "obsolete technical machinery," because it was afraid of the hard work and difficulties involved in producing new models. He accused those who refused to pay attention to foreign advances of "conceit" and arrogance, and demanded that "everything new in world science and technology must be under constant study."

Nor was Bulganin happier when he turned to other aspects of Soviet industry. He assailed the lack of specialization, asserting that some key plants were really "universal production factories." As an example he cited the Gorky automobile plant which produced, in addition to motor vehicles, such other products as bicycles, machine tools, welding equipment, farm machinery, small electrical apparatus, and even tens of thousands of oil cans monthly. Such a motley range of output clearly made it difficult or impossible to introduce cost cutting assembly line methods and automatic production equipment. Bulganin was furious about the widespread use of manual labor, pointing out that 69 per cent of all work in construction, 68 per cent in the lumber industry, 44 per cent in the coal industry, and 35 per cent in the iron and steel industry was done by hand workers. Making the situation worse, he pointed out, was the fact that a large fraction of available machinery was not used. More than one billion rubles' worth of idle equipment existed at the beginning of 1955, he declared, adding that in the coal industry one-third of the most complex machinery was not in use. The Soviet industrial wage system was thoroughly disorganized, he charged, leading to great inequality in the earnings of workers doing the same jobs in different plants. And the poor housing and living conditions in many areas, he asserted, had resulted in very great labor turnover. In 1954, he reported, more than 4,200,000 industrial and construction workers had quit their jobs. Since there were less than 20,000,000 workers in these two categories in 1954, Bulganin's data implied an annual labor turnover of more than 20 per cent.[14]

As was customary in such matters, Bulganin had concentrated on the negative aspects of Soviet industry in order to apply pressure for improvement. There was another side of the story, too. The West was to learn two years later, for example, how far ahead the Soviet Union was in rocket technology. Some visiting American industrial delegations—notably that representing the steel industry—discovered soon afterward that there were branches of industrial technology in which even the United States could learn from Moscow. Nor was Bulganin's address without fruit. A few years after he spoke, the West found that the Soviet Union had set up the most elaborate organization in the world to monitor all foreign progress in science and technology. Specific measures ordered in the light of the ills Bulganin recounted—for example, a new system of bank credits to help finance the introduction of improved technology—also helped many branches of Soviet industry to improve. In the years after Bulganin spoke, too, a comprehensive reorganization of the Soviet wage system was carried out, one aimed at simplifying its structure and bringing order out of the chaos the Soviet Premier had described. But even almost a decade after his comprehensive review, many of the problems he referred to still plague Soviet industry and are still the subjects of repeated official complaint. Fundamentally many of the ills of Soviet industry arise from the absence of the kind of competition which forces the Western industrialist to be alert to technical improvements and cost-cutting innovations, as well as to the development of new materials and new products that can be sold profitably. Experience has shown that in most industries Soviet leaders' exhortations are a poor substitute for the whip of competition.

At the 20th Communist party Congress, the subject of Soviet technical backwardness was still very much on the agenda, and the usefulness of having the United States and Western Europe available for comparison was again evident. Khrushchev's main report attacked the transportation authorities for their devotion to steam locomotives and their neglect of more economical electric and diesel traction power for railroads. He announced an ambitious program aimed at electrifying some 24,000 miles of Soviet rail line over a period of fifteen years, and an accompanying program for replacing steam locomotives by diesel and electric locomotives. Bulganin at the same meeting emphasized the importance of the decision to shift the fuel economy of the country from primary reliance on coal to stress on oil and gas as the future chief sources of energy. He also announced the government decision to build a large network of oil pipelines. Later Soviet discussions made clear that these shifts of policy were inspired largely by study of Western experience.

The Sixth Five Year Plan for 1956–1960 embodied these and

other decisions. Its section on industrial goals suggested a compromise solution had been reached on the issue of heavy versus consumer goods industry. As against a total five year industrial output expansion goal of 65 per cent, it called for a 70 per cent heavy industry production increase and a 60 per cent rise in consumer goods output. This plan's most spectacular feature was a provision calling for the Soviet Union to seize world leadership in atomic power. By 1960, the plan provided, the Soviet Union was to have atomic power generating capacity of between 2,000,-000 and 2,500,000 kilowatts, or much more than the rest of the world combined was likely to have by that time. In this and other respects the document exemplified its guiding principle, the belief stated in its preface that "the Soviet land now has all the requisites necessary for solving, through peaceful economic competition and in an historically short time, the U.S.S.R.'s principal economic task—to overtake and surpass the most highly developed capitalist countries in per capita output."

As 1956 progressed, the Soviet economy seemed to be going smoothly. Such attention as it got from the outside world was usually provoked by positive phenomena like the news of action designed to implement the promised increases in minimum wages and the reductions in working hours. But political events soon overshadowed economic developments as the world learned the contents of Khrushchev's originally secret denunciation of Stalin. The train of events set off by the speech culminated in the Hungarian Revolution and its violent repression by the Soviet Army. After the Eastern European unrest had been quelled, some Western economists began to calculate the substantial cost to the Soviet economy of the emergency aid provided to the Kadar regime in Hungary and of the concessions that were being made to other Eastern European countries to appease discontent there. But few if any in the West were prepared for the thunderclap of Christmas Day, 1956: Soviet publication of news equivalent to admission that the Sixth Five Year Plan was in serious trouble.

A closed meeting of the Central Committee had taken place, the Soviet press reported, and had decided questions regarding the alteration of the Sixth Five Year Plan in order to make its goals "more specific." The changes in production targets decided at this meeting sought "to eliminate excess strain in the plan for some industries and to bring production goals and the volume of capital investment into line with material resources." The Central Committee resolution instructed those assigned to "complete" the plan "to reduce the volume of capital investments and to make the lists of construction projects more specific with a view toward reducing their number, primarily at the expense of new construction projects; to prevent the dispersal of funds over a large number of construction projects by concentrating material and funds at major construction projects and installations ready to go into operation . . . to revise the plan targets for individual industries which have not been supplied with sufficient materials . . ."[15]

In a public lecture the following summer, a Soviet economist, I. A. Kulev, told part of what had happened behind the scenes at this meeting: the Central Committee had met and been informed it faced a major capital investment crisis. To fulfill the goals of the Sixth Five Year Plan, Soviet economic administrators had presented requests for capital investment allocations totalling 24,000,000,000 rubles for 1957 and over 136,000,000,000 rubles for the entire 1956–1960 period. But the original plan had only allocated 17,000,000,000 rubles for 1957 and only 99,000,000,000 rubles for the entire period. The Central Committee was also informed that some 4,000 major investment projects were under way in the country as a whole, and that many new ones had been started in 1956 despite the fact that large numbers of old ones were still unfinished. Finally the Central Committee heard that some of the newest industrial plants in the country had some of the highest production costs in the land and were showing huge losses. Unable to revise the plan because of inadequate data, Mr. Kulev said, the Central Committee decided to order retrenchment in capital construction and to launch an investigation that uncovered large scale waste throughout the economy.[16] Most important, the Central Committee made Mikhail G. Pervukhin virtual dictator of the Soviet economy, naming him head of the State Economic Commission for Current Planning of the National Economy. This agency was assigned "the function of operative solution of current problems connected with fulfillment of the state plan and responsibility for seeing to it that the necessary material resources are provided for assignments envisaged in the plan." The naming of a group of leading Soviet economic

administrators to assist Pervukhin emphasized the importance of
his assignment.

This was of course not the first capital investment crisis the
Soviet government had ever encountered. Time and again in the
1930's resources were not adequate to meet all goals of the five
year plans of that period. But under Stalin the solution had been
simple: resources had simply been diverted away from housing
or consumer goods expansion and concentrated primarily on increasing heavy industry production. But in the post-Stalin era
such a simple solution was no longer possible, especially after the
warning the Hungarian Revolution had given of what popular
discontent could produce. Now heavy industry also had to share
in the needed cutbacks.

Before concluding this discussion, we should note one feature
of this December 1956 crisis meeting: the complete lack of reference in the official statements to Communist party First Secretary
Nikita S. Khrushchev. Had he urged an alternative solution for
these problems and been defeated? Was an attempt under way to
try to make him the scapegoat for the bad planning which had
brought on the crisis? Was this temporary obscurity of the ebullient Khrushchev the result of responsibility attached to him for
the Hungarian Revolution? Subsequent events suggested that if
we knew all the facts we would answer at least some of these
questions positively.

Less than two months later, in mid-February 1957, there came
more astonishing news. Another Central Committee meeting had
been held, this one addressed by Khrushchev, who had spoken on
needed reorganization of industry and agriculture. He had found
a new culprit for the economy's problems: the system of centralized ministries which directed most of the economy. The
Central Committee resolution, adopted after Khrushchev spoke,
accused the ministries of taking a narrow departmental view of
economic activity, and thereby of weakening the links connect-
ing different branches of the economy throughout the country.
The ministries' mode of operation was said to have produced
great waste of resources, the build-up of parallel bureaucratic
structures, incomplete utilization of existing productive facilities,
irrational hauling and cross-hauling of freight, and a series of
other economic losses. To eliminate these weaknesses, the Central
Committee ordered a major reorganization to bring economic

administration closer to the grass roots in each major area of the country through a partial decentralization of authority.

A striking result of this meeting was the reversal of the December 1956 decision to concentrate enormous economic authority in the State Economic Commission. Now the Central Committee called for a reorganization of that body "to simplify its structure and make it less unwieldy." The Commission was told it must not duplicate the work of the State Planning Committee or other groups and it must "not interfere in the functioning of administrative bodies."[17] The shift was most drastic, indicating that a bitter political struggle had taken place. In December Premier Bulganin and the professional managers of the Soviet economy had been on top, and their proposed solution had been to strengthen the centralized powers in their hands. In February, the evidence suggests, Khrushchev, then only First Secretary of the party, and the regional party bosses had won a victory: if economic organization were decentralized, then in each region economic administrators would have less influence than party chiefs in the same area. Two years later Mikhail G. Pervukhin, whose tenure as head of the State Economic Commission and tsar of the Soviet economy was cut short by the February 1957 reversal, admitted he had opposed the reorganization. "My erroneous position in this very important matter and my discontent led me to commit a major political mistake," he said, revealing he had supported the unsuccessful plot in June 1957 to purge Khrushchev from his post as party First Secretary.[18]

The case made by those who opposed the industrial administration reform was summarized in December 1958 by N. A. Bulganin in the course of a speech confessing his sins in opposing Khrushchev:

> I well recall the fierce fight conducted by Molotov, Kaganovich, Malenkov and Shepilov against the reorganization of the management of industry and construction, against widening the powers of the republics and of local party and government agencies. These proposals were raised in the central committee by Comrade Khrushchev. Wasn't this the reason that Malenkov, Kaganovich and Shepilov opposed these ideas? Because of this fact they had no wish even to hear about these proposals. Then Molotov, Malenkov, Kaganovich and Shepilov asserted that there would be anarchy in the administration of industry

and construction. They even claimed that widening the powers of the republic and of local party and state agencies and particularly granting planning powers to the republics and shifting to them some of the functions of the State Planning Committee would contradict Lenin.[19]

The differences in the top leadership about this idea created conditions in which it was possible for a vast public "discussion" about the proposed reorganization to take place during March and April 1957. Numerous articles exposed the inefficiencies and irrationalities of the existing system. They emphasized the frequency with which decisions were taken from the point of view of one or another ministry's advantage with little or no regard for the national interest. A typical account told of a river which had two fleets of steamers on it, each owned by a different ministry. Because of the peculiarity of each ministry's interests, one fleet of steamers sailed loaded up the river and empty down the river; the other fleet sailed empty up the river and loaded down the river.[20] Typical of these accounts was the tale Khrushchev told the Supreme Soviet in May of the situation in Krasnoyarsk territory to which some ministries were sending prefabricated houses from distant points of manufacture. At the same time other ministries were manufacturing similar prefabricated houses in Krasnoyarsk and exporting them to distant points.[21]

The decision finally taken by the Supreme Soviet in May 1957 represented a major victory for Khrushchev. It was the most radical reorganization of Soviet economic administration since before World War II. Some 25 major economic ministries were simply abolished; the few economic ministries that survived were mainly engaged in the production of military equipment. A network of 105 regional economic units directed by Councils of the National Economy or *sovnarkhozy* was set up; in most cases a separate *sovnarkhoz* was created for each province. In each of the 15 republics of the Soviet Union, the regional *sovnarkhozy* were made subordinate to the republic authorities, and each republic's Council of Ministers supervised its *sovnarkhozy*. At the national level, coordination was placed in the hands of the State Planning Committee (*Gosplan*), which was charged with current and long term planning, with working out a unified and centralized economic development policy for the country as a whole, and with

ORGANIZATION OF THE VOLGA-VYATSK NATIONAL ECONOMIC
COUNCIL AS OF EARLY 1964.

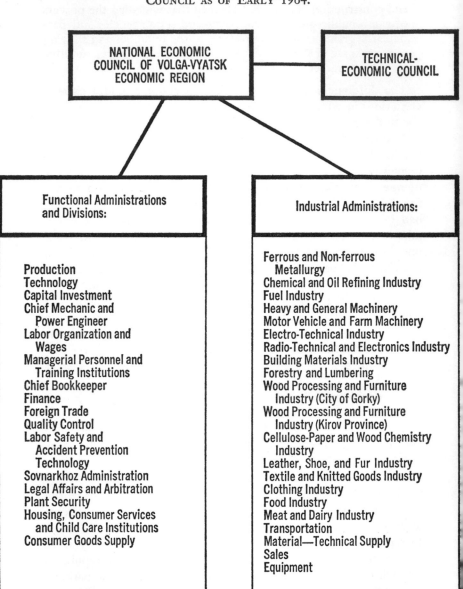

NATIONAL ECONOMIC
COUNCIL OF VOLGA-VYATSK
ECONOMIC REGION

TECHNICAL-
ECONOMIC COUNCIL

Functional Administrations and Divisions:

Production
Technology
Capital Investment
Chief Mechanic and
  Power Engineer
Labor Organization and
  Wages
Managerial Personnel and
  Training Institutions
Chief Bookkeeper
Finance
Foreign Trade
Quality Control
Labor Safety and
  Accident Prevention
  Technology
Sovnarkhoz Administration
Legal Affairs and Arbitration
Plant Security
Housing, Consumer Services
  and Child Care Institutions
Consumer Goods Supply

Industrial Administrations:

Ferrous and Non-ferrous
  Metallurgy
Chemical and Oil Refining Industry
Fuel Industry
Heavy and General Machinery
Motor Vehicle and Farm Machinery
Electro-Technical Industry
Radio-Technical and Electronics Industry
Building Materials Industry
Forestry and Lumbering
Wood Processing and Furniture
  Industry (City of Gorky)
Wood Processing and Furniture
  Industry (Kirov Province)
Cellulose-Paper and Wood Chemistry
  Industry
Leather, Shoe, and Fur Industry
Textile and Knitted Goods Industry
Clothing Industry
Food Industry
Meat and Dairy Industry
Transportation
Material—Technical Supply
Sales
Equipment

over-all responsibility for planning and supervising the whole industrial supply system of the nation. The State Economic Commission, which had ridden so high six months earlier, was simply abolished.[22]

It may help to understand the extent of the administrative revolution which had taken place if the change is stated in American terms. Such major industrial corporations as General Motors, Westinghouse, General Electric, Ford Motor Company, General Foods, Dow Chemical Company, and DuPont operate plants in many different states. Each company ultimately controls all its activities from a single center. If we regard these as the closest American analogues of the Soviet ministries, we have to think next of having all these major corporations abolished and all their plants in each state, New York or California or Texas, put under the control of state boards with wide ranging powers to control the activities of the many varied enterprises (local plants of General Motors, Westinghouse, General Electric, etc.) made subordinate to them. To go back to Soviet terms, the initial result was that 105 new economic governing bodies were set up, each charged with guidance and direction of a combination of the most varied enterprises within its geographic area. Each *sovnarkhoz* could combine organizations or separate them, redistribute functions and equipment among different plants, hire and fire executive personnel. Each *sovnarkhoz* had a chairman responsible for its activities but under him there was a more or less complex organization (depending upon the number and variety of plants in the area ruled by the *sovnarkhoz* in question) to provide detailed supervision and control. This revolutionary shift involved a violent upheaval for thousands of Soviet ministerial executives who had been accustomed to live and work in Moscow or in the capitals of other republics. With the abolition of the ministries, their jobs were gone and they had usually to accept reassignment to a *sovnarkhoz* or plant somewhere in the provinces. For many it was a most unpleasant readjustment.

Even before this administrative revolution had been approved, Khrushchev foresaw that new problems might arise with the new organization, problems summarized by the Russian word *mestnichestvo* (localism). Khrushchev stated these forebodings as he presented his radical proposal to the Supreme Soviet:

It may be that there will arise tendencies toward autarchy based on a desire to build a closed economy within a province or republic. This possibility is not without basis and must not be forgotten. Localistic tendencies may show themselves in efforts to develop raw material bases on the site of natural deposits whose exploitation may be less profitable than similar deposits elsewhere, or in a desire to have within a region the production of various equipment and auxiliary items that could more advantageously be produced in another region's specialized plants . . . Some workers in a particular area may try to use for the satisfaction of local needs more resources than the state can allocate for that purpose, thus harming industrial development important to the nation as a whole . . . The State Planning Committee must carefully study the economic wisdom of the capital investments planned by the regions and fight any efforts to employ funds contrary to state interests by those wishing to build up an autarchic economy in a particular area.[23]

Khrushchev was warning that, if improperly handled, the new organization might simply result in the exchange of one set of problems for another. The weaknesses exposed in the ministerial system arose in general because each ministry had tended to put its own interests first, to seek self-sufficiency for its own branch of the economy. Might not each region behave similarly, with similar detriment to the national interest as many different areas each sought territorial self-sufficiency? The most obvious danger was that factories in each economic district might favor customers under the same *sovnarkhoz,* and make "foreign" enterprises suffer the brunt of any shortfalls in production. Any major tendency toward such behavior could badly disrupt the national economy. In April 1958, less than a year after the new organization had gone into effect, enough disturbing incidents of this sort had occurred to persuade the government to issue a decree providing criminal penalties for officials engaging in this particular variety of *mestnichestvo.*[24]

A few months later the Central Committee angrily denounced another form of localism. Some directors of *sovnarkhozy* were diverting capital funds made available for major industrial investment projects and using these funds for local needs instead. In Karaganda province, for example, the *sovnarkhoz* chairman, a Comrade Onika, had taken funds away from a major iron and steel combine project and employed them to build a circus, a dramatic theatre, rest homes, two swimming pools, and similar non-productive installations. Continuation of such practices, the Central Committee, declared, "can disorganize our planned socialist economy."[25]

The sensitivity to the question of capital investment revealed in this Central Committee decision reflected the continued pressure of the discrepancy between all the things the Soviet regime wanted to do and the resources it had available to do them with. A price was paid in 1957 for the hurried and forced revision of economic plans to cope with the problems revealed at the December 1956 plenum. The price was a dramatic drop in the rates of growth of some key commodities. The continuing shortage of capital made it impossible to raise all these declining rates even in 1958. The slowdown which occurred is shown in Table 11.

Table 11. ANNUAL PERCENTAGE INCREASES IN
PRODUCTION OF SOME MAJOR
COMMODITIES, 1955–1958

Commodity	1955	1956	1957	1958
Pig iron	11	7	4	7
Steel	9	7	5	7
Coal	13	10	8	7
Electricity	13	13	9	11
Sulphuric acid	15	14	6	5
Mineral fertilizers	20	13	8	5

SOURCE: Official annual Soviet economic reports.

The 1957 slowdown in production of the key items shown above, as well as the continuing capital shortage, made it clear that the Sixth Five Year Plan could not be fulfilled. The decision to abandon that plan and to order the preparation of a longer range Seven Year Plan for 1959–1965 was finally made public in September 1957. The announcement revealed that a revised Sixth Five Year Plan had been submitted to the government by the *Gosplan* during the previous April, but that this revision was rejected because in it "there were not provided sufficient measures for the quickest liquidation of existing disproportions in the national economy, there was still not guaranteed the necessary concentration of capital construction, and also measures for exploiting the natural wealth of the country's eastern regions were not sufficiently worked out." Soviet geologists had discovered great new sources of raw materials and power in recent years, the announcement declared, and these could be used to create great new enterprises and industrial centers which the Sixth Five Year Plan had not provided for. But it would take five to seven years to complete these great new tasks, and hence a seven year plan was advisable.[26] It was all an object lesson in how to turn a real setback into an apparent victory.

Earlier that same year, however, the Soviet people had gotten a broad hint of the capital investment problems of the Soviet regime in an area that affected them immediately: the purchase of state bonds. In the preceding chapter we noted that one of the early post-Stalin concessions of 1953 had been to halve the amount of bond purchases required of the population. The diminution continued in 1954, but in 1955 and 1956 the concession was withdrawn. In the latter year, the total of bonds purchased soared to 3,400,000,000 rubles, suggesting compulsion had been stepped up. As Khrushchev explained at several public meetings in the spring of 1957, the Soviet regime's outstanding indebtedness had reached 26,000,000,000 rubles, and the annual cost of interest and bond redemption was climbing toward 2,000,000,000 rubles. Thus the net gain from forced bond sales was declining. The bonds themselves were, of course, very unpopular with Soviet workers who could think of many uses for the money taken from their pay. Khrushchev put a proposition to the workers in several audiences: would they accept a 20 year postponement, without interest, of repayment of the bonds already outstanding if the forced bond purchases were drastically reduced in 1957 and ended thereafter? According to the Soviet press, those asked the question roared their approval. Soon afterward the corresponding decree was issued. For all practical purposes this was, of course, a complete repudiation by the Soviet state of its indebtedness to its people. One Western observer has estimated that the average Soviet family at the time owned bonds with a face value of 600 or 700 rubles, an amount equal to roughly half its annual income.[27]

Khrushchev could, however, emphasize the positive addressing the Moscow celebration of the 40th anniversary of the Bolshevik

Revolution in November 1957, shortly after the first sputnik flew
into orbit. The Soviet Union had enormous natural resources, he
boasted. The newly opened iron ore deposits of the Kursk Magnetic Anomaly near Moscow would provide iron ore for cen-
turies; in Siberia large deposits of diamonds, tin, molybdenum,
gold, iron ore, and other minerals had been discovered; in
Kazakhstan geologists had found "enormous deposits of iron ore,
coal, chrome ores, high quality bauxites, all kinds of nonferrous
and rare metals and many other mineral raw materials"; in the
Ukraine major new sources of coal and natural gas had been
located. The Soviet Union was still behind the United States,
Khrushchev admitted, and then added, "At the same time, it
should be said that now the level of production in the United
States is no longer beyond our reach as it may have seemed to
some people 25 or 30 years ago." To buttress his point he gave
these figures on Soviet 1957 output of some key commodities and
the Soviet production levels he anticipated for 1972:

Table 12. PRODUCTION OF SOME MAJOR
COMMODITIES, 1957, AND 1972 GOALS

Commodity	Unit	1957	1972 Goal
Steel	million metric tons	51	100–120
Coal	million metric tons	462	650–750
Oil	million metric tons	98	350–400
Electricity	billion kilowatt-hours	210	800–900
Cement	million metric tons	29	90–110
Leather shoes	million pair	315	600–700

SOURCE: *Pravda*, November 7, 1957.

But the problem of capital had not been forgotten by any
means. Soviet economists were working intensively on the question of how to use capital most efficiently. They could not openly
use the concept of the rate of interest to measure the differential
profitability of alternative investments because Marxist economic
theory sees all value coming from labor alone and regards interest
on capital as illegitimate. But they could and did get around the
problem by using a related concept, that of measuring the recoupment period. Faced by alternative proposals for a given capital
investment, they could calculate the number of years necessary

for the additional value of output or the savings in production cost to recover or recoup the total investment. The alternative with the shortest expected recoupment period—or pay-off period as American businessmen might call it—was best. But one had simply to take the reciprocal of the recoupment period to get a "coefficient of capital effectiveness" which was not too dissimilar in concept from rate of interest.[28]

Khrushchev himself gave this trend toward greater rationality in capital investment a major boost in August 1958, when he opened the world's largest hydroelectric station in Kuibyshev province. His audience probably expected him to boast about another "victory" over capitalism. Instead, he hinted that the building of this huge installation—spread over seven years—might have been a mistake. He concentrated on the element of time, on the need to use resources so that investments would produce results as soon as possible.

In a capitalist economy the factor of time is taken into account by means of the interest charge on capital, a charge that clearly reflects the cost of tying up resources for a long time in a complex project such as a hydroelectric plant. Soviet calculations of cost do not include an explicit interest charge. This omission results in a systematic bias in cost calculation that makes Soviet economists and planners underestimate the real cost of production of goods which require heavy capital investment. The true interest cost is particularly high in the Soviet Union because of its chronic acute capital shortage. Khrushchev's speech at the Kuibyshev Dam—and a speech later that month in Smolensk, from which we quote below—was historic because he recognized the economic importance of the factor of time in a way that produced conclusions not unlike those that would have been arrived at if an interest charge on investment had been employed. Here is Khrushchev's position:

> The need arises to postpone a bit the schedule for hydroelectric station construction. Why? These stations now being built need a great deal of labor, time and money. Once a hydroelectric station is completed, it yields only profits because it can be operated cheaply. But the time factor must be considered. We must gain time in the competition with capitalism so as to overtake the United States in per capita output as soon as possible.

We built the 2,300,000 kilowatt Lenin Volga Hydroelectric Station in seven years. . . . But with the same money we could have built in less time several thermal power plants with a total capacity of 11,000,000 kilowatts. True, the electricity of thermal power plants will cost more, but on the other hand these plants will supply power to our factories much earlier; we will expand output and lower costs, thus compensating for the higher cost per unit of electricity.[29]

Khrushchev's words caused a sensation. The supporters of hydroelectric power counterattacked vigorously, with the result that the cutback in hydroelectric power station construction was not as large as Khrushchev apparently had intended. But the significant point is that the Soviet leader was calling for the introduction of the time factor into Soviet cost calculations. If he had been able to use a rate of interest concept, he could have presented his point more clearly. He could have argued that if interest costs on capital were taken into account, then at least some Soviet hydroelectric plants generated electricity more expensively than thermal plants. These considerations, of course, applied also to atomic power plants. At that time these also offered seemingly attractive low costs of power generation, if interest costs were ignored. It is not surprising, in view of Khrushchev's speeches at Kuibyshev and Smolensk, that in this period the boasting about ambitious Soviet plans for world leadership in atomic power by 1960 also ceased. The whole program for building 2,000,000–2,500,000 kilowatts of atomic power capacity by that year was quietly reduced very drastically. In the mid-1960's, realization of that target is still distant.

Khrushchev was particularly anxious for the most economical and most rational use of capital because by that time he knew that one of his boldest gambits to ease the capital shortage had failed—a formal, public request to the United States for a large loan.

The Soviet leaders realized that their country was far behind the West in the field of chemical production, particularly in the output of synthetic fibers, plastics, and synthetic resins. Even before World War II, the Soviet Union had been a world pioneer and leader in synthetic rubber production because of the material's key importance for military purposes. The motivation had been Stalin's fear that his country might be cut off from all natural rubber imports in the event of war. But many other chemical products—plastics, fibers, and the like—were used primarily in clothing, footwear, and other consumer goods that did not rank high in the Stalinist scale of values, and therefore got little attention. But by May 1958, Khrushchev was ready to call for a major effort in the chemical field. Chemical output had enjoyed so little prominence up to that time that Khrushchev, in addressing the Central Committee, felt he had to explain elementary concepts in chemistry to his audience. He emphasized how backward the Soviet Union was in the field of petro-chemicals and the opportunity that existed for expanding this field because of the increasing availability of Soviet oil and gas. The Central Committee approved the plan. It adopted a resolution calling for building capacity to increase output of artificial and synthetic fibers 4.6 times by 1965 over 1957, to raise production of plastics and synthetic resins eight times in the same period, and to multiply the amount of synthetic rubber turned out annually by 3.4 times. This would make possible, the Central Committee told the Soviet people, production of greatly expanded quantities of textiles made of synthetic fibers, of almost 100,000,000 pair of shoes made with artificial leather, and of large amounts of other needed consumer goods. Khrushchev explained in his speech that this program would require the building or expansion of 257 enterprises at a capital investment of more than 10,000,000,000 rubles. Khrushchev indicated he looked forward to getting substantial aid, on commercial terms, from the United States, West Germany, and Britain. He recalled nostalgically that "before the war we had good relations with American industrialists, such as Ford, and with such big American companies as General Electric and International Harvester."[30]

A month later Khrushchev made clear what he had in mind. He sent a letter to President Eisenhower suggesting that the Soviet Union would like to buy billions of dollars' worth of American machinery to help realize its chemical program and also to build up a whole series of Soviet consumer goods industries. The Soviet Union could pay by shipping raw materials, he wrote, but it might take time to build up sales of Soviet goods in the United States. He declared that American firms were interested in getting Soviet orders immediately, and that the Soviet Union was therefore prepared "in the first years to buy more American goods than we sell of our own. In this connection, in particular, the question arises of possible time payments and the granting of long term credits on customary terms."[31]

This request for American credits came at a time when American public opinion was still in a cold war mood, when Americans were still outraged at the brutal, bloody suppression of the Hungarian Revolution by Soviet troops. One can only wonder how Khrushchev could have been so ill-advised as to believe he might get such credits. The one clue here is the fact that in the first months of 1958 United States industrial production was declining. Khrushchev may have thought that the long hoped for (in Moscow, at any rate) American depression had arrived, a depression that would make the United States eager to get Soviet orders even at the price of extending credits. When President Eisenhower corrected Premier Khrushchev's misconception, it is not surprising that Khrushchev thought of saving capital by shifting from very expensive hydroelectric to relatively cheaper thermal power stations.

But even with the pressure of the capital shortage, one area could not be tampered with: housing. But where was the requisite capital to be found? One answer was given by a decree issued in October 1958. This in effect reversed a policy Stalin had followed when he built the elaborate Moscow subway before World War II and the expensive Moscow skyscrapers in the years just before his death, giving priority to show projects over badly needed housing. This new decree ordered that plans to build expensive administrative buildings, stadiums, palaces of culture, dachas, circuses, clubs, swimming pools, and the like be suspended wherever possible and the funds diverted to building houses, schools, hospitals, and children's institutions. The decree accused bureaucrats of putting on airs: "Excessively large offices, reception rooms and conference rooms are being permitted in administrative buildings, and there are also excesses in decorating them with costly furniture, television sets, radios, and similar equipment." *Pravda* complained that in the city of Vladimir the authorities in charge of junk collection were putting up a building for which they had no real need, that the officials of the Mordvinian *sovnarkhoz* were building summer homes for themselves with money allocated for public housing construction, and that authorities in Baku were building a luxurious new theater at a cost of 1,500,000 rubles though existing theaters were adequate.[32]

Along with problems of capital investment, Soviet leaders dealt during this period with many problems connected with their labor force. The rise in labor productivity was a constant preoccupation, as was the effort to assure an adequate number of workers for the growing complex of factories, mines, stores, transport facilities, and other installations being created. We have already noted the changes made in 1956 when the old laws providing criminal penalties to freeze workers in their jobs were revoked, minimum wages and pensions were raised, and a beginning was made in shortening the work week. All through 1957 and 1958, decrees were issued shifting particular industries from an eight to a seven hour work day, a figure reduced to six hours for workers in underground or especially hazardous occupations. The basic six-day work week was retained, however.

In this period, too, the State Committee on Labor and Wages made substantial progress toward a massive reform of the whole Soviet wage system. The former departmental and ministerial organization of the Soviet economy had spawned literally thousands of wage scales in different factories and industries; as a result, many workers doing the same work received different levels of wages. Also, in many cases basic wage rates had not been altered for years, despite the general inflation of prices since the early years of Soviet industrialization. To assure workers of wages they would accept, therefore, the practice became widespread of setting low work norms so that large bonuses could be paid for overfulfilling those norms. As a result, it was commonplace in many Soviet factories for base wages to account for only 30–40 per cent of workers' normal monthly earnings. The reform begun in the mid-1950's and continued into the early 1960's sought to simplify this complex structure, to replace the many existing wage structures by a small number, and to raise basic wage rates so they would account for the bulk of earnings. One important goal was to assure so far as possible that workers of a given occupation could receive the same wages regardless of where they were employed. The policy makers tried, too, to narrow the spread between the lowest and highest wage rates, to link the wage reform and its increased basic wage rates with a system of higher work norms, and, in most cases, to set up wage structures with only six grades.

Workers in the most important industries were to be paid higher wages and workers laboring under difficult or harmful conditions were to receive favorable differentials. In the Soviet machinery industries for example, two wage structures were set up.

The more generous pay scale was established for the aviation, motor vehicle, electronics, and related priority industries and the less generous for lower priority branches. For those working under ordinary conditions, wages in the first group of industries ranged from 27.5 to 55 kopeks an hour, and in the second group of industries from 26.3 to 52.6 kopeks per hour. For workers laboring under especially difficult or harmful conditions, wages in the first group of industries ranged from 39 to 78 kopeks an hour; in the second group of industries from 37.8 to 75.6 kopeks an hour.[33]

In the mid-1950's, to recapitulate, Soviet workers' earnings were influenced mainly by three factors: the first was the effort to raise the wages of the lowest paid workers; the second was the wage reform which sought, among other goals, to make the wage system more effective in providing the needed incentives for higher worker productivity; and the third was the steady rise in labor productivity which tended in turn to be reflected in earnings. The combined upward influence of these factors on money earnings is illustrated by the following estimates of industrial workers' average annual incomes:[34]

Year	Earnings (rubles)	Year	Earnings (rubles)
1950	925	1957	1100
1953	971	1958	1130
1954	1010	1959	1160
1955	1020	1960	1190
1956	1040	1961	1240

These data, however, do not show the average earnings of all Soviet workers, since they exclude workers in agriculture, trade, and other nonindustrial branches of the economy. Average earn-

ings for government employes during these years were well below the industrial workers' averages shown above. Action to
rectify this inequity by raising the wages of such government
workers as teachers, doctors, and store clerks, among others, was
not announced until mid-1964, while much of its implementation
was scheduled for 1965.

Soviet trade unions began to receive increased attention, too,
in this period. After the reorganization of the industrial administration in the spring of 1957, the trade unions themselves were
reorganized. Formerly there had been a large number of unions,
essentially one for the workers in each ministry. Now, with the
ministries abolished and the emphasis placed upon more local
administration through the *sovnarkhozy* in each area, the formerly large number of unions was drastically reduced through a
process of consolidation. New emphasis was placed upon the
activities of local, territorial trade union bodies.[35]

More important, action was taken in the spirit of Khrushchev's
words at the 20th party Congress urging the unions to be more
active in defending their members' rights and in enforcing those
rights under the collective agreements. A Central Committee
meeting in late 1957 examined the situation and ordered two
major changes: an expansion of the powers of the local union
factory committee in each enterprise and the establishment in
each enterprise of a permanent production conference empowered to exert worker influence upon the management of the
plant. These reforms did not—and were not intended to—make
Soviet unions all-out defenders of their members' interests against
management, as they are in capitalist nations. Nor were the
permanent production conferences intended to exert the kind of
direct and major influence upon enterprise administration that, in
theory at least, workers' councils exercise in Yugoslavia. Nevertheless, these moves were intended to change the situation from
Stalin's day, improving the usefulness of the unions by increasing
their prestige.

The Central Committee resolution was not as openly critical of
the supine nature of Soviet unions as Khrushchev had been, but
it did note that unions suffered from "violations of democracy
and of the norms of trade union life." It assailed the trade unions'
practice of meeting irregularly and their lack of interest in pro-
moting to responsible union posts "young, energetic workers

who have proven themselves in production and in social life and who have the confidence of the workers."

The resolution also gave some indication of the kinds of abuses that were rampant because of the unions' weaknesses:

> . . . some managers care little about improving the laborer's working conditions, are allowing violations of labor laws, and are not fully utilizing the resources available for improving working conditions. At some enterprises no proper struggle is conducted for observance of labor safety laws, machinery is not properly shielded, and ventilation is poor. There are many instances in which factories and shops are put into operation with serious deficiencies in safety devices and with sanitary facilities lacking. There are serious deficiencies in the supply of special clothing and footwear and of safety equipment for workers.

To raise the prestige of the national trade union movement, the decree ordered that henceforth all important decisions of the State Committee on Labor and Wages, which decided basic labor policy for the Soviet state, had also to be approved by the national trade union leadership.[36] At least in theory this gave the unions a voice in national wage and hours policy, though, of course, all really basic policy was decided by the Communist party leadership to which both the State Committee and the unions were subordinate.

The new regulations for factory trade union committees gave them, on paper at least, additional functions. Management was prohibited from firing any worker without union consent. The committees were empowered to review, and if necessary to revoke or change, decisions on disputes between individual workers and management made originally by the labor disputes commission in each enterprise. The same groups were authorized to call for removal or punishment of production executives who failed to carry out obligations under collective agreements, and management was ordered to take union opinion into account in making new managerial appointments within an enterprise. The committees were also to be consulted over a wide range of other matters, from distribution of bonuses to the establishment of wage categories for different jobs.[37] The charter of rights was sufficiently wide so that an energetic union committee could exert much influence on behalf of its members. But in the Soviet

Union, as elsewhere, formal rights are one thing and actual behavior another. And Soviet trade unions had and have a long tradition of cooperating with management to maximize production.

The July 1958 regulations on the permanent production conferences defined them as a means of drawing workers into production management with the objective of helping enterprises fulfill and overfulfill state plans, raise productivity, utilize production reserves, and improve management of enterprises and construction projects. Members representing workers are elected at general meetings of the work force, while representatives of the Communist party, the Young Communist League, and other enterprise organizations are elected by their members. Management is also represented. Each conference helps draw up the plans for its enterprise, considers questions of production and labor organization, and discusses a broad range of other questions affecting the work of the enterprise. Conferences meet at least once or twice a quarter in a factory, at least once a month in a shop. Each has a presidium which is responsible for its work between meetings. All this is obviously vague, but it does attempt to set up an organization in which workers' representatives can have some say in the running of an enterprise. How this actually works out in practice must vary from plant to plant, but this was clearly a beginning toward something resembling the Yugoslav system.[38] The Soviet leaders' hope, of course, has been that these conferences will help raise output by improving worker morale through worker participation in management.

The problem of providing adequate labor for the non-agricultural economy was also worrisome in these years. The rapid rise of the scale of industrial production and construction created ever higher labor requirements. There was also need for additional workers because of the reductions in working hours introduced during this period. Most of the additional workers came to urban areas from the countryside, but another major source was the armed forces. Khrushchev revealed in early 1960 that between 1955 and 1958 a series of demobilizations reduced the size of the Soviet armed forces from 5,763,000 men to 3,623,000, a reduction of 2,140,000.[39] This was helpful, but as Soviet leaders examined their labor needs for the years following 1958, they could see a major problem approaching. This was the prospect of a sharp drop in new entrants to the labor force. The young people coming of age in the late 1950's and early 1960's were the products of the very small baby crop born during and immediately after World War II. The census of 1959 found, for example, that as of January 1959 there were only 17,100,000 young people aged 10–15 years, while the size of the next older age group, aged 16–21, was approximately 23,000,000. What should be done to compensate for the predictable sharp drop in the number of young people becoming available for work as the members of this 10–15 year group came of age in the years immediately following 1959?

A solution was announced by Khrushchev in late 1958 as he sparked a radical reform of the Soviet educational system. This reform abandoned the then-existing Soviet goal of universal ten-year secondary education for its young people, replacing it with the goal of universal education through the eighth grade. More important from the point of view of the labor force, this reform reorganized Soviet education so as to facilitate the entrance of younger people, 15–18, into the employed Soviet labor force while supporting an expansion of part-time education facilities for these young people so they could continue to improve their knowledge and skills.[40] As part of this 1958 reform, the ten-year secondary schools were made into eleven-year schools so that the older pupils could work part-time and receive training on their jobs. In mid-1964, the Soviet press announced a decision to scrap the eleven-year schools. The announcements indicated that the time saved would be at the expense of the vocational training program, much of which had proved a "useless waste of time," according to the Russian Republic Minister of Education.[40a]

During the years considered here, agriculture, too, was shaken by major policy and institutional innovations. It is to these that we turn now. At the Central Committee meeting in January 1955, Khrushchev's speech on agriculture was the principal item on the agenda. Though nominally concerned with increasing livestock output, his emphasis was again on the need to raise grain production. Population was growing by more than 3,000,-000 people annually, he explained; urban population was increasing particularly rapidly; and all these people had to be fed. He hinted that the state grain reserves had been depleted, and asserted that the reductions of consumer prices in 1953 and 1954 had increased the demand for grain products and foods derived from grain. To meet the nation's needs, he declared, grain production had to be raised to 10,000,000,000 poods (about 165,000,000 metric tons) by 1960 or 1961. He did not add—since 1954 grain production was then being kept secret—that this amounted to almost doubling Soviet grain production in five or six years. The goal could be achieved by action along three lines, he maintained: by increasing grain yields per hectare, and in this connection he noted how little fertilizer his country used as compared with "many capitalist countries"; by further increases in virgin and fallow lands areas planted to grain; and by a sharp increase in the area planted to corn. The last was a most radical, new suggestion. Khrushchev was ordering that this unfamiliar crop, hitherto confined entirely to southern regions of the country, be planted throughout the country. He had an answer for those who objected that Soviet summers were too short and too cold to permit Iowa farm practices to be applied in Russia: "Experience has shown that corn can reach lactic maturity wherever wheat can be grown. Even if there are some years when the corn fails to ripen, the collective or state farm will still get a considerable amount of green silage. In such a case the farm would not suffer a loss." It was an audacious gamble, for Khrushchev demanded that the area planted to corn be raised from 3,500,000 hectares in 1953 to 28,000,000 hectares in 1960. With the vast increase in grain production that his virgin lands and corn programs would bring, Khrushchev predicted, great gains could be made in meat, milk, and other livestock output. By 1960, he said, beef production should be increased 70 per cent above that of 1954; poultry output should be 2.5 to 3 times that of 1954; and egg output should be 2.2 times that of 1954. Over-all, output of meat and animal fat as well as milk in 1960 was to be double that of 1954. The blueprint had been laid down, in short, for what was hoped to be a speedy and major improvement in the nation's diet.[41]

The resources and energy put behind these agricultural programs were soon reflected on the farms. In 1954, for example, the Soviet Union had planted only about 4,300,000 hectares to corn; in 1955 this area jumped to almost 18,000,000 hectares and in 1956 to 24,000,000 hectares. A great deal of valuable additional green fodder was undoubtedly made available by this expansion. The amount of grain and grain equivalent contributed by corn is estimated in Soviet statistics to have quadrupled between 1953 and 1956. Soviet farmers might be dubious and even unenthusiastic about this new crop, and they might gibe at the party First Secretary, calling him Nikita *Kukuruznik* (Nikita the corn man), but they generally obeyed his orders. A similar explosive expansion of wheat planting took place in the basic virgin lands areas in Kazakhstan and Siberia. In Kazakhstan, the key area of this effort, 4,600,000 hectares were planted to wheat in 1953, 18,300,-000 hectares in 1956, and 19,300,000 hectares in 1958. Just between 1954 and 1956, the total Soviet crop area increased by about 90,000,000 acres, more than 20 per cent, an amount almost equal to the combined arable land of France, West Germany, and Britain.

During the years considered here, the fates were kind to Khrushchev. The rains came to the virgin lands areas in 1956 and 1958, producing bumper crops that helped to make up for the disappointments of 1955 and 1957. But even then the extreme variability of the virgin lands harvest gave warning of the dangers that might lie ahead if the rains came less frequently. The official data show both the growth and the variability of the Soviet grain crops during the first six post-Stalin harvests in the country as a whole, in the regions where most of the virgin lands expansion took place, and in the rest of the country:

Table 13. SOVIET GRAIN PRODUCTION, 1953–1958

Year	Total Grain Harvest	Basic Virgin Lands Areas*	Rest of Country
		(millions of metric tons)	
1953	82.5	26.9	55.6
1954	85.6	37.3	48.3
1955	106.8	27.7	79.1
1956	127.6	63.3	64.3
1957	105.0	38.1	66.9
1958	141.2	58.4	82.8

* Includes Kazakhstan, the Urals, Siberia, and part of the Volga region.
SOURCE: *Selskoye Khozyaistvo SSSR*, p. 227.

Some Western specialists have suggested that these harvest data are exaggerated for particular years, and that in 1956 the grain harvest may have been only 115,000,000 tons and in 1958 only 125,000,000 tons.[42]

But production data alone fail to show the full significance of the virgin lands program for the Soviet state and its policies. We must consider procurement data for added light on another dimension. Through 1953, the Soviet state was primarily dependent upon European Russia for the bulk of the grain it needed to feed the cities and for other purposes. In that year only about 10,800,000 metric tons, roughly one-third the total, of all grain procurements came from the regions where the virgin and fallow lands expansion took place in the next several years, primarily from Kazakhstan and Siberia. But in 1954, 1956, and 1958, more than half of all state grain procurements came from these latter regions. In 1956, more than two-thirds of all government grain procurements came from these regions, 36,700,000 metric tons in all.[43] In densely populated European Russia, with an agriculture based primarily on collective farms, it was relatively hard to squeeze grain out of a peasantry which wanted more bread for itself and more feed for its livestock. The task was far easier in sparsely settled Siberia and Kazakhstan where the virgin lands were being farmed in government-owned state farms. We may surmise that this easing of the grain procurement problem, which was one of the virgin lands' most attractive features in Premier Khrushchev's eyes, helped induce him to persist in later years even as drought and low yields struck these areas more frequently.

Returning now to our consideration of over-all grain production, the generally rising trend of 1953–1958 output is clear. So is the extreme year to year variability of Soviet harvests, both regionally and over the country as a whole. In 1955 the virgin lands did poorly and European Russia saved the day. The situation was reversed in 1956. In 1957 the virgin lands' output was only mediocre and that of European Russia was only fair. But in 1958 both parts of the country enjoyed excellent weather and a record crop resulted.

The rich 1958 harvest delighted Premier Khrushchev, and he began to anticipate the time when the country might even have a surplus of grain. Here is the way he painted the perspectives at this high point in Soviet agricultural fortunes:

> This year we are procuring a large quantity of grain which will not only permit us to supply the nation's grain needs but also to lay in a reserve. If a good harvest is gathered next year—and the conditions exist for this—we will raise reserves still more in order to insure the nation against any adverse conditions. With sufficient stocks and a good harvest, the state will buy less grain in the future than this year. Now we buy from all the collective farms. Clearly the time will come when the state will buy grain from those collective farms that sell it at a lower price. Therefore those collective farms that produce high cost grain will find themselves in serious marketing troubles. The government will not buy expensive grain and there will presumably be no market demand for it.[44]

Such optimistic calculations were to be rudely disappointed in the years that followed, but it was such anticipations that determined the subsequent Soviet farm planning.

With increased grain available, the number of livestock and the production of livestock products also began to show increases, though not always as rapidly as Khrushchev had hoped. Meat and related animal fat production rose slowly from 6,300,000 metric tons in 1954 to 7,700,000 tons in 1958. Milk output rose more rapidly, from 38,200,000 to 58,700,000 tons over the same period. Egg production went from 17,000,000,000 to 23,000,-000,000.[45]

In May 1957, Khrushchev suddenly raised his earlier goals for progress in livestock production. The Soviet Union, he declared, must "catch up with the United States in the near future in per capita production of meat, butter and milk." And by the near future, he made clear, he meant 1958 for milk and, in the case of meat, 1960 or at latest 1961. To catch up, he said later, the Soviet Union would have to produce 70,000,000 tons of milk in 1958 and 20–21,000,000 tons of meat in 1960 or 1961. The actual 1956 output had been 49,100,000 tons of milk and 6,600,000 tons of meat. He ridiculed economists who had predicted the Soviet Union could only catch up with the United States in meat production by 1975. These economists, Khrushchev claimed, had failed to understand the significance of the fact that some "collective farms have literally increased their production 10, 15 and

20 times in the space of two or three years. How can all this be reckoned in an arithmetical computation. This is a political phenomenon." This was a sort of Khrushchevian precursor to what the Chinese soon afterward called the "great leap forward." Did Khrushchev really believe he was setting practical goals? Or was this part of the obscure intrigue that preceded the political explosion of June 1957 in which Khrushchev almost lost his political life before he vanquished his opponents?

What is certain is that the whole complex of agricultural reform measures adopted in the mid-1950's played an important role in the political struggle between Khrushchev and those who, after their defeat in mid-1957, were given the title of "the anti-party group." Here is the way Bulganin summarized this aspect of the Stalin succession rivalry during his *mea culpa* to the Central Committee in December 1958:

> Comrade Khrushchev's report stated correctly that the anti-party group opposed the party's policy on raising the virgin lands, the new system of agricultural planning, and the patriotic movement . . . to solve the problem of equalling the United States in per capita production of livestock products in the shortest possible time. . . .

> I well remember the situation in the Presidium of the Central Committee when Comrade Khrushchev raised the problem of cultivating the virgin lands and when he suggested—almost at the same time—a new system of planning in agriculture. 'This is adventurism,' said Molotov. 'We shall be left without grain,' said Molotov, Malenkov and Kaganovich. 'We must squash the movement for the slogan of overtaking the United States in per capita output of livestock products; we do not have enough livestock feed,' they said.

The bitterness which surrounded this struggle and the organizational in-fighting it led to is suggested by the statement at the same meeting by the Communist party chief of Altai territory, in the virgin lands area:

> Malenkov and other members of the anti-party group who opposed developing virgin lands in the Altai have been defeated completely. You will recall, Nikita Sergeyevich, that in the summer of 1954 you visited us and saw the grain growing on the state farms set up in the virgin lands. Just at that time, Malenkov, then Premier, signed a decree reprimanding us for

organizing the virgin lands state farms. We were ordered not to set up new state farms.[46]

Khrushchev hoped to use the meat and milk programs to win a spectacular and rapid economic triumph over the United States. Thus, when he called for equalling American meat output in three years, he declared: "This victory of ours will be stronger than the hydrogen bomb." He added, "We do not intend to blow up the capitalist world with bombs. If we catch up to the United States level of meat, milk and butter we shall have shot a highly powerful torpedo at the underpinnings of capitalism." But the essence of the arrogant attitude that dominated this speech was best expressed in this passage:

> We have dared to challenge America to peaceful competition in a most important economic field, that same America whose money bags make all the capitalist states tremble and grovel. The United States throws this one a little moldy wheat, that one some stale lard, and the third one gets some other bit of goods that can't be sold at home.
>
> They all go about on tiptoe as though they were afraid of offending her. But we have always walked proudly. We refuse to recognize the greatness and superiority of imperialist America and have ground to believe in the greatness and superiority of our own socialist country . . . In 1953 . . . certain American officials dangled some bait before us. If the Soviet Union would give them some strategic goods or some gold, they might perhaps sell the Soviet Union some surplus lard, meat, or other similar foods.
>
> We told them that we might sell them some strategic raw materials but not on such enslaving terms as to give away valuable raw materials and gold in return for rancid butter. We told them without any doubt that the Soviet government would have enough of its own butter, meat, and other similar foods. It will be interesting now to see what the American imperialists have to say when they read that the U.S.S.R. is planning to exceed them soon in per capita output of meat, milk, and butter.[47]

By late 1963, of course, Khrushchev had changed his tune. The Soviet Union was selling large quantities of gold abroad to finance the purchase of wheat from Canada and the United States. But even before this humiliating denouement, the evident gap between the disappointing reality of later developments and the immoderation of Khrushchev's 1957 boasting had led the Soviet leader quietly to bury these promises, eliminating them even from the published volumes of his speeches on agriculture.

Despite the disappointment of the most soaring Khrushchev hopes, Soviet agriculture did make extraordinarily good progress during 1955–1958. What other factors, besides the good weather of 1956 and 1958, help explain this improvement? The sharply increased capital investment in agriculture of the post-Stalin period is part of the story. Khrushchev noted in 1958 that during the previous four years about 1,000,000,000 rubles more had been invested by the government in Soviet agriculture than had been invested altogether in the 16 earlier peace time years since 1932.[48] In the five years following 1953, the number of tractors in Soviet agriculture rose about one-third, from 744,000 to over 1,000,000; the number of grain combines increased almost 60 per cent and the number of trucks available for agriculture almost 75 per cent, from 424,000 to 700,000. The number of agricultural specialists (agronomists, livestock experts, and veterinaries) engaged directly in farm work increased from 96,000 in mid-1953 to 281,000 by December 1957. Finally, and by no means least important, the higher prices being paid by the government were increasing the incomes of collective farms and permitting better pay for work on the collective farm fields. In 1953 the total money income of all Soviet collective farms had been less than 5,000,000,000 rubles; in 1958 that money income exceeded 13,000,000,000 rubles, reflecting the post-Stalinist increases in prices and output.[49]

This rapid rise in collective farm incomes, however, was no sign that anything resembling affluence had been attained. Rather it would be more accurate to say that the general poverty of the countryside was somewhat alleviated. Dr. Lazar Volin has put these developments into perspective:

> After Stalin's death, the new leadership instituted a contrary policy of reducing taxes and substantially raising the very low prices hitherto paid by the state for farm products. As a consequence of this and of increased farm output, the cash income of the collectives more than doubled, from 4.28 billion rubles to 9.5 billion, between 1952 and 1956–57. This in turn made possible cash payments to the peasants in many collectives where such distribution had formerly been negligible. The

cash payments, in fact, more than trebled between 1952 and 1956, increasing from 1.24 billion to 4.22 billion.

Yet even the greatly increased volume of cash distributed in 1956 represented an average cash income of only something over 210 rubles per peasant family on the collective farms, a sum roughly equivalent to a little more than $200 at a realistic rate of exchange. In 1952 the average had been as little as 62.3 rubles, equivalent—with higher prices—to less than $60 per peasant household. Moreover, since the cash distributions in some areas of intensive crop production (such as the growing of cotton, sugar beets, etc.) were considerably above the average rate, many peasant families in the less prosperous collectives obviously received much less than the average.[50]

A number of institutional changes in Soviet agriculture during the years considered here also affected its operation. The process of consolidating collective farms into larger units continued. A new policy of converting the poorest collective farms into state farms was also begun during this period. As a result of both processes, the number of collectives declined from 93,256 at the end of 1953 to 69,129 at the end of 1958. The number of state farms grew from 4,857 at the end of 1953 to 6,002 five years later, mainly because of the decision to rely primarily on state farms to work the vast new areas in the virgin lands territory.

A major effort was made during 1955–1958 to improve the quality of agricultural planning. A decree issued March 9, 1955 denounced the defects of the old planning system which had aimed at complete control of all agricultural enterprises from the center. Such planning, the decree commented, "caused incorrect distribution of crops and failed to take proper account of the economic, soil and climatic conditions of the collective farms. It contradicted the accumulated experience of the farms, violated established farming practices, and failed to produce higher harvests." No longer should collective farms be told how much to plant of each crop or the number of head of livestock they should produce. Instead the collectives were to be told what the state would require them to deliver, and then it would be up to them, in consultation with the Machine Tractor Stations, to determine what they would plant, how many acres they would plant, and the number and kind of livestock they would raise.[51] The avowed objective of the move was to give freer play to local initiative on the collective farms, to enable them to conduct their operations in the light of their members' knowledge of local conditions. But of course the government's ability to prescribe deliveries exercised great influence on each farm's planning. No less important, as time went on much experience showed that local government and Communist party officials tended often to ignore the spirit of the 1955 decree, to meddle in collective farm affairs by imposing their own ideas of what those farms should grow and of how many acres they should plant. The legal loophole which gave the entering wedge for such official meddling was a clause in the 1955 decree requiring each collective farm to submit its plan to local authorities for checking. Not until 1964, nine years later, was this loophole closed.

Along with this first effort, Khrushchev tried to spur better planning at the center. He encouraged attempts to study farm production costs scientifically so that the government would have meaningful cost data on which to base its farm price policy. The impression given by Soviet discussion on the last point is that Stalin paid no attention at all to the question of farm production costs and discouraged his economists from making such studies. Certainly a spirited debate went on among Soviet agricultural economists in the middle and late 1950's over the correct bases for computing collective farm production costs. In all this and other related activity, Khrushchev's goal appears to have been to replace the old system of arbitrary bureaucratic control of agriculture by a system based on rational criteria and financial levers to enlist the self-interest of the collective farmers.

The problem of providing more incentives for Soviet farmers received much attention during 1955–1958, as did the related problem of trying to discourage their excessive attention to private garden plots. Both matters were treated at length in a decree issued in March 1956.[52] On the positive side, the most important move was an order for a new system of payment for collective farmers. The decree pointed out that the old method under which most of the farmers' income from the collective was paid out at the end of the year did not increase the members' material interest in raising production. To remedy this, the decree recommended that collective farms institute a wage system permitting collective farmers to receive monthly monetary payments. No doubt this move tended to increase incentives but many farms introducing this system soon fell into financial difficulties because they simply did not have the working capital required to pay their members in the months before the crops were harvested and sold. These difficulties occurred even though the decree ordered procurement agencies to advance the farms funds before deliveries were made. Additionally, the decree ordered the collective farms to try to reduce the size of garden plots, and particularly to make the size of these private plots dependent upon the amount of work members of each farmer's family actually put in on the collective fields. Tighter limits on the number of livestock permitted each farm family and establishment of higher numbers of minimum workdays required of each collective farm member were also suggested. All this, of course, was a marked shift in policy from a few years earlier, when both Khrushchev and Malenkov had praised private ownership of livestock and taken moves to make the private garden plots more profitable by cutting the compulsory deliveries to the state required from these plots. But this tightening up must have had negative political consequences, probably encouraging grumbling and discontent. This is certainly suggested by the fact that in May 1957 Khrushchev appeared publicly as the advocate of complete abolition of required compulsory deliveries from the garden plots. One of the first decrees issued after Khrushchev won his fight against his political opponents in June 1957 was an order abolishing these compulsory deliveries.[53] Forty years after the Bolshevik Revolution, it was still proving difficult to eliminate the attractiveness of private property from the consciousness and interests of Soviet peasants.

The most important institutional change in agriculture during this period came in early 1958, when one of the basic features of the Stalinist farm system, the Machine Tractor Station, was ordered abolished. Under Stalin, the government-owned MTS had had a monopoly on all important farm machinery used upon the collective farms. The latter had to turn to the MTS for the services of tractors, grain combines, similar equipment, and their operators; in return for the services of this equipment, the MTS were paid a portion of the harvest. This separation of machinery users from machinery owners made for an unwieldy system full of opportunities for friction between farm and MTS officials and personnel. Moreover, the system of payments for MTS workers usually made them concerned primarily with attaining good indices showing large amounts of work done, in terms of acres plowed or the like. In many cases, concern for quantity of performance caused a loss of interest in quality, with unhappy effects upon the size of the harvest. While Soviet officials were undoubtedly well aware earlier of the MTS weaknesses, they had a non-economic reason for supporting this institution: in each area the MTS was also a political watchdog over the local peasantry, and its monopoly of the machinery for harvesting grain and other crops enabled it to play an important role in assuring that the farms delivered the required portions of their harvest to the state.

Yet even before Stalin's death, the transfer of the MTS machinery to the collective farms had been suggested. In his last major theoretical work, Stalin had given an emphatic no to this suggestion by two Soviet economists, A. V. Sanina and V. G. Venzher. He argued that the collective farms could not afford to buy the expensive machinery, and only the state had the financial capacity for this. More important, he argued that such a transfer would be a step away from full socialism and communism, since it would strengthen an institution, the collective farm, which was not fully socialized. The correct line of change, Stalin indicated, was toward making the collective farms fully the property of the state, rather than turning state property over to them.[54]

Against this background, Khrushchev inflicted a major shock on many Soviet citizens when, without any advance warning, he suddenly spoke out in public in January 1958 to urge that the MTS be abolished, their machinery sold to the collective farms, and the MTS themselves converted to farm machinery repair stations. He advanced a series of reasons for the change: the MTS had become uneconomic, he argued, because the cost of grain secured by the state in payment for their services was greater than the cost of grain bought directly from the collective farms. The MTS no longer played or needed to play an important political role in the countryside. And the separate existence of the MTS, he asserted, created needless costs and inefficiencies in agriculture because "We have two masters on the same land—the collective farm chairman and the MTS director. And where there are two masters there can be no good management. . . . The collective farm chairman has to argue and coordinate with the

MTS director on even such matters as where to put a tractor. All this leads to irrational utilization of machinery and harms the interests of the state and the collective farms."[55]

Khrushchev's proposal apparently provoked a major debate in the Soviet leadership, where it is clear some people secretly opposed it. We know some of the themes of the debate from the remarks Khrushchev made before the Supreme Soviet in late March 1958, the session at which he was named Premier of the Soviet Union. One argument brought up was Stalin's rejection of this idea in 1952. In effect Khrushchev was asked why, if sale of machinery to collective farms was wrong in 1952, it suddenly became correct in 1958.

Khrushchev's answer did not mention Stalin, but implied he had supported Stalin's rejection of the idea in 1952. The proposal was wrong then, Khrushchev asserted, "because the collective farms were economically weak. They would not have been able to buy the equipment and use it properly. We would have seriously weakened our agriculture." To support his thesis he cited the poverty of the collective farm in his native village of Kalinovka. In 1945, he said, that collective was so poor it had refused to accept free of charge horses offered by the Soviet army, because it could not afford to care for and feed those horses.

But this did not answer the objections of those who pointed to Stalin's warning that sale of the machinery to collective farms would strengthen the collectives and impede the progress of further nationalization. Khrushchev's answer was a significant change of ideological emphasis. It was incorrect, he argued, to stress the idea that nationalized property was superior to collective farm property. Both were forms of socialist property, and both served the interests of the nation, he asserted, so that there was no reason to be afraid of strengthening the collective farms. All this, of course, was diametrically opposed to the point of view Stalin had asserted five years before.[56]

The Supreme Soviet approved the proposed change. By the end of 1958 most of the MTS machinery had been sold to the collective farms for more than 2,000,000,000 rubles, while most of the MTS had been converted into RTS (Repair and Technical Service Stations). The Communist party Central Committee ordered in late 1958 that the business of winding up the MTS and transferring their machinery to the collective farms be speeded up and completed. The substantial sums paid by the collective farms for the machinery depleted their treasuries, of course. But from the government's point of view this helped curb inflationary trends born of the rising farm incomes, and provided an additional important source of funds to meet the state's need for capital investment resources.

With the MTS out of the way, the road was open for a reform of the complicated Soviet price and purchase system for agricultural products. As Khrushchev pointed out in his speech to the Central Committee in June 1958, farm products were bought at one price if sold to the state as part of the compulsory delivery quota, at another if part of the above-quota sale, at still another if delivered to the MTS as payment in kind. In addition, some raw material crops were bought on a complex system of contracts with many bonus and other provisions. Khrushchev described the consequences of this:

> As a result the same commodity delivered to the state through different channels brought different prices to the collective farms. Some farms received several times more than the base price for a particular product, especially a technical crop, because of the bonus. This gave rise to incorrect tendencies in agriculture: Some farms tried to have low plans set so that a large part of their output could be delivered at high prices above the plan. These farms received substantial sums for a small quantity of produce and planned their farming for maximum profit. Simultaneously, average farms and particularly the economically weak farms were at a very great disadvantage. They were required to deliver most of their output at low compulsory delivery prices, which did not always cover their production outlays. . . .

> Under existing delivery terms and prices, a comparatively small number of collective farms have received particularly high incomes. These are the collective farms in the cotton, flax, and hemp areas, those specializing in dairy farming and located close to the large cities and industrial centers, and those growing citrus fruits and some other crops. But even in these areas only those collective farms that provided a great deal of produce above the planned level and therefore got large bonus payments had such incomes . . . Most collective farms, which

delivered a large part of their commercial production to the state primarily as compulsory deliveries and payments in kind for MTS work, everywhere had considerably smaller incomes.[57]

The solution adopted was the institution of a system of one price for each product grown in a particular area. This is sometimes referred to as the abolition of compulsory deliveries, but under the new system collective farms were still required to deliver a portion of their produce, calculated as before on the basis of their acreage. The change was simply that instead of two or more state prices for deliveries, the farms were paid one uniform price which was generally higher than the low former compulsory delivery price and lower than the former premium price paid for above-quota deliveries. The objective was a redistribution of income, giving less total income to the farms that had formerly been able to profit from the high premium prices and improving the average prices received by the remaining farms. In carrying out this reform, the Soviet regime was concerned that the farm produce it bought should not cost more in total than it had formerly spent both in buying farm produce and in paying for the MTS through which, as we have seen, it had also collected a significant portion of farm produce. As part of this total reform, Khrushchev instituted a policy of charging the same wholesale prices for farm machinery and many other production essentials to both state and collective farms. Earlier, the collective farms had been charged much higher prices than the state farms for agricultural production essentials.

The new price system for different crops and products was differentiated by zones. The Soviet government hoped to keep the new prices relatively stable for a number of years, though it warned that in times of good harvests prices might be lowered somewhat and in times of poor harvests they might be raised somewhat. The average prices the government would pay over the nation as a whole were fixed as follows for some key farm products (in post-1960 rubles per 100 kilograms or other unit as indicated):

Grain—7.4; sunflower seed—17.2; potatoes—4; sugar beet—2.35; raw cotton—34; flax fiber No. 8—230; hemp No. 5—230; cattle of average fatness—61.9; sheep of average fatness—53.6; pork pigs—78.6; bacon pigs—108.1; lard pigs—82.6; hens and chicks—89.5;

ducks and geese—73.8; milk—11.5; eggs (per ten)—.6; fine unwashed wool—410; coarse unwashed wool—237.

The impact of this change on the system of farm procurements
and pricing was very substantial, altering the relative prices
offered for different foods and agricultural raw materials more
than a little in many cases. These changes, as well as the more
general trend toward higher farm prices paid by the government,
are evident from the data in Table 14 showing indexes of average
state prices paid for procurements from collective farms, collective farmers, and other workers and employes:[58]

Table 14. INDEXES OF FARM PRICES PAID BY
THE SOVIET GOVERNMENT, 1954–1958

| | | (1952 = 100) | |
Product	1954	1956	1958
All farm products	207	251	296
All crops	171	207	203
Wheat	752	647	621
Rye	730	625	1047
Corn	564	572	819
Rice	243	887	957
Cotton	102	114	106
Flax fiber	166	213	239
Sugar beets	111	229	219
Sunflower	626	928	774
Potatoes	369	814	789
All livestock products	307	371	546
Cattle	476	508	1147
Hogs	786	976	1156
Milk and milk products	289	334	404
Eggs	135	155	297
Wool	146	246	352

SOURCE: *Selskoye Khozyaistvo SSSR*, p. 117.

CHAPTER V

Economic Factors in Khrushchev's Downfall

ON OCTOBER 15, 1964, a startled world learned that Nikita S. Khrushchev had been removed from his posts as First Secretary of the Communist party, member of the party's ruling Presidium, and Premier of the Soviet Union. Two days later *Pravda* appeared with an editorial assailing "harebrained scheming, immature conclusions and hasty decisions and actions divorced from reality, bragging and phrasemongering, commandism, unwillingness to take into account the achievements of science and practical experience." Though Khrushchev's name was not mentioned, it was clear that his conduct as Soviet leader was the target of these adjectives, and that in large part this indictment was intended to characterize his direction of the Soviet economy. On October 21, 1964, Soviet authorities released the report on their country's economic perfomance during the first nine months of that year, revealing that industrial production growth during that period had been little more than 7 per cent over the corresponding period of 1963. This was the slowest rate of industrial advance claimed for the Soviet economy since 1946, almost a generation earlier. There could be little doubt that this slowdown in growth and Khrushchev's downfall were closely related. But beyond this immediate sign of trouble, Khrushchev's purge was the consequence in large part of the far from glorious record written by the Soviet economy under his direction during 1959–1964. This record of unsatisfactory economic progress helped undermine Khrushchev's position. We turn now to an examination of the developments of these six years.

Few periods of Soviet economic history have been—on balance—so full of disappointments for the Soviet leaders and the

121

Soviet people as the years since 1958. The nation's prospects had seemed very bright in early 1959 when the new Seven Year Plan for 1959–1965 was adopted. In 1958 both industry and agriculture had set new production records. It was in character for the men in the Kremlin to assume that all these new high marks would soon be exceeded. The economy had successfully overcome all the difficulties created in the mid-1950's by such varied factors as the struggle for power among Stalin's heirs and the Hungarian Revolution. It seemed hardly likely that sterner tests lay ahead. Abroad, Soviet leaders noted with glee, concern with Soviet economic growth and the possibility of Soviet victory in the economic race had become common in the West. If the once-skeptical capitalists and their analysts were worried about the future, why should not good Communists be optimistic? In this atmosphere of euphoria, it was easy to make generous promises. But sad experience was to show how much harder it was to fulfill those promises.

The high hopes prevailing then were reflected in Premier Khrushchev's keynote speech to the 21st Soviet Communist party Congress in January 1959. Now Khrushchev was ready to offer a precise timetable for Soviet and Communist economic victory over capitalism. By 1970, he assured his auditors, Soviet industry and agriculture both would be outproducing the United States on a per capita basis as well as in total output. And by 1965, he indicated, he expected that the Communist bloc as a whole would be producing more than half of the world's industrial output, though it had only one-third of the world's population. He rattled off glibly the impressive percentages by which he expected the Soviet economy to grow under the new plan. By 1965, he predicted, Soviet national income would be 62–65 per cent higher than in 1958, industrial production would be 80 per cent more, and agricultural output would be 70 per cent above the base figure.

The Soviet people were assured that these gains would be translated into improvements in their everyday life. "The food consumption of the population will be considerably improved, especially as regards such items as milk, butter, meat, sugar, vegetables and fruit . . . Soviet people will be adequately provided with good and attractive clothing and shoes . . . There will be a basic improvement in the people's housing situation." So went the promises in the Seven Year Plan directives approved by the Congress. Khrushchev himself put the glittering perspectives this way:

> As a result of higher money wages, pensions and grants, and a reduction in restaurant prices, the real income per worker and employe will increase 40 per cent by the end of the seven year period. It is also planned to raise the minimum wages of low-paid workers and employes from the present 27–35 rubles to between 50 and 60 rubles a month. Real earnings of collective farmers will similarly rise at least 40 per cent . . . In these circumstances, taxes from the population will no longer be necessary . . . We will be able to discontinue taxation of the public in the next few years. . . .

> Workers and employes with a seven hour work day will be shifted to a forty hour week in 1962. Starting in 1964, personnel in underground work or in jobs with harmful working conditions will gradually change to a 30-hour week, and all other workers to a 35 hour week. Thus if there is one day off a week, the working day will be five or six hours, depending on the nature of the work. Inasmuch as for most persons it is more convenient to have two days off each week, it is intended to introduce a five day work week with a six or seven hour day.

> The shift to a shorter work day and work week will be carried out in our nation not only without reducing wages, but while substantial increases are being granted. The Soviet Union is to have the shortest work day and the shortest work week in the world, while at the same time there is a rise in the welfare of the people.

Khrushchev emphasized that the perspectives he was describing were no mere fantasies. "The Seven Year Plan was drawn up so as to be capable of fulfillment without strain," he assured his audience. He even allowed himself to speculate that the plan might be overfulfilled and that there might be even more brilliant perspectives ahead by 1965 than the plan envisaged.[1]

The passage of time proved these bright promises to be delusions that never came close to being fully realized as the Seven Year Plan period neared its close. Under the pressure of repeated economic setbacks during the first half of the 1960's, especially of disappointments and setbacks in agriculture, the Soviet leaders quietly abandoned most of the promises Khrushchev had trumpeted so loudly in 1959. Near the Seven Year Plan period's end, the Soviet people had neither the shortest work day nor the shortest work week in the world, and most of them labored 41 hours a week, not 35 as Khrushchev had promised. Soviet workers still paid income taxes since the plan to abolish these taxes had had to be abandoned in 1962. By the end of 1964, the lowest paid Soviet workers looked forward to a minimum wage of 40–45 rubles a month, not the 50–60 rubles a month Khrushchev had promised. Even worse, retail prices on meat and butter had been raised 30 and 25 per cent respectively in June 1962, provoking violent discontent in some areas. By late 1963 and early 1964, the Soviet people were subject to what amounted to informal bread rationing, but even that relatively mild deprivation was possible only because the Soviet Union had been able to buy 12,000,000 tons of grain from abroad, mostly from Canada and the United States. Moreover, the fluctuation of prices during 1962 and 1963 in the collective farm markets, where food prices are subject to supply and demand factors, showed clearly that substantial inflationary pressures were operating. In 1962, when the food situation was better than it would be a year later, the price index of food sold in such urban markets was 16 per cent above the 1958 level, most of the increase having taken place in 1962.[2]

Table 15. ANNUAL SOVIET INDUSTRIAL PRODUCTION GROWTH RATES, 1954 AND 1958–1964

Year	All industry	Heavy industry	Consumer goods
		(annual percentage increases)	
1954	13	14	13
1958	10	11	8
1959	11	12	10
1960	10	11	7
1961	9	10	7
1962	9.5	11	7
1963	8.5	10	5
1964, 1st half	7.5	over 10	2

SOURCES: *Narodnoye Khozyaistvo SSSR v 1962 godu*, p. 119; *Pravda*, January 24 and July 23, 1964.

There was another side to this coin, of course: the much better performance of industry—particularly heavy industry—than of agriculture. But even here was evident the action of powerful forces tending to slow down the growth of production, particularly to reduce the rate of growth of consumer goods output. The official Soviet data on annual rates of industrial production growth, presented in Table 15 above, show this tendency clearly.

These data imply that Soviet heavy industrial output was more than 50 per cent higher in 1963 than in 1958. Whatever technical deficiencies there may be in the Soviet index, it is clear that among all areas of the Soviet economy, heavy industry turned in the best production performance during these years. The magnitude of this feat is best suggested by looking at the production growth of the basic industrial raw materials of Soviet heavy industry during this period:

Table 16. OUTPUT OF KEY SOVIET INDUSTRIAL COMMODITIES, 1958, 1963, AND 1964

Commodity	Unit	1958	1963	1964 (estimated)
Pig iron	million metric tons	39.6	58.7	62.0
Steel	million metric tons	54.9	80.2	84.5
Oil	million metric tons	113.2	206.0	225
Electricity	billion kilowatt-hours	235.4	412.0	455
Cement	million metric tons	33.3	61.0	63

SOURCES: The same as for Table 5.

The record shown by these data can be summarized simply: pig iron and steel production in the Soviet Union increased more than 50 per cent during 1958–1964; oil, electricity, and cement output almost doubled in the same period.

As a result of this brilliant production performance, and the capital investment priority behind it, Soviet heavy industry accounted for almost 75 per cent of all Soviet industrial production in 1963. In 1952, Stalin's last full year of power, the corresponding proportion was less than 70 per cent.

In January 1961 Khrushchev began to indicate that he was troubled by this trend. He pointed out that if steel production continued to increase at the same tempo as during the first years

of the Seven Year Plan period, steel output could exceed 100,000,-
000 metric tons by 1965, though the formal goal for that year
was in the range of 86–91,000,000 tons. He then declared:

> Obviously, however, we shall not follow a policy of developing
> ferrous metallurgy as much as possible. Obviously we shall shift
> part of the capital investments to agriculture and light industry.
> It is impossible to build communism by offering only machines
> and ferrous and non-ferrous metals. People must be able to eat
> and clothe themselves well, to have housing and other material
> and cultural conditions.
>
> This is not a revision of our general line, but a reasonable em-
> ployment of our possibilities. When we were encircled by
> enemies and our industry was weaker than that of the capitalist
> nations, we economized on everything, even, as Lenin said, on
> schools. We are in a different situation now. We have a power-
> ful industry and our armed forces have the most modern
> weapons. Why should we deny people what they can receive
> without harm to the further development of our socialist
> society?[3]

By May 1961, he sounded like Malenkov when he declared
publicly—in remarks that, significantly, were not reported in the
Soviet press—that light and heavy industries could in the future
develop at equal rates of speed since "the industrial base of the
country is built."[4]

It is reasonable to assume that in this period a new battle was
raging behind the scenes on economic policy. Khrushchev presumably sought a more balanced pattern of development, but
other powerful figures insisted on the continued primacy of
heavy industry and the policy of building up military and space
capabilities as rapidly as possible. The outcome of this debate
appears to have been decided by President Kennedy's decision
in this period to step up the volume of United States military
spending because of the tension over Berlin. That American
decision was quickly followed in early July by Khrushchev's
announcement that Soviet military spending would also be increased substantially. Then came the building of the Berlin Wall
by the East Germans and international tension mounted still
further.

Thus it was quite a different spirit Khrushchev voiced when
he spoke in October 1961 at the 22nd Congress of the Soviet

Communist party. Now his emphasis was on the Soviet Union's possibilities for increasing 1965 production of key heavy industrial products beyond the original targets of the Seven Year Plan. Here are the revisions he presented:

Commodity	Unit	Original 1965 goal	Revised 1965 goal
Pig iron	million metric tons	65–70	72–73
Steel	million metric tons	86–91	95–97 "or more"
Oil	million metric tons	230–240	over 240
Electricity	billion kilowatt-hours	500–520	over 520

The most significant upward revision he gave, however, was for the field of machinery and metal working. The output in these fields, he said, would now be raised to 56–67,000,000,000 rubles by 1965 rather than the 49,000,000,000 rubles originally planned. It is this category, of course, into which Soviet arms production falls.[5]

But anyone who thought in October 1961 that Khrushchev's revised goals had set the path for the rest of the Seven Year Plan period to 1965 was profoundly mistaken. Within two years decisions were taken—in large part because of agricultural difficulties —that amounted to scrapping much of the Seven Year Plan and its 1961 revision. This may be most vividly shown by comparing the data given above with the new set of corresponding 1965 goals set by the special Two Year Plan announced in December 1963.[6] (The data below are in the same units as those above.)

Commodity	Original 1965 goal	1961 Revised 1965 goal	1963 Revised 1965 goal
Pig iron	65–70	72–73	65.7
Steel	86–91	95–97 "or more"	89.3
Oil	230–240	over 240	240
Electricity	500–520	over 520	508

The 1965 goal for machinery construction was stated in late 1963 to be 240 per cent of the 1958 output, not 200 per cent as the Seven Year Plan had originally envisaged. The possibility seems strong that the 1961 plans for further expansion of arms output were not substantially reduced by the 1963 revisions which slowed down pig iron and steel expansion so drastically. Behind this 1963 set of revised goals were the needs for a new pattern of capital investment created by the ambitious program for expanding Soviet chemical production announced in late 1963.

Let us turn now to the experience of consumer goods production, postponing to a later point detailed examination of the factors that caused the radical changes of plans in 1962 and 1963. The picture in this area is complex. Some of the best performances were achieved in the field of durable consumer goods. Thus fewer than 1,000,000 television sets were turned out in 1958, but in 1963 this output reached 2,500,000 and in 1964 it neared 3,000,000 sets. Refrigerator production was 911,000 units in 1963, and appeared likely to exceed 1,000,000 units in 1964. Both figures were far above the 359,600 turned out in 1958. In a few commodities output mounted so rapidly that there began to be sales difficulties. Consequently, production of some items had to be kept roughly constant for several years, as in the case of clocks and watches. The same problem of surplus stocks forced a drastic reduction in the output of sewing machines during 1963. The introduction of a limited system of short term installment credit during this period was partially the result of increasing difficulty in selling some high priced consumer durables, though much of the credit actually used by consumers was for the purchase of clothing. But even in 1964, after substantial increases in production, such key commodities as television sets, refrigerators, and washing machines were still in very short supply in much of the Soviet Union. Another outstanding accomplishment was the rapid expansion of the fishing fleet and of the fish catch to help offset partially the disappointing increase in meat output. By 1963, the catch of fish and marine animals was roughly 60 per cent above the 1958 mark and higher than the 1965 target. In size of fleet, size of catch, and high level of technology employed, the Soviet fishing industry was one of the world's leaders in the mid-1960's.

Much more disappointing was the performance in basic food and clothing items. In the case of cotton textiles, for example, output increased only about 20 per cent between 1958 and 1963 and there seemed little chance that the 1965 goal of a 33–38 per cent rise would be fulfilled; the picture was similar in the case of wool textiles. Hosiery output increased about 25 per cent between 1958 and 1963, indicating that there was some chance of the planned 40 per cent increase being achieved by 1965. The output of leather shoes increased appreciably during 1959–1961, and then grew hardly at all during 1962 and 1963. There was little surprise, therefore, when in late 1963 a new 1965 shoe production target, well below the original 1965 goal, was announced. Granulated sugar production in 1963, from domestic sugar beets, was little more than it had been in 1958. These data confirm the picture shown by the over-all statistics that the growth of consumer goods production during 1959–1963 was much less impressive than the growth of heavy industrial output. The poorer performance reflected the relative parsimony of Soviet capital investment and other resource allocation to this field as well as the impact of disappointing agricultural production upon the supply of agricultural raw materials for consumer goods production. Moreover, much of the Soviet consumer goods production was of poor quality. In mid-1964, it was revealed the Soviet Union had accumulated 2.5 billion rubles of excess inventory consisting of expensive, poor quality textiles, clothes, and shoes that consumers refused to buy.[7]

Urban housing construction after 1958 also suffered setbacks. The Seven Year Plan had called for building a total of 650,000,000 to 660,000,000 square meters of such housing during 1959–1965, or an average of over 90,000,000 square meters annually. The record of what was achieved during 1959–1963 and what was planned for 1964–1965 shows the major disappointment suffered here:[8]

Year	New Housing Completed (million square meters)
1958	71.2
1959	80.7
1960	82.8
1961	80.2
1962	80.5
1963	77.4
1964 goal	77.5*
1965 goal	77.5*

* Estimated as the annual average of 155,000,000 square meter goal announced for 1964 and 1965 together.

Assuming the reduced 1964 and 1965 goals are achieved, the total volume of housing built during 1959–1965 will have been slightly more than 550,000,000 square meters, or about 100,000,000 square meters below the planned total. Since the Soviet urban population has grown more rapidly since 1958 than expected, the housing situation in Soviet cities and towns in the mid-1960's is substantially more crowded than the planners had anticipated it would be when they drew up the Seven Year Plan in 1958. What must have made this disappointment worse was the fact that up to the last minute, in a sense, the Soviet regime kept promising better performance in housing. Thus the 1963 economic plan outlined to the Supreme Soviet called for 91,000,000 square meters of new housing to be built that year, or more than 10 per cent over the 1962 amount. The actual new housing built in 1963 was only 77,000,000 square meters, 5 per cent less than in 1962.[9]

We turn now to the agricultural debacle of 1959–1963. In 1958, it will be recalled, Soviet farmers had gathered a record harvest. The authors of the Seven Year Plan assumed that this could soon be surpassed. They called for total farm production in 1965 to be 70 per cent above that of 1958. Table 17 shows the picture official Soviet data drew of what actually happened to farm production after 1958:

Table 17. INDEXES OF SOVIET AGRICULTURAL
OUTPUT, 1958–1963, AND 1965 GOAL

Year	Total gross farm output	Crop output (1958 = 100)	Livestock output
1958	100	100	100
1959	100	95	108
1960	102	100	107
1961	105	101	111
1962	107	101	114
1963 (est.)	96	86	110
1965 goal	170	*	*

* Not available.
Sources: Data for 1958–1962 recalculated to 1958 base from *Narodnoye Khozyaistvo SSSR v 1962 godu*, p. 227. Data for 1963 estimated on basis of material in *Pravda*, January 13, 1964 and other sources. 1965 goal from Seven Year Plan directives.

The basic phenomenon behind this disappointing picture was the failure of the Soviet grain crop to rise substantially above the 1958 record level. Without a much larger grain output, the supply of feed was inadequate for the much greater number of livestock needed to secure the dramatic increase in meat production Premier Khrushchev had promised. And behind the failure to secure large grain production increases was the continued inability of the virgin lands areas to equal their 1958 output, let alone exceed it substantially. This is apparent from the official data below, which probably reflect the geographic pattern of production with some accuracy, though there is reason to suspect they may exaggerate the over-all level of grain production:

Table 18. SOVIET GRAIN OUTPUT, 1958–1962,
AND 1965 GOAL

Year	Total Grain Harvest	Basic Virgin Lands Areas*	Rest of Country
		(millions of metric tons)	
1958	141.2	58.4	82.8
1959	125.9	55.3	70.6
1960	134.4	59.2	75.2
1961	138.0	51.3	86.7
1962	148.2	56.4	91.8
1965 goal	164–180	†	†

* Kazakhstan, Siberia, the Urals and part of the Volga region.
† Not available.
SOURCES: Data for 1958–1962 taken from official Soviet statistical handbooks.

These data overestimate the performance of the virgin lands in the sense that the region termed "basic virgin lands area" includes much farm land cultivated before the Khrushchev drive to plow up new lands began in 1954. For a clearer picture of the uneven, and in the most recent years increasingly unsatisfactory, production record in the new lands, it is worth looking at the output of the virgin lands territory of Kazakhstan, a region which may be regarded as the core of the whole Khrushchev program. Here are the data in millions of metric tons of grain: 1954–4.6; 1955–3.1;

1956—17.7; 1957—6.7; 1958—14.3; 1959—13.9; 1960—12.9; 1961—10.3; 1962—10.1. In 1963 this region presumably saw its production plunge down toward or even below the 1957 level. It is hard to avoid the conclusion that such gains as were made from plowing up these lands were largely the result of "mining" the moisture and soil fertility accumulated from the past when these areas were used only for grazing. As recurrent planting of the same crop and repeated drought seriously depleted this accumulated moisture and fertility, the likelihood of getting good crops decreased. As time passed, moreover, the appearance of repeated dust storms and other signs of serious erosion made clear that high costs were being incurred. Similar warnings were given by the reports of heavy weed infestation in many of the area's fields.

Clearly Khrushchev's hopes that these lands would provide a long term solution to Soviet grain problems have proved illusory. At best this program provided a temporary and high cost means of easing the Soviet grain problem during part of the 1954–1963 period. Here, as in some other cases, opponents of Khrushchev's policy were proved essentially correct. By the time their predictions were realized, however, they had been politically defeated and had no chance to point out the correctness of their views. Khrushchev, of course, liked to "prove" the profitability of the virgin lands experiment by comparing the direct cost of opening these lands to cultivation with government profits from the grain raised on them. The weakness in this calculation arises from the deliberate failure to consider two important factors: (1) the losses incurred because these lands were not used to pasture livestock and thus help produce meat, and (2) the probably greater losses incurred because the capital invested in the virgin lands was not employed in more profitable uses, specifically for intensifying agriculture in the lands with dependable rainfall by making available to them more fertilizer, more farm machinery, and the like.

Since many of the data have already been presented in an earlier chapter, we shall not discuss the development of other areas of agricultural production here. The central fact that actual growth of farm output through 1963 fell considerably short of the hoped-for gains may be illustrated, however, by comparing 1963 production of key commodities with the corresponding 1965 goals of the Seven Year Plan:

Table 19. PRODUCTION OF KEY AGRICULTURAL
COMMODITIES IN 1963 AND 1965 GOALS

Commodity	Unit	1963 Output	1965 Goal
Cotton	million metric tons	5.2	5.7–6.1
Sugar beets	million metric tons	44.0*	76–81
Potatoes	million metric tons	88.0*	147
Meat	million metric tons	10.2	16
Milk	million metric tons	61.2	100–105
Eggs	billions	28.8	37
Wool	thousand metric tons	374	548

* Estimated on basis of government purchases for year.
SOURCES: 1963 data taken from *Pravda*, January 24, 1964. Where only government purchases were given, actual output was estimated by using available past data on relationship between government purchases and actual output. Data on 1965 goals from Seven Year Plan directives.

In the summer of 1964, preliminary Soviet reports implied strongly that weather that year had been much improved over 1963 and that a substantially larger grain crop was being harvested. Reports from Kazakhstan indicated that one of the largest grain crops ever had been grown in that area, but concern was expressed about whether all the crop could be harvested before heavy snowfalls arrived. Though most of the credit for the improvement was given to increased rainfall, Soviet reports claimed that the greater availability of insecticides, herbicides (for weed control), and fertilizers also made a significant contribution. The outlook for meat production in 1964 seemed poor because of the need to rebuild livestock herds after the drastic slaughter of animals in late 1963.

The review given above suggests that when 1965 is concluded, the pattern of fulfillment of the Seven Year Plan, as originally outlined, is likely to be extremely uneven. On the one hand, output of heavy industry is likely to be above the original targets. On the other hand, production of consumer goods and agricultural products, as well as the volume of new housing, are likely to be well below their goals. In some respects, particularly the military capability deriving from the most modern and most expensive weapons, the Soviet Union is likely to be much stronger at the end of 1965 than was originally envisaged in early 1959. On the other hand, it is also clear that the Soviet people's diet, clothing supply, and housing situation will be substantially poorer than was hoped for when the Seven Year Plan was announced. This pattern of fulfillment has striking similarities to those of the Stalinist five year plans.

What forces produced this pattern of development? How did the Soviet regime try to meet the problems that have arisen in the years since 1958? Let us consider these questions now.

One major element influencing Soviet economic development all through this period has been the state of international relations, particularly of Soviet relations with the United States. In retrospect it seems likely that one of the reasons Premier Khrushchev sought to improve relations with the United States in 1959—the year that he and Deputy Premiers Frol R. Kozlov and Anastas I. Mikoyan visited Washington at different times—was the Premier's awareness of how crucially dependent the Seven Year Plan was upon a relaxation of tension. The extremely ambitious and unprecedentedly large capital investment program envisaged by this plan would clearly require maximal mobilization of the nation's resources; any worsening of international relations that would require increased defense spending would threaten the program. In January 1960, Premier Khrushchev sought to harvest some economic gain from the improved atmosphere generated by his Camp David conference with President Eisenhower the previous September. He declared that the Soviet armed forces had numbered 11,365,000 men in May 1945, 2,874,000 men in 1948, 5,763,000 men in 1955, and 3,623,000 at the time he spoke. He called for approval, which he got, of a proposal to reduce these forces to 2,423,000 men, justifying this by the improvement in the international situation and by the great nuclear weapon and rocket strength of the Soviet Union.[10]

Barely a year and a half later, as we have seen, Khrushchev felt compelled to raise military spending sharply and to stop the release of men from the Soviet armed forces. We may speculate that this turn of policy signified primarily a much greater than planned effort to increase the number of Soviet nuclear weapons and rockets, and to build the very expensive hardened underground installations for rockets which would make such weapons invulnerable to all but direct nuclear hits. The cost of this shift must have been high for other parts of the economy, especially since these sophisticated military weapons and measures require the highest grades of resources, both material and human. In early 1964, six months after the signing of the 1963 limited nuclear test ban treaty, Khrushchev and other Soviet spokesmen indicated Soviet military spending and the size of Soviet armed forces were again being reduced somewhat. But by that time the damage to the original Seven Year Plan had been done. A vivid insight into the magnitude of the Soviet military preparedness program in the mid-1960's was given on April 20, 1964, when Premier Khrushchev announced he would halt the building of two large scale nuclear reactors for producing plutonium. That the Soviet Union at that late date—almost fifteen years after the first detection of a Soviet atomic bomb explosion—should still have been increasing its capacity for producing fissionable materials is a sobering thought indeed.

The need to spend more than originally planned on military preparedness plus the recurrent shortfalls in agricultural production were key factors creating the virtually chronic capital shortage which plagued Soviet leaders during 1959–1963 and even afterward. Khrushchev had claimed in presenting the Seven Year Plan that its targets had been set so they could be attained without strain and without creating disproportions. The reality was a constant state of strain and the creation of many disproportions.

The Soviet leaders have sought to meet the capital shortage problem in three main ways. They have tried to utilize the available capital more efficiently and thus, in a sense, to "stretch" it to compensate at least partially for the deficit. They have attempted to increase the supply of capital by getting increased output which could be diverted to investment. And they have cut back on capital investment in some areas of the economy, notably housing and consumer goods industry. A fourth method, the borrowing of capital abroad, played only a minor role through the end of 1963. But in 1964 there were increasing signs of Western European and Japanese willingness to extend credits of 7–10 years or longer to finance Soviet imports of machinery and other capital goods. The 15-year loan Britain extended to the Soviet Union in mid-1964 to purchase chemical production equipment raised the possibility of a competition among Western powers to win Soviet orders through ever more generous credit terms.

The problem of using capital more efficiently was acute all during this period not only because of the unexpected demands on Soviet resources, but also because of the customary tendency of the Soviet system to spread capital thinly over an excessive number of projects. Much capital tends to be frozen unproductively, as a result, but to the individual executive responsible this does not seem a cost since he and his organization are not paying interest on this frozen capital. The rapidly rising dimensions of the problem are evident from the data in Table 20:

Table 20.   CAPITAL INVESTED IN UNFINISHED
PROJECTS, 1958–1962

At End of Year	Capital Invested in Unfinished Projects (billion rubles)	This Capital as Per Cent of Year's Total Investment
1958	17.5	73
1959	19.0	70
1960	21.4	69
1961	24.8	76
1962	26.1	75

SOURCE: *Narodnoye Khozyaistvo SSSR v 1962 godu,* p. 438.

At the Central Committee meeting in June 1959, Premier Khrushchev was already expressing his dissatisfaction with the inefficient use of capital. Hundreds of millions of rubles' worth of expensive equipment was being bought abroad, he complained, and then permitted to lie around—sometimes until it even began to rust. He called this situation "criminal." Then he went on to talk about the more basic problem: "We still continue to disperse funds among many projects and don't take care to finish new enterprises as quickly as possible. . . . We often drag out construction and thus postpone output. This is senseless. Capitalists can't do that. They would go bankrupt. But on occasion, we take 10 to 15 years to build a plant."[11]

Even before Khrushchev voiced these complaints, an important step had been taken to centralize and tighten control over capital investment funds. A decree of April 7, 1959 abolished the investment banking system which had existed since 1932, which had consisted of the *Prombank* (industrial bank), *Selkhozbank* (agricultural bank), *Torgbank* (bank for trade and cooperatives), and the *Tsekombank* (communal and housing bank). Most of their functions were transferred to the new *Stroibank*, the All-Union Bank for Financing Capital Investment, which took over the disbursing of state grants for capital investment in state enterprises as well as the issuance of credits, at low interest rates, to collective farms, cooperatives, and other borrowers.[12] By November 1959, the Soviet leaders had apparently decided this centralization of control over long term investment was inadequate. To tighten control further, they compiled a list of 271 specially important construction projects whose completion in 1960 was to receive highest priority in the allocation of materials and other resources.[13]

That these and related moves did not solve the problem became evident at the 22nd party Congress in October 1961. Khrushchev emphasized that the "question of questions is capital construction," a field in which, he charged, great confusion and many delays prevailed. He declared, "By January 1, 1961 there were millions of square meters of completed production areas that were not provided with equipment, and at the same time hundreds of millions of rubles worth of equipment had no production areas assigned."[14] He boasted that the Soviet Union was overfulfilling the capital investment plan, but then he described the situation in these terms and made this radical proposal:

> There are now more than 100,000 building sites in the country. . . . With the simultaneous construction of such an enormous number of projects, material and monetary resources are dissipated; many enterprises are commissioned two or three years later than technical facilities permit. Allocated funds are kept frozen for a long time . . .
>
> Why does this happen? In this case the desire for more becomes the enemy of what is sensible and realistic. Not infrequently, behind apparently plausible pretexts of concern for state interests, there is concealed outright sectionalism. . . . Republic councils of ministers, sovnarkhozes, ministries, and

local party organs seek funds to start building as many projects as possible, taking no account of how they are to be supplied with building materials, manpower, and equipment. Meanwhile, planning organs do not halt such anti-state activities. This results in time lags, low labor productivity, delayed completion dates, additional expenses, and increased building costs.

. . . Obviously, one should adopt the policy of stopping for some time, let us say for a year, laying foundations for new enterprises, while all the funds which accumulate during that period are turned to the speediest completion of the projects already started. Exceptions may be allowed only for especially important building projects.[15]

Almost two years later, in June 1963, Premier Khrushchev had the unhappy task of announcing what was in effect the decision to abandon the Seven Year Plan, two years before the period's end. He did this by declaring that the government had found it necessary to order a new plan drawn up to cover 1964 and 1965. He did not give the reasons explicitly, but the subject he emphasized above all was capital investment. "In many cases," he complained bitterly, "capital investments are still being used irrationally. The dispersion, theft, and freezing of financial and material resources is permitted, rather than securing the concentrated and intelligent use of these resources." Some projects had been under construction a decade or longer, though they could have been completed in three or four years, he charged. He gave this prescription for improving the situation:

Even a large allocation of capital investments may fail to achieve a large increase in operating capacity if the investments are spread over an enormous number of projects. Such an approach is senseless and inflicts enormous damage on the state.

At present the most important construction projects must be chosen and capital investments concentrated on them so they may go into production in the shortest time technically possible.

In preparing the capital construction plan we must scrutinize every project which is now under way or which is scheduled. . . . Funds must not be divided up among the individual branches of industry according to the existing proportions. Nor should the percentage growth for each branch be maintained at the average percentage of growth for the entire economy as has been the practice up to now. The chief thing is to allocate funds for developing the main, progressive branches among which the chemical industry is first and foremost . . .

We must look closely at all projects under way, estimate the importance of each in the national economic plan, and calculate how many of them our material resources will cover. . . . We must determine how many of the new projects we can supply with equipment, so that the building and equipping of new enterprises will be completed together and there will be no delay, no time wasted before they start to give the country returns of finished products and thus repay more quickly the funds spent on their building.

Under no circumstances must we begin projects that cannot be provided with material resources. We must not repeat the erroneous practice that has existed to date. If calculations show that we do not have the needed material resources, then we must not hesitate to halt work on some projects already started so that we may carry others through to completion more quickly.[16]

What emerges from the above is not only the chaos that must have existed in the capital investment field then, but the tremendous complication introduced into this area by continued agricultural setbacks. By the time Khrushchev made this last speech it had already been decided that the policy of developing an extensive agriculture, represented by the virgin lands program, had failed. Instead, agriculture had to be developed intensively, i.e., by seeking to secure higher yields per acre instead of merely increasing the number of acres sown. But this goal can be reached only by providing additional irrigated area as well as large quantities of fertilizer, herbicides, and insecticides. But the Soviet economy had normally given the expansion of irrigation and the effort to increase the output of agricultural chemicals low priority in the past. The chemical industry, in fact, had been one of those most badly hurt by earlier decisions to cut back on investments. As Khrushchev put it in that same 1963 speech, "The Seven Year Plan is being more than fulfilled in metallurgy but it is not even being fulfilled in the chemical industry." The 1958 chemical expansion plan had long since been buried, and now Khrushchev was faced with the problem of finding large new sums to invest in the chemical industry. We can understand why he had to scrap the Seven Year Plan and why he assailed his economic planners in these terms:

> With such planning there is no money available for new branches of industry whose swift growth is called for by life itself. And this is true at a time when these branches could yield major economic gains quickly. Because of these practices, everything new and progressive is still growing slowly in our land since the basic funds and material resources are being allocated according to previously established proportions.

An innocent listener might be forgiven if he did not suspect that Khrushchev himself had helped set the "established proportions" earlier and had played a key role in every stage of the planning he now condemned.

Another major theme of economic policy during this period has been the persistent drive to get better performance in the operation of the Soviet industrial and agricultural production apparatus. The measures employed for this purpose have ranged from incessant exhortation to far-reaching reorganization of the entire managerial structure of the Soviet economy and even reorganization of the party's own structure. The frequency of these reorganizations is perhaps the best evidence of continued dissatisfaction and the need to search for better means of securing improved performance. Perhaps most radical has been the new leeway given Soviet economists to suggest even drastic changes from old methods and old techniques to stimulate better production. As of mid-1964, these economists' most fundamental proposals have not been adopted, but their wide public discussion raises the possibility these ideas may yet be implemented.

Tighter control over the operations of the Soviet economy has been one favored technique. As early as June 1959 Premier Khrushchev revealed a decision to set up party control commissions in industrial and trade enterprises. He defined the functions of the control commissions as checking on the punctual fulfillment of production quotas and delivery schedules and assuring that the staffs of these enterprises "strictly maintain state discipline and fight all signs of local selfish interest or narrow departmental approach" in their work. The commissions were empowered to lodge protests against management decisions and to report to outside authorities on illegal actions in the plants.[17] We shall see below how this effort to intensify control was broadened still further in the massive 1962 reorganization of the Soviet economy's administrative system.

Another approach has been an effort to alter the incentive system for management so as to create greater interest in efficiency, cost reduction, and rational use of resources. Traditionally the Soviet manager's personal fortunes and the size of his bonuses have depended upon his success in fulfilling or overfulfilling his gross production target, almost regardless of how he did it. The kinds of abuses this leads to were vividly described by Premier Khrushchev in 1959:

> It has become the tradition to produce not beautiful chandeliers to adorn homes, but the heaviest chandeliers possible. This is because the heavier the chandeliers produced, the more a factory gets since its output is calculated in tons. So the factories make chandeliers weighing hundreds of kilograms and fulfill the plan. But who needs such a plan? . . .
>
> Many consumers often don't want to purchase our Soviet-made furniture. They look for foreign furniture because it is more rational. The plan for furniture factories is stated in rubles. Consequently the factories find it more advantageous to make a massive armchair since the heavier the chair the more expensive it is. Formally the plan is thus fulfilled since the furniture makers add this and that to the armchair and make it cost more money. But who needs such armchairs? If they were to manufacture ordinary chairs, do you realize how many would have to be made to fulfill the plan? The factories ponder: armchairs or ordinary chairs? The weight of the armchairs finally decides the issue in their favor. Everybody knows this. Everybody talks a good deal about this, but still the armchairs win.[18]

An effort to get more rational incentives was taken in the early 1960's when the success indicators for determining managerial bonuses in non-priority industries were changed. Instead of being primarily based upon a manager's success in reaching or exceeding his output goal, bonuses were made dependent primarily upon a manager's ability to reach his cost production targets, or to lower costs even below these targets. More attention was also focused upon managerial ability to turn out high quality goods, to deliver commodities on time, and other similar qualitative aspects of his work. But the habit of striving above all for maximum production, almost regardless of cost, is deeply ingrained in the psychology of Soviet managers and hard to eradicate.[19]

This small reform does not begin to compare with the bold proposals which have been put forward by a number of Soviet economists and mathematicians whose ideas have been given great publicity. In 1962, for example, great publicity and much public discussion were devoted to the ideas of Professor Yevsei G. Liberman of Kharkov. Professor Liberman seems to have started from the observation that there are at least two major sources of inefficiency in Soviet industrial management: one is the fact that since bonuses are given for fulfillment or overfulfillment of the plan, each enterprise has a great incentive to try to get the lowest and easiest possible plan. To achieve this, managers even try to conceal from superior authority the full extent of their plants' production capabilities. A second weakness is the fact that the Soviet manager's complete plan gives him orders on a great variety of matters: what items—and the quantities of each—he shall produce, the amounts of labor, raw materials, and other resources he may use, the cost of production he is permitted, the amount of profit he must make, etc. These directives are sometimes inconsistent and mutually contradictory. In any case, they tend to inhibit the manager's freedom of action and hinder his ability to make the best use of the resources at his disposal.

Professor Liberman offered a scheme designed to replace this confusion and complexity with simplicity, while at the same time creating a situation in which it would be to each manager's and enterprise's advantage both to have the most ambitious plan possible and to use available resources most efficiently and economically. Professor Liberman proposed that incentive payments be based upon one indicator: the rate of profit earned on total capital invested in an enterprise. He suggested arranging the incentive payments in such a way that the higher the rate of profit planned for by an enterprise and then realized, the higher would be the bonus received. In this way the enterprise would have no incentive to seek a plan based on a low rate of profit, because if it got such a plan and made more profit, the incentive payment would be less than it would have received if the plan had called for the higher rate of profit actually received. Managers, in Liberman's scheme, would receive from above only a minimum of plan orders, primarily those concerned with amount of output, the breakdown of that output into specific goods, and a schedule of delivery dates. The formal resemblance between this scheme and the normal system in a private enterprise economy where the entrepreneur seeks to maximize the rate of return on his invested capital is clear, a fact which caused a good deal of trepidation among Soviet economists who saw this idea as a departure from Marxism.[20]

Through the middle of 1964, the Liberman proposals had not been adopted except as the basis for experiments in some areas. But the attack on them did produce a Khrushchev defense of the profit concept:

> If we take our socialist economic system as a whole, the economic category of profit does not have the same social meaning as does profit in capitalist society. . . . Our industry produces goods not to obtain profit but because all of society needs these goods.

> But the individual enterprise is a different matter. In the enterprise profit is very significant as an economic index of the efficiency of its operation. It is very important whether an enterprise functions at a loss, thus consuming public funds, or at a profit, increasing those funds. Unless profit is calculated, it is impossible to ascertain the level at which an enterprise is operating and what contribution it is making to the public fund.[21]

The discussion of the Liberman proposals quickly exposed one key problem: if profits were to serve as the guide for rational conduct of Soviet enterprises, those profits had to be based on prices that were themselves meaningful, that actually reflected supply and demand conditions for the different commodities. But the arbitrary character of Soviet prices is well known, as is the fact that many of them offer no economically rational guide for choices among alternatives. The confusion in the Soviet price system is traditional and monumental. How shall the Soviet price system be reformed? At this point proposals advanced by Soviet mathematical economists, particularly by Leonid V. Kantorovich, come on the stage. Professor Kantorovich, using the method of linear programming which he discovered before World War II,

has in effect worked out a means of securing economically meaningful prices, the quantities he terms "objectively conditioned
indicators." Soviet mathematical economists would reform the
Soviet economic system by basing pricing and resource allocation
upon such mathematical formulations as linear programming, input-output analysis, and similar techniques. Put another way,
these mathematical methods and the electronic computers required for these methods offer a way in which the Soviet
economy might compensate for the absence of a meaningful market such as that in which many free world prices are determined
by the interplay of supply and demand.[22]

The extremes among the would-be reformers of the Soviet
planning system are to be found, on the one hand, among those
Soviet economists who would like to abandon centralized planning of all but the most important Soviet economic indexes. They
would introduce something akin to the Yugoslav system of
market-determined prices and inter-enterprise competition. At
the other extreme are some economists and mathematicians who
would retain detailed central planning, but who think this planning can be done much better by extensive use of electronic computers employing giant input-output tables and other types of
mathematical techniques such as linear and dynamic programming. One can find many other positions as well in the cacophony
of voices that the Soviet debates in this area have permitted to be
heard.

The diversity of opinions among Soviet specialists in this field
may be seen from a sampling of statements at a 1964 conference
on cybernetics and economic planning. Here, for example, is a
summary of mathematician Sergei Sobolev's position:

> It is a Marxist axiom that labor is the only source of wealth.
> Hence the principal task of socialist planning is to achieve the
> greatest abundance with the least expenditure of labor.

> What are the researches of Leonid Kantorovich and Victor
> Novozhilov concerned with? With proving that the best use
> of resources is made when distribution aims at the gross output
> reaching the highest possible level with a given assortment [of
> resources]. From classical mathematics we know that any
> deviation from this distribution, no matter how slight, must
> conform to the same ratio as holds for the most advantageous
> investment of capital. This results in quantitative relations ap-

proximating those used by the "theory of maximum utility." Fixing prices in accordance with these relations on a national scale on the basis of "objectively conditioned indicators" would be advantageous, since it would make the interests of the individual enterprises coincident with those of the nation as a whole.

Bitterly opposed to the trend toward centralizing economic planning with computer-operated mathematical techniques was the vice chairman of the Soviet Central Statistical Board, Ivan Malyshev:

We have eight million different prices. Taking into account the various links between them, there are hundreds of millions of prices—even billions, if the technological links are added.

A machine could possibly be built with a high speed response of a billion by a billion. But the question is, what good would it do us? Do you mathematicians expect to be able to see from the Main Computing Center all of our vast territory . . . all the innumerable technological processes—how people sow and reap, how every chemical installation functions, how every machine operates? . . .

You imagine that with the help of computing centers you will be able to press buttons, and, in response to your command, the processes of production, exchange, distribution, accumulation and consumption—in all their multiple economic, technical and organizational forms—will begin to run smoothly without a hitch or complication. And if you suddenly received a signal that something had gone wrong, say in Khabarovsk, all you would have to do would be to press a button and things would straighten themselves out. A strange Utopia! Society is not a sum of mathematical zeros and digits; it is a living, creative body of men, comprehensively developed, with a mind and will, successfully building communism.

Can all this be programmed? Central planning should give the general objective, the direction of movement, letting the workers themselves find and apply the best solutions for specific problems. Under such conditions there will be no need for the central computing centers to absorb and to weigh daily thousands of millions of pieces of information, quite possibly less than a hundred will do.

What we need is one general index.

Academician Khachaturov rejected the notion that any single index could effectively govern the Soviet economy:

> If we were to take price as that single index, for example, we would be forced to the conclusion that when there is a bread shortage the price of bread ought to be raised. An impossible conclusion for us. Or take fertilizers. We are short of them now. Do we remedy the situation by raising the price? Obviously not.[23]

Special interest attaches to a comprehensive plan for reorganizing Soviet planning advanced in early 1964 by Academician Vasili Nemchinov. The interest derives both from the author's eminence among Soviet economists and from the fact that his proposal appeared in the Communist party's theoretical organ, implying influential support in the party hierarchy. The key features of the Nemchinov proposal may be outlined as follows:[24]

1. The system of handing down production assignments to enterprises would be ended. Instead he seems to propose a competition among enterprises, each of which would offer the terms on which it would be prepared to fulfill different plan assignments. Planning agencies would then pick the enterprises proposing the most advantageous conditions and sign what he calls "plan-contracts" with them. He envisages that the price set would be mutually acceptable to both the planning agency and the enterprise, and the agency would guarantee the purchase of the contracted output by a specific economic body.

2. In general he would favor central planning of stable prices that change infrequently only for a limited number of important goods determining the population's standard of living or determining the level of production costs. He would permit other prices to fluctuate within a limited range.

3. He would encourage enterprises to make the goods most in demand by permitting those which did to divert a relatively large share of their profits to the enterprise's own use for paying bonuses, building facilities for the enterprise's workers, etc. Enterprises producing goods that enjoyed little or no demand would be permitted to divert very little or none of their profits for their own use.

4. He would introduce into Soviet cost accounting "obligatory standard charges on the fixed and working capital that society has

placed at the disposal of the enterprise," i.e., he would introduce interest on capital as an obligatory element of cost.

5. He would set up an automated electronic system of administering the economy, consisting of a system for collecting and processing economic information and also one for calculating economic and plan accounts to serve as the basis of planning decisions. He would run this through a system of long term norms governing, for example, such matters as the division of profits between the state budget and the enterprise. The combination of these norms and of the new set of prices would seek to assure that it would be advantageous for enterprises to carry out the directives and goals of the national economic plan. His expectation is that if this is done properly the enterprises would naturally strive, out of self-interest, to get contracts from planning and economic agencies precisely for the types and quantities of goods that the national economic plan wants produced.

As of the summer of 1964, nothing this ambitious and comprehensive has yet been tried out in practice, but a series of interesting experiments has been attempted by Soviet planners and economic managers.

One involves the use of a new measure of enterprise output, the "normative value of processing" (NVP) to replace gross output. The NVP is akin to the Western concept of value added by manufacture since it omits that portion of gross output representing the value of raw materials and parts bought by an enterprise for inclusion in its final product. The NVP seeks to express the net value of the enterprise's output by adding planned (or "normed") labor costs, the cost of production essentials such as electricity, and the relevant depreciation of fixed capital. Thus it seeks to remove the temptation for a plant manager to increase his seeming gross output by using more outside materials. NVP has been used for several years in the garment, printing, canning, and some other industries, as well as in all enterprises of the former Tatar *sovnarkhoz*.[25]

In early 1964 several consumer goods factories were given the right to act with greater independence, to determine their output and prices by negotiation with their customers rather than being governed by plans and prices handed down by higher authority. In another experiment being tried in 1964 in more than 80 enterprises of different industries, an effort was being made to combine some of Professor Liberman's ideas with continued central planning. The essence of this last experiment is a new bonus system based upon the combination of four major indices: the increase in output, growth in labor productivity, reduction in cost, and improvement in product quality. Bonus arrangements are set so that an enterprise gets a higher percentage premium for fulfilling planned indicators of progress, i.e., for each planned percentage of production growth or each planned one-tenth of one per cent cost reduction, than for the equivalent percentage overfulfillment of the plan. This, of course, incorporates the device Professor Liberman employed when he suggested offering material incentives to an enterprise to plan for the highest possible profit rate. As noted earlier, traditional Soviet incentive systems have tended to induce enterprises to seek the easiest possible plan because it was most profitable to do better than had been planned. The more traditional system may be illustrated by the arrangements for rewarding managers on the basis of the cost reduction index adopted in 1959. For fulfilling the cost reduction plan, managers receive 8–15 per cent of their salary. Then for overfulfilling that plan they receive 8–15 per cent of salary for *each per cent* of overfulfillment with the maximum bonus being 40–60 per cent of salary.[26]

To mid-1964 Premier Khrushchev had proved unwilling to adopt generally any of these radically novel proposals to improve the efficiency of Soviet industry. Instead he had placed his faith on efforts to reorganize that industry's administration. During the early 1960's signs of high level discontent with the operation of the 100 or so regional economic councils (*sovnarkhozy*) multiplied. At first this dissatisfaction showed in the creation of new higher bodies with coordinating functions. Thus in mid-1960 republic *sovnarkhozy* were formed in the Russian republic, the Ukraine, and Kazakhstan. These new groups must, in the nature of bureaucratic systems, have taken over much of the power formerly residing in the local councils. In May 1961, seventeen "Councils for Coordination and Planning" were set up, each given wide powers over a "large economic region" consisting, on the average, of six or seven ordinary *sovnarkhozy*. In addition there existed by this time some eleven USSR State Committees for different key industries and for construction. Unlike the old ministries, these new bodies apparently focused mainly on problems of technology and investment policy. The trend toward a recentralization of industrial administration seemed clear.[27]

The intensive Soviet press discussion of Professor Liberman's ideas during the late summer and early fall of 1962 seemed to suggest good prospects for increased reliance on economic levers of one sort or another as the next major innovation in Soviet industrial administration. The press discussion of those months proved a poor guide, however. Premier Khrushchev chose quite a different alternative in November 1962 when he unveiled the newest, and in some ways the most radical, reorganization of Soviet economic administration.

Khrushchev's address to the Central Committee was a wide-ranging indictment of the operation of many features of the Soviet economy. The changes it recommended, which were adopted, were geared to the specific weaknesses the Premier had pointed out. Below, therefore, we summarize both Khrushchev's bill of complaints and the measures taken to meet them:

First, he asserted that experience had shown that many of the existing economic regions were too small for efficient operation. Their multiplicity created problems, moreover, when major natural resources and the industries based on them were so located as to be administered by two or more different *sovnarkhozy*. He cited the iron ore deposits of the Kursk Magnetic Anomaly "divided quite unnaturally between the Kursk and Belgorod *sovnarkhozy*" as an example. His solution was to merge small economic regions. When this was done the former 100 or so *sovnarkhozy* were reduced to below 50, the biggest change coming in the Russian republic whose 67 economic regions were cut to 24. In Central Asia the republic economic councils for the Uzbek, Kirgiz, Turkmen, and Tadzhik republics were combined into one Central Asian Inter-Republic *sovnarkhoz*.

Second, Khrushchev attacked the existing territorial organization of the Communist party as unsuitable. Party leaders in a given province or district, he complained, were responsible for both industry and agriculture. This meant in practice, he argued, that at some times of the year they were concerned primarily with industry and paid little attention to agriculture while at other times the reverse was true. His solution was radical: the

NEW ECO

NOMIC REGIONS

SOVIET ECONOMIC ADMINISTRATIVE REGIONS AS OF EARLY 1964.

Translation from The Current Digest of the Soviet Press, *published weekly at Columbia University by the Joint Committee on Slavic Studies, appointed by the American Council of Learned Societies and the Social Science Research Council. Copyright 1963, 1964; by permission.*

Communist party should in effect be broken into two, one set of members and leaders at the local, provincial and republican levels exclusively and constantly concerned with agriculture, and the other set of members and leaders with industry. Thus each province would have a First and Second Secretary for industry and a similar set of officials for agriculture; in farm areas only what might be called the "agricultural Communist party" would function; in industrial areas only what might be called the "industrial Communist party." Moreover, Khrushchev suggested and secured the division of the provincial Soviet governments into similar "agricultural" and "industrial" governments. Nothing like this had ever been seen in the Soviet Union before. Dissatisfaction with the existing party control over the economy was implicit in this radical reorganization. And what was also clear was the existence of disagreement at the top over details. Khrushchev had called originally only for the formation of agricultural and industrial bureaus of the Central Committee. The decision actually taken provided for three economic bureaus, one for industry and construction, one for agriculture, and one for the chemical and light industries. A Central Asian party bureau was also set up to supervise the Central Asian *sovnarkhoz* mentioned earlier.

Third, the Soviet Premier assailed bitterly the confusion and lack of adequate central direction in Soviet industry's technical and design policy. He spoke enviously about the difference between the centralized design and technology of the American automobile industry's three major firms as against the diversity and duplication in Soviet industry. Here is a portion of his indictment:

> Who can calculate how many scientists and staff members of design bureaus are simultaneously designing similar farm machines or similar machine tools! Dozens or hundreds of design organizations duplicate each other's work, starting each project from the beginning almost as if no one else worked on it . . .

> Each of our furniture factories has its own designs and furniture. We have real freedom for bureaucrats who can each decide his own office style. Furniture is manufactured by about 4,000 enterprises, most of them small and poorly equipped. These enterprises are not specialized and some turn out more than 20 kinds of furniture. This disorganization causes the production of a good deal of inconvenient, expensive, ugly and

fragile furniture. The *sovnarkhozy* of the Russian republic alone turn out 156 types of chairs, 116 types of dining tables, 222 types of wardrobes, and even 217 types of beds.

Khrushchev's solution for these problems was a new centralization of authority over activity related to designing and new technology. The system of USSR State Committees was extended to cover all branches of industry, and these committees were given authority over this area of industrial decision-making. In Khrushchev's phrase, "The industrial committees must be the law makers of new technology."

Fourth, Khrushchev attacked the entire system of planning and executing the capital construction program. He charged that the plans provided often for building projects for which there were no designs and for which materials, manpower, and equipment were not assured. At times, he said, these plans called for locating plants in areas without adequate labor supply or raw materials. The solution, he declared, was to make the State Construction Committee the prime authority over the capital investment program, the agency to approve new projects, to assure that such projects had proper designs and resources required to build them, and to make certain that as far as possible all Soviet building is done from standard designs. Centralization of authority in this agency, he said, "will avoid the possibility of graft or localism in capital construction and will assure that projects not supplied with designs, money or material resources will be kept off the lists of approved projects." All questions of construction, he stressed, must be removed from the jurisdiction of the economic councils which could only appear before the construction industry as clients contracting for specific projects.

Fifth, he berated the nation's planners for incompetence. He accused the planners of being infatuated with the idea of increasing steel production and failing to see the need of raising polyethylene output instead. Everyone in the State Planning Committee cared only about his own little department and few were interested in drawing up a harmonious over-all plan with proper proportions, Khrushchev declared. To make his point he told this story:

A great many motor vehicles have been immobilized by the lack of tires. Many commissions have been organized to solve

Organization of a Typical U.S.S.R. State Production Committee as of Early 1964.

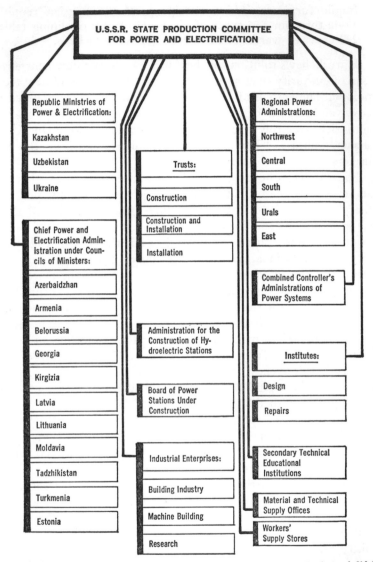

U.S.S.R. STATE PRODUCTION COMMITTEE FOR POWER AND ELECTRIFICATION

Republic Ministries of Power & Electrification:

Kazakhstan

Uzbekistan

Ukraine

Chief Power and Electrification Administration under Councils of Ministers:

Azerbaidzhan

Armenia

Belorussia

Georgia

Kirgizia

Latvia

Lithuania

Moldavia

Tadzhikistan

Turkmenia

Estonia

Trusts:

Construction

Construction and Installation

Installation

Administration for the Construction of Hydroelectric Stations

Board of Power Stations Under Construction

Industrial Enterprises:

Building Industry

Machine Building

Research

Regional Power Administrations:

Northwest

Central

South

Urals

East

Combined Controller's Administrations of Power Systems

Institutes:

Design

Repairs

Secondary Technical Educational Institutions

Material and Technical Supply Offices

Workers' Supply Stores

Addenda to the Chart: (1) The republic Ministries of Power and Electrification and Chief Power and Electrification Administrations are subordinate to the U.S.S.R. State Production Committee for Power and Electrification and are at the same time agencies of the Union-republic Councils of Ministers; (2) the functions of the Ministry of Power and Electrification of the Russian Republic (abolished in the spring of 1963) are performed by the U.S.S.R. State Production Committee for Power and Electrification.

Translation from The Current Digest of the Soviet Press, *published weekly at Columbia University by the Joint Committee on Slavic Studies, appointed by the American Council of Learned Societies and the Social Science Research Council. Copyright 1963, 1964; by permission.*

this "tire problem." . . . It was proposed that tire output be increased by a certain amount by a certain time. Independently, however, decisions were made to increase the production of motor vehicles. The result was that the entire increase in the production of tires went to equipping the additional motor vehicles, while many drivers can only stroll around their immobilized vehicles rather than drive them.

What sense does this make? They say resources are lacking. If so, cut the metal expenditure for motor vehicle output, produce fewer cars and trucks and allocate more resources to increasing tire output. Then more freight can be carried with the same number of vehicles.

Many planners, Khrushchev complained, get their jobs through "friendship and nepotism," have no "production experience, do not know management fundamentals, work organization, or the accounting system."

His proposal in this area was that the State Planning Committee be converted into the Council of the National Economy which would have managerial powers so it could settle problems that arose in the realization of a plan. The State Scientific-Economic Council, he suggested, should be renamed the State Planning Committee and instructed to concentrate on long range planning.

Finally, Khrushchev assailed different types of corruption, theft, embezzlement, and swindling in the Soviet economy. Thievery from state enterprises detected during the first half of 1962 and made the subject of court cases, he revealed, amounted to 56,000,000 rubles. Padding of accounts and misrepresentation of different kinds were rife on Soviet farms, he declared, while bribery had penetrated Soviet institutions and had even infected executives belonging to the Communist party. As a result, he declared, "state goods are wasted, apartments assigned illegally, land plots given away, pensions granted, students allowed to enter higher educational institutions and even diplomas granted, all for bribes."

The solution must be, Khrushchev declared, the mobilization of the masses to detect and punish those responsible for these evils, and thus to discourage other potential law breakers. To do this he called for creation of a Party-State Control Committee which would have units all through the country, units working with groups of ordinary people to uncover all possible kinds of abuses. A vast national organization for prying into every aspect of Soviet life would thus be created. Like the other Khrushchev proposals, this one, too, was adopted.[28]

Khrushchev's speech should not be viewed out of perspective. He focused on the ills of the Soviet economy because he wanted measures adopted to improve matters. But not everything was poorly planned, wasteful, or subject to illegal manipulation. Yet even after allowance is made for the one-sidedness of much of the speech, it is clear that Khrushchev was addressing himself to major problems. Certainly very little remained of the original *sovnarkhoz* system of 1957 after his reforms were adopted, and the Communist party's organization was altered more radically than ever before in its history.

One might have thought that such thoroughgoing changes would be given time to be implemented and to show whether they were adequate to meet the problems. But in early 1963, less than four months after Khrushchev's speech, a major new body was created: the Supreme Council of the National Economy. This was given all powers needed to direct the entire industry and construction of the Soviet Union, including authority over the State Planning Committee, the USSR Council of the National Economy, the State Construction Committee, all the production committees formed to guide technological policy, and, of course, all the regional *sovnarkhozy*. Centralization of authority had reached a new peak since 1957, suggesting that the additional centralization created the previous November had already proved inadequate. No explanation for this move was made. The only visible clue was the fact that the man named head of the new Supreme Council of the National Economy was Dmitry F. Ustinov, an individual known earlier as the head of the Soviet armaments industry. This raised the presumption, though not the certainty, that he had been given his post in the hope that he could raise all of Soviet industry and construction to the height of efficiency attained in military production. Another possibility, of course, was that the formation of this new agency and Mr. Ustinov's appointment were signs of a victory for those Soviet leaders who wanted more attention paid to military output and preparedness. The truth is, however, that we do not know the full meaning or motivation for this move.

One more change in the organization of Soviet industry during

ORGANIZATION OF CENTRAL SOVIET ECONOMIC MANAGEMENT AGENCIES AS OF EARLY 1964.

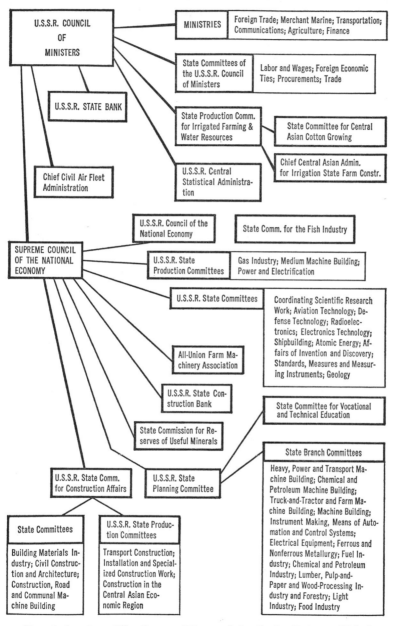

Translation from The Current Digest of the Soviet Press, *published weekly at Columbia University by the Joint Committee on Slavic Studies, appointed by the American Council of Learned Societies and the Social Science Research Council. Copyright 1963, 1964; by permission.*

the first half of the 1960's should be mentioned. This is the growing number of Soviet "firms." These are formed by aggregating small related enterprises into one larger complex. The aim is to economize on managerial costs, to form units large enough so that specialized technical and other personnel can profitably be employed, and to increase efficiency by having each of the small sub-units in the large "firm" specialize in one or another aspect of the productive process. A firm may be formed, for example, by combining a group of small shoe or clothing factories in the same city, or, alternatively, by combining several small enterprises dealing with successive stages of the same productive process. This movement began in the Ukraine and by 1964 had spread modestly to other parts of the Soviet Union.

In July 1964 Premier Khrushchev delivered a speech suggesting that he intended to carry out a far-reaching reorganization of the Soviet consumer goods industry to make it far more responsive to consumer demand expressed in the market than it could ever be under the traditional system of central planning. The Premier had evidently been badly disturbed by the realization that some 2,500,000,000 rubles of unsaleable consumer goods cluttered up Soviet warehouses, dismaying evidence of how little consumer wants influenced production. Here is the solution he proposed:

> We must have a system under which the costs arising because goods produced by some factory or other can't be sold will be borne by the enterprise that provided them. The fulfillment of plans by enterprises must be evaluated not only by gross output or by the variety of goods turned out, but also by taking account of the saleability of merchandise, of how people buy different goods.

> Evidently the necessity has arisen to change the order of planning and evaluating the work of enterprises producing consumer goods. Output of these goods must actually be based on the orders of trade organizations. Then the workers of industry and of trade will be more responsible before the people. . . .

> Factories and plants producing consumer goods must receive orders from stores, and stores must take into account the desires of the population and give orders for goods in correspondence with this demand. If a trade organization has ordered goods of a certain fashion, color and size and if these goods are not saleable, then responsibility should be not on the factory but on the trade organization that gave the order for this produc-

tion. In such cases the trade organizations must carry the material costs since the responsibility lies on those who ordered, not on those who fulfilled the order.

The Soviet leader was ordering, in short, introduction of a "feedback" system in which production of consumer goods might reflect actual consumer demand.[29]

The need for such a radical reform had been indicated three months earlier by a Leningrad Communist party official who proposed this major change in the operation of the system for consumer goods production and sale:

> One thing is clear: The system of planning consumer goods production is imperfect. Life demands it be changed. We propose to plan for such enterprises only the accumulation [apparently profit, HS] and average wages. And that's all! Let the director of the factory or plant himself ponder what and how to produce. With this we cease objectively to push managers to produce goods for which there is no demand, and we will compel them to agree on an assortment of goods with the trade organizations.

> Actually who, if not the trade network, must define or even dictate output and assortment plans for consumer goods! However, in order to realize this in practice, one must exclude the serious deficiencies in the forms of mutual relations between industry and trade.

> What are those forms now? They are extremely imperfect and at times carry a formal character. Stores make up requests for goods, send them to the wholesale offices of their own organizations and then the orders go to the Chief Trade Administration. From there they go to the headquarters of, let us say, the Russian Clothing Trade Organization, where summary orders for many stores are prepared. Then the Administration of the Clothing Industry "cuts" these orders in the light of its own production possibilities. The clothing manufacturers then go out to buy cloth. At this point the textile makers introduce their own limitations. Practically the result is that demand does not dictate supply, but rather that demand is "adjusted" to what can be supplied.[30]

As we turn to the development of Soviet agriculture after 1958, attention should be called to the quiet but major organizational revolution carried out in those years. At the beginning of 1959 there were 67,700 collective farms with 18,800,000 families, or 276 families per farm. Five years later, at the start of 1964, the number of collective farms was only 38,829 and they included only 16,200,000 families, an average of 411 families per farm. Presumably part of this change reflected the continued trend toward enlarging the individual collectives through mergers of two or more neighboring farms. But the other part of the story—helping explain the disappearance of 2,600,000 families from the collective farm statistics—is the growth of the state farms. At the beginning of 1959 there had been 6,002 state farms with a total work force averaging 3,835,000 persons during the preceding year. When 1964 began there were 9,175 state farms and they had employed over 7,000,000 persons on the average during the preceding year. The great bulk of this increase undoubtedly reflected the brisk pace at which collective farms were turned into state farms after 1958. The Soviet Union is still far from wiping out the collective farm system and making all collective farmers state employes. But if this process of conversion of collective into state farms continues at this pace very much longer, the end of the collectives could be closer than had earlier appeared likely.

We have seen that from the beginning of the Seven Year Plan in 1959 agricultural output proved disappointing. The first year Soviet leaders were not very alarmed. At the December 1959 Central Committee meeting which reviewed the results, Premier Khrushchev called the output reasonably good. He concentrated his criticism on the leaders of Kazakhstan—the key virgin lands territory—and accused them of responsibility for having failed to gather the good crop that, he said, had been grown there. About four million acres, Khrushchev charged, had not been harvested. He rejected the excuse that some of this grain had not ripened, attributing this to late sowing caused by the fact that 18,000 tractors in the area had not been repaired and thus were not available. And he revealed that 64,000 grain harvesting machines had also stood idle during the harvest season.[31]

But as 1960 neared its end, and it became apparent that the desired substantial increase in farm output had again failed to materialize, the Soviet leadership really became alarmed. At the end of October, the Premier submitted a memorandum—secret at the time but later published—to the party Presidium. In this he called attention to existing milk and other livestock product shortages and warned of the dangers these posed. The population was getting some 30,000,000,000 rubles more purchasing power annually than it had received in 1956, he pointed out, and much of this money was seeking food. He expressed the gravity of his concern in these words:

> Comrades, it is necessary for all of us to be fully conscious that the people's requirements have grown so much that a shortage of livestock products has arisen even at the current output level. Serious conclusions must be drawn from this situation. Need one speak of the difficulties that can arise if the current volume of agricultural production—and especially of livestock products—is maintained and no annual growth of production of these products is obtained? I think everyone understands the importance of these problems.[32]

It was an angry Khrushchev who faced the Central Committee meeting in January 1961, therefore. There had been "some growth in agricultural production," he conceded. "But this growth cannot satisfy us since it does not correspond to the people's growing needs." Much of his speech was a bitter attack on deficiencies that had been found. There was widespread thievery at grain warehouses; local party officials were trying to hoodwink the government by padding accounts and by delivering even essential seed grain to the state; millions of livestock were dying of cold and hunger in some areas. Most significant, in the light of later developments, were his complaints about the many areas that were turning to the government with requests for grain to meet their needs. Here, it seems likely, was a sign of official sensitivity about drains on the state's grain reserves.

Khrushchev offered two main solutions. One was a large expansion of irrigation so as to make key areas independent of rainfall. In his memorandum the previous October he had already expressed regret to his colleagues in the leadership that capital investments for irrigation had been cut by over 1,000,000,000 rubles. In his January speech he projected a broad irrigation program, and pointed out that a mistake had been made in building the huge Bratsk hydroelectric station in Siberia. In Central Asia, he asserted, such a huge installation would have permitted irrigation of vast sunny areas.

His second solution was a radical reorganization of the entire governmental apparatus concerned with agriculture. As implemented by subsequent decrees, this reorganization in early 1961 involved the following measures:

First, the Ministry of Agriculture was made primarily an agency for carrying out scientific research in agriculture and seeing to it that improved farm technology was actually put to work in the fields. Obviously influenced by the American example, the creation of a system of provincial agricultural experiment stations was ordered along with the creation of model experimental farms in localities throughout the country. Each model farm was to have priority claim on new machinery, fertilizers, insecticides, and the like, so as to carry out its main job: the encouragement of the most efficient methods and latest scientific techniques on all farms in its area.

Second, a new agricultural procurement system was set up under the leadership of a newly-created State Procurements Committee. The new body, through its local organs, was to handle all state agricultural procurement on the basis of a system of advance contracts with collective and state farms. The agency was also provided with a nationwide network of inspectors who were charged, in effect, with supervision of all Soviet agriculture at the local level, and empowered to bring pressure—through Communist party and government channels—against any farm management whose activities did not satisfy the inspectors.

Third, a new centralized system of supplying state and collective farms with machinery, spare parts, fertilizer and other production essentials was created, the government's All-Union Farm Machinery Association (*Soyuzselkhoztekhnika*). In effect this was to be the central link between agriculture and industry, receiving orders from the farms, and getting the factories to supply what the farms wanted. The intention was to cope with the new problems created by the fact that there were no more machine tractor stations. Since the collective farms owned the farm machinery, they had become direct customers for many additional industrial products. The collective farms, as customers, were choosier than the old MTS had been, and the better farm chairmen wanted to be sure they got their money's worth. It was the new organization's job to make industry meet the farms' needs, rather than continuing the bad habits born when equipment was simply allocated centrally to the MTS. The new organization

also inherited the farm machinery repair centers in the countryside.

In theory, at least, this arrangement had great promise. The
Ministry of Agriculture and its subordinate bodies would bring
science down to the individual farm, much as the state agricultural colleges and county agents do in the United States. The
new farm machinery organization would make sure the farms got
what they wanted and needed in the way of equipment and production essentials. And the procurement agents and inspectors
would not only arrange for state purchase contracts, but also
make sure that what was contracted for would be actually produced. Nikita Khrushchev, in another secret memorandum to the
party Presidium in March 1961, hailed the procurement agency
as "our controller." Its local agents, he wrote, would check
matters at the local level so that through them "we will reach
literally to each collective farm, to each state farm, and even to
each brigade."[33]

But neither the new organization nor the nation-wide speaking
tour of agricultural areas Premier Khrushchev made in early 1961
helped a great deal that year. The Ukraine put in an improved
performance and sold significantly more grain to the state than
it had in the disastrous year before. But, over all, the official data
claimed less than a 3 per cent gain either in total farm output or
in the grain harvest. As 1961 closed, the Soviet leadership was
faced by the hard fact that three of the Seven Year Plan years
had gone into history, and almost no progress had been made
toward reaching that program's farm goals.

Something like panic seems to have seized Premier Khrushchev.
He clearly cast about for some expedient that would surely give
the country an immediate and appreciable increase in farm production, particularly grain production. What he wanted was a
measure that would improve farm output in 1962, regardless of
long term consequences. At the 22nd Communist party Congress
in October 1961, Premier Khrushchev unveiled his newest
panacea. The Soviet Union, he declared, must radically revise its
structure of sown areas and abandon the grass-crop rotation
system that, he charged, Stalin had foolishly foisted upon Soviet
agriculture. The acreage of fallow lands and of lands planted to
oats and to annual and perennial grasses should be cut drastically,
and the acreage planted to corn and to such legumes as peas and

fodder beans should be increased sharply. In the virgin lands, he ordered, 20,000,000 more acres should be brought into cultivation within the next few years. His strategy was plain: increase the area under grain as much and as fast as possible. Only in the virgin lands area, where the planting of wheat year after year had resulted in huge areas infested with and overwhelmed by weeds, did he suggest that there be clean fallow. In early 1962, Khrushchev again went barnstorming throughout the Soviet Union to sell his new recipe to farmers and to denounce those who continued to defend the system of crop rotation that had been standard for roughly a quarter of a century. At one point, a leading agronomist complained about the attacks on him for defending the old rotation system. After all, he had simply followed the party's orders, he pointed out. Khrushchev turned on the agronomist in fury, telling him it was his job to tell the party and him, Khrushchev personally, the truth when they went wrong, not simply to be a toady.[34] The impact of this campaign upon the pattern of Soviet sown areas was immediately apparent in 1962 and 1963.

Table 21. DISTRIBUTION OF SOVIET SOWN AREA, 1961–1963

| Crop | Sown Area | | |
	1961	1962	1963
		(million hectares)	
Total sown area	204.6	216.0	218.5
Grain	128.3	135.9	133.8
Corn	25.7	37.1	34.2
Oats	11.5	6.9	5.7
Legumes	4.3	7.2	10.8
Annual grasses	16.7	11.7	17.5
Perennial grasses	19.4	15.6	13.6
Fallow	16.1	7.4	6.3

SOURCES: Official Soviet statistical handbooks.

Khrushchev emphasized the seriousness of the situation when the Central Committee met in March 1962. He bluntly declared that the Seven Year Plan's agricultural goals were in serious danger, and pointed out explicitly how far actual 1961 production of grain, meat, and milk had fallen below that year's targets. Soviet citizens who thought that existing local meat shortages were the result of the distribution system's errors were wrong, he said: there simply was not enough meat to satisfy the demand.

There was no real control over agricultural production in the rural areas, Khrushchev said, implying that the system of procurement inspectors set up a year earlier had failed to accomplish its purpose. He demanded a really stringent control organization that would penetrate to the grass roots and actually improve production. The result was the creation of a new farm administrative mechanism replacing the procurement committees, and their inspectors, set up in 1961. This mechanism consisted of so-called territorial production administrations having authority over all the collective and state farms in a given area, usually a region consisting of several local government districts.

The responsibilities given the new administrations were impressive. They were charged with supervising the implementation of government farm decisions on output and procurement, with "guiding the organization of output and of procurement of farm products," with the planning, accounting, and statistical functions for their areas, and the like. They were enjoined correctly "to organize production, norm setting and labor payments" on the farms in their jurisdiction, and empowered to select managerial personnel and specialists for these farms. The administrations were ordered to work through inspector-organizers who would cooperate closely with collective farm chairmen and state farm directors, but who were told not to supplant these officials. Each local administration was also assigned Communist party and Young Communist League organizers who, with their assistants, would supervise political work in each area.

The powers given these administrations made them in effect the bosses of each area's agriculture. Despite the 1955 decree giving collective farms the right to carry out their own production planning, the new administrations had the practical power to issue orders to the collective and state farms under their jurisdiction. This new organization immediately introduced great possibilities for conflict between the inspector-organizers and the farm officials who would in many cases naturally seek to preserve such independence as they could. This situation reflected the schizophrenia resulting from the leadership's desire to have simultaneously the benefits of local initiative and freedom and also maximum control over what actually went on. But how much difference the new organization actually made is conjectural, especially since in the nature of things many of the same administrative personnel must have been used in each region in each reorganization. And many of these personnel must have kept on doing much the same thing regardless of how different the organizational charts drawn up in Moscow may have seemed.

Khrushchev's speech at the March 1962 Central Committee meeting emphasized that the existing problems were not all created by organizational deficiencies. He charged that those responsible for supplying the farms with fertilizer, insecticides, and herbicides had shown "full irresponsibility," and that the plans in this area were not being fulfilled. Moreover, he pointed out, Soviet farms lacked much needed machinery. He cited estimates showing, for example, that the nation's farms required almost 2,700,000 tractors but had less than half that number, that they required 1,650,000 trucks, but had fewer than 800,000, etc. Farm machinery output had to be doubled, he declared, and for that purpose large new factories producing this equipment had to be built and existing plants had to be increased in capacity. His implication was clearly that increased capital investments had to be provided for this purpose. This must have met strong and effective opposition. This conclusion follows from the fact that when Khrushchev spoke again at the very end of the Central Committee meeting he hastened immediately to make clear that agriculture would not be aided "at the expense of industrial development and the strengthening of the country's defense."[35]

But while the Soviet people waited to see whether the new measures would improve agricultural output, they continued their relentless pressure for more meat and butter. We may suspect the Soviet leaders feared that the situation here was getting out of hand. Certainly on June 1, 1962 they announced what must have been politically the most painful economic decision of the post-Stalin years, a rise in the retail prices of meat and butter. Increases of 30 per cent in meat prices and 25 per cent in butter prices were required, the announcement argued, in order to permit a 35 per cent rise in the prices paid farmers by the state for meat. The previous prices paid farmers for meat had been so low, the announcement said, that many collective farms had actually lost money on every kilogram of meat they sold, a situation which provided no incentive for increasing production. The retail prices being raised, it was argued, had been so low that the state, too, lost money on its meat and butter sales to the public. The Soviet state had no alternative to this step, the Soviet people were told, because funds could not be diverted from industrial expansion or armaments. The increases were only temporary, the Soviet people were assured, and in the "not too distant future" farm production costs would come down and it would be possible to lower prices.[36]

This was a particularly hard blow for the Soviet people because for most of the preceding year they had been deluged with a flood of propaganda about the new Communist party Program's plan for achieving full Communist abundance within the next few decades. Discontent at this sacrifice appeared all over the country, even within the Communist party. Thus Khrushchev declared at the end of June:

> We know that even some Communists talk this way at times: "So at the 22nd party Congress we adopted a program for building communism. And then meat prices went up. Where are we moving, forward or backward?" Only those who look backward reason in this manner. Forward looking people know quite well that we are moving ahead.[37]

More dangerous was the spirit of open rebellion the price increases generated. The facts are best known about the pitched battles which took place in the city of Novocherkassk, near Rostov, where hundreds were apparently killed before rioting was put down. A Western observer has summarized the national reaction in these words:

> The price increases had, in fact, been greeted everywhere with demonstrative anger. Sit-down strikes, mass protest demonstrations on factory premises, street demonstrations, and here and there riots involving bloodshed occurred throughout the Soviet Union. Some of the places from which evidence at hand speaks about such occurrences include Grozny, Krasnodar, Donetsk, Yaroslavl, Zhdanov, Gorky and even Moscow itself (reportedly a mass protest meeting took place in the "Moskvich" Automobile Plant). And, despite guarded official denials, reports about street demonstrations and widespread looting of food stores in the Kemerovo area are solidly based. An outside observer cannot judge the intensity nor the extent of the various

local disorders; neither can he affirm with certainty that Novocherkassk was the worst and bloodiest.[38]

Soviet statistics—which are doubted by many abroad—claim that Khrushchev secured one main 1962 farm production objective: grain output rose dramatically by 10,000,000 tons to the highest level known in Soviet history. But, curiously, state grain procurements in 1962 increased very little above the level of 1958 though the grain crop was reported to be 7,000,000 tons higher. Whatever the reality of the official grain figure, the composite farm production index made clear that on balance Khrushchev had again failed to make a rapid and sharp improvement in agricultural output. The sharp decline in 1962 potato production was the worst blow, but the output of cotton and some other important crops also declined. The official agricultural index made clear that total farm output in 1962 was a mere 2 per cent more than in 1961. And even more ominous, 1962 total farm output was only 7 per cent above that of 1958, as against the 70 per cent increase called for by 1965.

This was the agricultural background to the November 1962 Central Committee meeting that decided to split the party organization and the provincial governments into industrial and agricultural organizations. The collective farm-state farm territorial production administrations had justified themselves since their formation the preceding March, Khrushchev said, but some had been found to be too large and unwieldy. Hence instead of the 961 originally formed, their number would be increased to 1,500. At the same time the rural party organizations in the Soviet equivalent of the county, the *rayon*, would be abolished and the rural party organization concentrated in groups centered about the territorial production administrations. Khrushchev gave this explanation:

> This is done so that the party committees may occupy themselves above all in guiding agricultural production. Emphasis on production must be foremost. Party committee workers must live by concern for this primary activity, must maintain constant alertness, bearing in mind that the chief thing in communist construction is economics, production . . .[39]

With the attention of the entire rural Communist party thus concentrated on the necessity for raising production, Khrushchev made clear that he would be satisfied in 1963 only if the state could raise its grain purchases to 70–75,000,000 metric tons. He asserted that even the record amount of grain collected in 1962 by the state "is not enough for our present grain needs. Therefore there arises the urgent requirement to find means to raise the output and procurement of grain in 1963 and following years."[40] The actual result, as we know, was nearly catastrophic. Bad weather, and we may also suspect poor work by many farmers, produced a 1963 grain crop so low that its size was kept secret well into 1964. The key statistic that was released told the story of the disaster, however: in 1963 the government had procured only 44,800,000 metric tons of grain, more than 20 per cent less than the 1962 procurements, and more than one-third below the 70–75,000,000 tons Khrushchev had called for. The results were swift and drastic: sharp limitations on bread sales were imposed in the Soviet Union and government buyers fanned out to the Western world to buy millions of tons of grain from the United States, Canada, and other Western nations. The Khrushchev agricultural program had resulted in a fiasco.

By late 1963, the decision had been made to scrap the previous policy line. Increasing the area under extensive farming would not suffice—it was now clear—to raise Soviet grain production to the 230–250,000,000 metric tons that would be needed by 1970. Khrushchev could not admit that the virgin lands program had basically failed, but when he appeared before the Central Committee in December 1963 to present a new program he gave this definition of the change of course, and this justification:

> Can we continue farther along the road of developing grain farming by expanding the sown area? It is clear we will not be able to follow this road in the future. We do have great possibilities for extending the planted area. However, we should have to spend very large amounts to make these lands suitable. We would have to engage in drainage, in clearing rocks and underbrush away, etc. Where is it more profitable to allocate resources now that the best lands are already being cultivated: into expanding the chemical industry or into expanding the sown area? Clearly it is more advantageous to allocate these funds for the development of chemistry, for the production of mineral fertilizers. The Soviet Union now has genuine opportunities to intensify its farming, to increase grain output per acre of arable land, to raise yields significantly.

We must develop chemistry rapidly and increase mineral fertilizer output in order to achieve dependable, guaranteed grain harvests and to harvest all the grain required for the full satisfaction of the country's needs.[41]

This was part of the huge chemical industry expansion program requiring 42,000,000,000 rubles in capital investment in order to triple chemical production in the seven years after 1963. Khrushchev called for production by 1970 of 70–80,000,000 tons of mineral fertilizers as against the 20,000,000 tons expected in 1963, and 1970 output of 450,000 tons of herbicides and insecticides as compared with the manufacture of 59,700 tons of such substances expected in 1963. The same program also called for large expansion of plastics, artificial fiber, and tire production. This new program went far beyond the unfulfilled 1958 chemical production expansion plan. Khrushchev also declared that to intensify agricultural production there would have to be more irrigation, but he indicated that, since capital was scarce, extension of irrigation canals would have to take second priority to growth of the chemical industry. The cutback in steel and related production goals noted earlier was forced by the need to find capital for the chemical program.

The great novelty in all this was not only the gross expansion planned for fertilizer production, but also the fact that a decision had been made to apply fertilizer in large quantities to grain crops. In the past the great bulk of Soviet fertilizer production had gone to crops such as cotton and flax providing industrial raw materials. But as Khrushchev and other Soviet leaders made clear, much of the fertilizer available in the past had been poorly used. Some had been left to deteriorate in the open for long periods at railroad stations and other points far from the fields. Some fertilizer had been used incorrectly without regard for local conditions of soil and weather. All these and other abuses had to be ended, Khrushchev demanded.

When the party Central Committee met again in February 1964 to consider agricultural problems, the decision had apparently been made to fight vigorously against agricultural slackness. The Agricultural Minister, I. P. Volovchenko, struck some telling blows. He implied, for example, that Khrushchev had gone too far earlier in his all-out campaigns for corn growing everywhere and for maximal elimination of grass sowings. The Soviet Premier himself had seemed to retreat at least slightly on these and other points in his concluding speech at the December 1963 meeting. Volovchenko assailed the careless treatment of Soviet farm land, and the resultant losses due to serious erosion, to excessive diversion of fertile farm land to non-agricultural use and the like. He denounced the high weed infestation on many Soviet fields, noting that unless weed infestation was combatted more effectively introduction of fertilizers might actually be harmful in some areas, since fertilizer would simply give a richer crop of weeds. The quality of much farm work was very poor, he indicated, with many farm operations not completed at optimum times because of the poor condition and poor utilization of farm machinery. He assailed Soviet state and collective farms for feeding 15.2 per cent of their 1962 milk production to young livestock. "No other country expends such a large amount of milk for livestock," he declared angrily. Other speakers at the same meeting told of areas in which up to 40 per cent of the farm machinery stood idle, of the need to turn every seventh new tractor back to the factory to repair its defects, and of the large amount of land provided with irrigation canals, but not irrigated.[41a]

When Khrushchev spoke before top Soviet officials in late February 1964, he, too, was in a bitter mood. He stressed the need to give farmers material incentives, and hinted that on some collective farms payment had no relation to the amount or quality of work but—as he said had been true earlier—still was made in proportion to the number of "mouths." He denied that low government prices were responsible for the existence of unprofitable farms, and cited the data in Table 22 as evidence.

His implication was plain: prices were high enough, and the solution was better distribution of farm incomes so that the most productive workers were paid adequately while the poor producers suffered. He devoted much of his speech, too, to denouncing the incompetent agricultural bureaucrats, citing case after case of the stupid decisions they imposed upon the farms. It was these ignoramuses, he implied, who were mainly responsible—along with bad weather—for the poor farm production of 1963.[42]

The impression that the grass-roots agricultural bureaucracy was being used as a scapegoat for the 1963 setback was strengthened the following month. In a disingenuous tone, as though it

Table 22. AVERAGE PRICES PAID COLLECTIVE FARMS,
1952 AND 1963, PER 100 KILOGRAMS OF PRODUCE

Commodity	1952	1963
	(rubles)	
Wheat	.97	7.56
Corn for grain	.54	7.66
Sugar beets	1.05	2.87
Raw cotton	31.88	38.30
Sunflower	1.92	18.10
Potatoes	.47	7.10
Beef*	2.03	79.90
Pork*	6.72	98.00
Milk	2.52	12.18
Eggs (per 1000)	19.90	70.00
Wool	106.80	378.67

* Live weight basis.
SOURCE: *Pravda*, March 7, 1964.

were revealing a solemn state secret, a decree piously denounced
the interference of local officials with individual collective and
state farms. The 1955 decree giving the farms themselves the
right to plan everything except the amounts they should deliver
to the state was being violated, the decree declared with sancti-
monious horror. The thrust of the many and complex changes in
Soviet agriculture's administration during the preceding years had
been aimed at getting more effective government and party control over the work in the countryside. Yet the decree declared
primly:

> Lately, however, some provinces, territories and republics have
> permitted stereotyped planning of production from above,
> which the party has long denounced. Plans setting out sown
> areas, crop yields, and the size and productivity of animal herds
> have been crudely thrust upon the farms so that the entire work
> of collective and state farms has been regimented by orders
> from above. This stifles the activity of farm leaders and spe-
> cialists and curbs the initiative of workers on collective and
> state farms.

> Some local agencies often show a scornful attitude toward the
> plans and proposals that have been worked out by the collec-

tive and state farms. Without reason, they force the farm directors to revise their plans, revisions which do not take into account real possibilities and economic expediency.

All this must stop, the decree demanded. The farmers must be allowed to plan their own production. And to show that this time the party and government really meant it, the decree wiped out the loophole in the 1955 enactment which had given local officials the legal right to intervene in farm planning. This was the provision that farm plans had to be reviewed by local authorities who could send them back to the farms for revision if they wished.[43] But could a mere decree end the long tradition of farm subservience to local officials? And did not the same incentives exist as before for those officials to intervene? After all, the party and government held them responsible if farm production in their districts was poor.

The following month, April 1964, Premier Khrushchev came forth with a memorandum containing still more ideas for rectifying the situation. Farmers and farm officials must be taught the best methods known for carrying on each type of production, he insisted. The issuance of textbooks containing this knowledge was of the highest priority, he asserted. He compared Soviet methods of producing chickens, eggs, and dairy products with those used abroad, and found them wanting. The United States and Western Europe were using industrialized methods with high productivity of labor and low costs. The Soviet Union must do the same, he declared in his memorandum to the Central Committee. And he returned bitterly to the poor quality of many agricultural officials. How could the Soviet Union keep on explaining its agricultural backwardness by the shortage of qualified personnel, he asked. In the preceding 10 years a whole generation of well trained people could have been raised. But this had not been done, he concluded sadly, and agriculture had been allowed to drift by itself.[44] These words came ominously close to admission that much of what he himself had tried to do in the preceding decade had failed. But his domination over Soviet farm policy seemed to be unshaken, for the Central Committee immediately appointed a very high level committee to submit within a month's time recommendations for implementing his specific proposals.

In July 1964, Premier Khrushchev proposed and the Supreme

Soviet voted the Soviet Union's first comprehensive social security system for collective farm members, one including old age pensions, disability payments, aid to dependent children, and maternity benefits. The pensions, scheduled to begin for some 6,500,000 collective farmers (men over 65 with 25 years' service and women over 60 with 20 years' service) on January 1, 1965, are to be financed jointly by collective farm and state contributions. They will depend upon the average earnings of each pensioner during his active work period, and can theoretically vary from a low of 12 rubles a month to a high of 102 rubles monthly. The formula employed is 50 per cent of the average earnings up to 50 rubles a month, and 25 per cent thereafter. The actual monthly pension in 1965 is likely to be about 14 rubles or less monthly. This is implied by Premier Khrushchev's revelation in February 1964 that total money earnings of collective farmers from the collective farms in 1963 amounted to 7.2 billion rubles, equivalent to 448 rubles a year for the average household, and 320 rubles annually for an average member. The 14 ruble monthly pension may be compared with the 30 ruble monthly figure which is the minimum pension for an urban worker. A special government decree after the pension law was adopted provided for the urban pension system to cover collective farm chairmen, mechanics, tractor drivers, and the like, thus tacitly admitting the huge differential between the pension system for peasants and the more generous one for urban workers. Nevertheless, the institution of even this limited social security system for the collective farms was a step forward.[45]

A month later, in August 1964, Premier Khrushchev was again touring the country's farming areas, and discussing a new reorganization of Soviet agriculture to be considered the following November at a Central Committee meeting. In speeches and talks with farmers, he sneered at the existing supervisory organization set up in 1962, comparing the local personnel unfavorably with American county agents. The Soviet local inspectors, he complained, only asked questions, while the needed system was one in which local officials would really make useful suggestions. Judging by his statements, at least four major policy changes were under consideration: (1) the setting up of a system analogous to that of American county agents; (2) the end of the existing system under which farm personnel are paid according to the number of acres plowed or weeded or harvested. Instead, he suggested, a group of peasants with appropriate equipment should be given a tract of land, made responsible for its care during the entire growing process, and then paid on the basis of what they actually produced. His praise for this system sounded remarkably like the arguments advocates of privately owned farms make for a family farm of the type common in the United States:

> Under this method the responsibility of each person for production is raised. One does not have to send a controller behind each tractor driver. The tractor driver or brigade leader who is responsible for the entire complex of work is himself a controller. He checks to make sure everything is done on time and in high quality fashion. He calculates correctly that if the work will be done on time . . . if the harvest will be gathered without loss, then more production will be received per hectare, and consequently he will guarantee himself higher earnings.[46]

Khrushchev indicated a few days later that his revelations had irked some of his colleagues, implying apparently that there was disagreement about this idea—with its marked resemblance to some features of capitalist agriculture—and other proposed changes. (3) He revealed that a new reorganization of agriculture was being considered, one that would set up a different administration for each major crop or animal product.[47] (4) He urged adoption of a large new program of capital investment in irrigation facilities for the corn-growing areas of southern European Russia. These proposals must also have helped increase the opposition to Khrushchev that finally deposed him two months later.

What have the gains and setbacks, the achievements and the failures of the Soviet economy during the Seven Year Plan period meant to the Soviet people? The simplest answer is that, as of the second half of 1964—a year before the plan period ends—the Soviet standard of living is higher than it was in 1958, but not as much higher as Premier Khrushchev had said it would be in the period of exuberant promises, when the Seven Year Plan was adopted in early 1959. To appreciate this more precisely, we may compare in detail the promises Khrushchev made then and the data on the real situation in the early and mid-1960's:

1. Khrushchev promised that by 1965 the real wages of work-

ers and employes—taking account of higher money wages, pensions, grants, and lower restaurant prices—would be 40 per cent higher than in 1958. The real earnings of collective farmers, he declared, "will similarly rise at least 40 per cent." Taking available official data at face value, the actual increases achieved have been the following:[48]

	1952	1958	1961	1963
Real incomes of workers and employes	100	142	155	158
Real incomes of peasants	100	168	182	198

These data indicate that during the first five years of the Seven Year Plan period the real income of workers and employes, even by Soviet reckoning, rose only about 11 per cent, while real income of peasants rose only about 17.8 per cent. On balance, therefore, it is difficult to see how the gains for either category by 1965 could be very much more than 20 per cent above the 1958 level, while they could be below that figure. The most reasonable estimate would seem to be that during the Seven Year Plan period, 1959–1965, Soviet real incomes will have increased only about half as much as Premier Khrushchev had promised they would during these years.

2. Premier Khrushchev promised that by 1965 minimum wages would be raised to 50–60 rubles a month. The minimum wage law actually adopted in July 1964 set the levels at 40–45 rubles a month.

3. Premier Khrushchev promised that by 1962 the mass of Soviet workers would be shifted to a 40 hour week, and that by 1964 most Soviet workers would start being transferred to a 35 hour week, while miners and others working in harmful conditions would start being shifted to a 30 hour week. As of October 1964, there was no evidence that any of this had happened.

4. Premier Khrushchev promised that by 1965 "taxes from the population will no longer be necessary," i.e., promising the abolition of the Soviet income tax. The effort to fulfill this promise turned into a fiasco.

Premier Khrushchev set the stage for the attempt to end Soviet income taxes when he delivered a major speech before the Supreme Soviet on May 6, 1960. The Soviet Union was now rich enough to discontinue the income tax on urban workers and employes, the Premier told his people, and this would be done by the end of 1965 in a series of six annual steps. The income tax on the lowest paid workers would be eliminated first and then other higher income groups would benefit. Workers receiving up to 100 rubles monthly—a group that Khrushchev's figures indicated included roughly 90 per cent of all urban wage earners—would get the full benefit of the eliminated tax. Workers earning between 100 and 200 rubles monthly—about 10 per cent of the government labor force, Khrushchev's data implied—would get only part of the saving, the percentage varying from 79 per cent for those in the 100.1–120 ruble bracket to only 10 per cent for those in the 180.1–200 ruble group. Those earning over 200 rubles monthly would gain nothing from the elimination of the income tax, but they constituted only .6 per cent of all government employes. However all those affected, regardless of income, would benefit from the simultaneous abolition of the special surtax levied on bachelors, childless couples, and families with few children.

Since the Soviet income tax rates were low, the savings per worker even if this program had been carried out would have been small. For the great majority of workers, the income tax rate varied from 4.3 per cent for those earning 37 rubles monthly to 8.2 per cent for those receiving 100 rubles monthly. Those who earned over 100 rubles were taxed at 13 per cent. However modest the prospective savings, they were clearly welcome, and the Soviet press met the announcement with its accustomed paroxysms of joy. Here is a typical *Pravda* comment at the time:

> The abolition of taxes from the earnings of the workers and salaried employes! Where, in which capitalist country can this be done, which bourgeois parliament can make such a decision? Such bourgeois countries and such parliaments in them have never and will never exist . . .

> Only a socialist country which has achieved a high level in its development and places the well being of the people above everything can completely abandon taxes on wages.[49]

The promised reductions for the lowest paid groups of workers were carried out on October 1, 1960 and the same date in 1961. But on September 25, 1962, *Izvestia* carried an announcement that the further elimination of the income tax had been "temporarily postponed." The move was necessary, the official announcement asserted, "in view of the important measures now being carried out . . . for a further rise in agriculture and industry, and for a substantial increase in the production of consumer goods as well as in housing construction, which call for additional budget allocations, and also in view of the intensification of the aggressive plots of imperialism and the need to strengthen the defensive ability of the Soviet Union." In the accompanying propaganda, the menace of war was stressed, and *Izvestia*'s editorial comment promised explicitly: "Needless to say when the international situation changes, the measures of the party and state for abolishing taxes on the population will be completed." More than two years later, the international situation had improved, but nothing more had been heard of eliminating Soviet income taxes.

A notable feature of Soviet policy during the years 1959–1964 was the changes in wages paid different categories of workers. Priority in the wage reform was given to workers engaged in industry whose production quotas could be increased at the same time as their wages rates were improved, as well as to workers engaged in construction, transportation, and on state farms. Premier Khrushchev said in July 1964 that during the preceding five years over 50,000,000 workers had received higher wages averaging 13–25 per cent in different fields. He put the additional cost of these earnings improvements at about 4.5 billion rubles annually.

Premier Khrushchev made these revelations at the same time he announced a comprehensive program for raising the wages of the poorest paid major category of Soviet workers—service personnel employed by the state as teachers, barbers, doctors, store clerks, apartment house superintendents, pharmacists, nurses, local government officials, public utility repair men, and the like. He announced a program of wage increases that, he said, would give 18,000,000 workers an average 21 per cent increase costing 3.3 billion rubles annually. This implies an average absolute increase of some 180 rubles or so annually, and indicates that the average base pay of these workers before the increase was about 900 rubles annually or 75 rubles monthly.

The low wages Premier Khrushchev revealed existed in these

fields helped explain some traditional features of Soviet life, for example, the perennial shortage of rural teachers, the reluctance of men to study medicine, and the tendency of Soviet store clerks to leave such work as soon as possible and, often, to supplement their incomes by theft or deception of one sort or another. Thus he revealed that a rural teacher in the first four grades was paid— during the first five years of work—only 52 rubles monthly, equivalent to less than $15 a week at the official exchange rate. This rate, the Premier announced, would rise to 80 rubles a month. But even after the increase goes in effect in November 1964, a teacher with higher education and more than 25 years' experience will receive only 160 rubles a month, or less than $50 a week. Young doctors working in urban clinics, Khrushchev said, were receiving 72.5 rubles monthly if they had less than five years' experience, or about $20 a week. This is to be raised to 90 rubles a month. After the wage increase, the highest pay provided for a doctor—a person with more than 30 years' experience, if working in a city, and having the highest competence rating possible—will be only 200 rubles a month, or less than $60 a week. Khrushchev gave no specific wage figures for store clerks. But he implied that these had been very low, saying that these clerks had gotten a 50 per cent wage increase in 1961, and that in 1965 they would get an additional increase whose absolute amount would be not very much less than the 1961 rise.[50]

There was a somber overtone to the words of Leonid I. Brezhnev, newly chosen First Secretary of the Communist party of the Soviet Union, when he delivered his first public speech after the ouster of his predecessor, Nikita S. Khrushchev. He said then, "We rejoice at the successes that have been attained, but we also understand well the real difficulties in our path. There is great work ahead. . . ." There were similar overtones that day in the speech of Alexei N. Kosygin, who had succeeded Khrushchev as Premier of the Soviet Union. He stressed the overriding importance of raising labor productivity and warned that "Communist abundance of material and spiritual goods does not fall from the sky." The speeches were delivered at Moscow's celebration of the feat of the "Sunrise" space ship in which, for the first time in history, three men orbited the earth. Yet the addresses of the two new post-Khrushchev leaders on this occasion had a muted quality, suggesting they were more oppressed by the problems they had inherited than joyful over this latest "victory in space."[51]

Against the background of the history described in this chapter, both the removal of Khrushchev and the sober attitude of his successors in office are very understandable. While the former Premier's downfall was caused by many factors, including some that were non-economic in nature, the contrast between his glowing promises of economic advance and the less brilliant reality must have played a key role. From the economic point of view, the surprise is perhaps only that he remained in power as long as he did and was not removed earlier, say in late 1963 after the grain production setback of that year. In 1964, as noted above, the grain harvest improved substantially. In late October 1964 it was reported that the Russian republic and Kazakhstan alone had already sold the Soviet state some 53,800,000 metric tons of grain, or 9,000,000 tons more than had been procured from the entire country the year before. The later news that the Ukraine had delivered almost 12,000,000 tons of grain confirmed earlier claims of record state grain receipts in 1964.[52]

But if the agricultural situation was brighter than it had been earlier, the slowdown in industrial production growth must have provided a potent argument for Khrushchev's foes. During the period of October 13–15 when the anti-Khrushchev coup was carried out, the Central Committee of the Soviet Communist party must already have known what was made public a few days later: that industrial output during the first nine months of 1964 had been little more than 7 per cent above the same period of 1963, the slowest growth rate in more than a decade and a half. And the Committee must have known too that during this nine-month period industrial labor productivity had increased only 4 per cent, a sharp decline from the 6 per cent rise for the same period in 1963.[53] Behind this decline in industrial labor productivity must have been such factors as worker discontent and the ineffective use of much of the vast new capital investment being made in Soviet industry. In the first half of 1964, the existence of poor worker morale had been obvious from complaints about the large number of laborers changing their jobs, but the proposed measures for tightening labor discipline were not enacted at that time.

We may conclude this discussion by summarizing some of the issues that emerged as subjects of Kremlin controversy in the summer and early fall of 1964, issues that appear likely to have played key roles in setting the stage for Khrushchev's fall from power and determining its precise timing:

First, there appear to have been major disputes over agriculture. During Khrushchev's tour of farm areas that summer, he unveiled proposals for new major changes, notably the reorganization of collective farms to make their operation analogous in some ways to private farms and his call for large capital investments to irrigate corn-growing areas. At the time he made these speeches, Khrushchev hinted broadly that he was meeting opposition, and that to counter this opposition he was appealing over the heads of his colleagues in the Soviet leadership to the Soviet people. Whatever their opinion of his proposals, his attempt to win public favor for his ideas and thus bring pressure upon his fellow Communist party hierarchs can hardly have endeared him to them.

Here is the way Khrushchev spoke on August 8, 1964 as he sought to mobilize public opinion behind his latest set of farm reform proposals:

> Some comrades have said to me: Perhaps these materials should not be made public. You are stating in advance what will be said in the report at the Central Committee plenary session. Yes, this is what we did earlier. Then not only the proposals for the calling of Central Committee meetings but even the materials of the meetings were kept secret. At times, even Communists were ignorant of what had been said in the report and speeches at the meeting. Now things have changed. We have gone back to Lenin's work style and are doing things in the way he taught us. And Lenin, even in those complex and hard conditions, always tried to acquaint the party and the people with the decisions of Central Committee meetings. He personally went to the factories, to the workers and peasants to tell them how and what the Central Committee had decided . . .

> Why should we make a secret of the fact that the Central Committee Presidium has decided to hold a meeting and discuss a report on the extension of specialized production and on its administration? . . . We will lose much time if we do not discuss the matter now. Otherwise it would happen that the meeting would agree with these suggestions and take the necessary

decision, but you would say: "It is good they took the important decision, but it would have been better to discuss it before-
hand so that beginnings might have been started as early as
next year."

So I am discussing this with you in advance. The meeting will
be held in November, but I have come to see you in August to
consult and give you advice. . . . Now you cannot reproach
me by saying that at the Central Committee meeting I spoke
about everything, but when I was on the collective farm I kept
silent.[54]

Second, Khrushchev suffered a further setback when, in August
1964, his radical reform of Soviet secondary education was abandoned. In 1958, the ten-year schools had been changed to eleven-
year schools to permit combining academic education with work
in factories, farms, and other enterprises. When the decision
was announced to return to a ten-year school system, and to save
most of the required time at the expense of work experience,
nothing was said publicly about Khrushchev's much publicized
role in originally introducing the reform.

Third, there seems great likelihood that Khrushchev in the
summer of 1964 was thinking of introducing major changes in
other areas of the Soviet economy besides agriculture. This
appears to be implied by the discussion that opened in *Pravda* in
mid-August 1964 and immediately got down to basic and important issues.

Academician V. A. Trapeznikov opened the discussion by re-
iterating the call for the use of profits as the main indicator of an
enterprise's success or failure, and denouncing as "obsolete" the
traditional management of the economy through a system of obligatory norms governing every type of resource used by an enterprise as well as every major type of expenditure. His description
of how the existing system produced damaging contradictions
between the interests of particular enterprises and those of the
economy as a whole was devastating:

Now, unhappily, the economic interests of the producing organization and of the national economy that consumes its output frequently turn out to be contradictory. For example, the
producing plant has no incentive to improve its product's

quality if this makes for increased unit cost, but the consumer wants improved product quality even if this is somewhat dearer.

The nation's economy desires the development of new types of output, but the producing enterprise has no such interest since the effort to secure this causes extra trouble and lowers its indexes of economic performance. To offset irregularities of materials supply, the producer has an incentive to accumulate large inventories of materials, but the national economy's interest is in reducing the freezing of funds and resources that are needed by other enterprises. Building organizations have an incentive to install expensive materials and equipment rapidly . . . long before they are needed to go into operation, since this increases the building organization's plan fulfillment as measured in terms of money. But the interest of the national economy is in having such materials put in place as late as possible and as close as possible to the time they are really needed so that capital is not tied up unduly.[55]

Even more radical proposals were put forth as the summer of 1964 wore on. O. Volkov, an automobile plant executive, proposed that the Soviet Union adopt a quasi-market economy. He urged that "enterprises, marketing and trading organizations have maximum independence on questions of concluding agreements to supply and sell their products, and also to some degree in setting the price of the goods being bought and sold" and called for prices to be negotiated between buyers and sellers. He declared: "Prices for one-of-a-kind products even now are negotiated with consumers. This system should be applied also to items that are mass produced or manufactured serially." He called for profit sharing to be a major factor in workers' wages, saying that bonuses from profits might be 30–40 per cent of a factory collective's wages funds, or even up to 80 per cent in some cases. A week later, a planning official, V. Shkatov, called for introducing differential economic rent explicitly into Soviet prices. He proposed setting up a system of charges and subsidies for enterprises based on the natural advantages or disadvantages they had because of the relative fertility of the soil they worked, of the different degrees of metal content in ores from mines they operated, and the like. He pointed out that because of the neglect of economic rent, enterprise profits under the existing system often reflected primarily the differential quality of land or mineral resources an

184 THE SOVIET ECONOMY SINCE STALIN

enterprise worked rather than the actual quality of its poduction performance. To solve the problem, he urged the introduction of what he called "polar ratings." He suggested that, on the basis of these ratings, payments be made to the state by enterprises endowed with relatively rich and advantageously located resources, and conversely that payments be made by the state to enterprises endowed with relatively poor or inconveniently located resources.[56]

Finally, however, the most important economic blow to Khrushchev's hold on power may well have been the one he himself delivered when—apparently in late September 1964—he spoke before the nation's Communist party, government, and planning leaders. In this speech he out-Malenkoved Malenkov. In a summary of the speech that appeared in the Soviet press two weeks before his purge, Khrushchev came out publicly for giving the highest priority in the Soviet economy to raising the Soviet standard of living. He implied that the nation's heavy industrial production and military strength were now high enough to get along on lower priorities. The threat this posed to powerful vested interests in Soviet society may well have encouraged the formation of the coalition that unseated Khrushchev; and many of the arguments used against him may have echoed those he himself had hurled at Malenkov in early 1955. Here is the way Khrushchev put his thesis, according to the official summary of the speech:

> In composing the perspective plan for the period immediately ahead . . . it is necessary to be directed by the thesis that the chief task of this plan is the further raising of the people's living standard. If, in the period of the first five year plans and in the postwar years, we placed basic emphasis upon the development of heavy industry as the foundation for the expansion of the economy of the entire country, for strengthening its defensive capability—then now, when we have a mighty industry, when the country's defense is at the necessary level, the party poses the task of quicker development of those branches producing consumer goods.

> We have now a mighty metallurgical industry, a contemporary developed machinery industry, highly developed energy, fuel and other branches of heavy industry. At the given stage of Communist construction our task consists in the further de-

velopment of the production of means of production for the broader production of the means of consumption. . . .

Now our country is at such a stage of its development that the satisfaction of the growing material and spiritual requirements of man must be advanced to first place in working out the perspective plan of development of our economy.

Behind the laconic phrases of the official summary there are also hints that he demanded major changes in many parts of the Soviet economy and its organization. He called for planning to give preference to improving the quality of Soviet goods over simply increasing the volume of output and accompanied this by an apparently bitter attack on the inferior quality of much Soviet industrial output and new housing construction. He put great stress on the need for getting maximum results with least expenditures, a section of his speech that conceivably may have called for adoption of some of the reforms urged in the earlier *Pravda* discussion. He attacked the continuing failure to take adequate account of foreign technical innovation, and asked that Soviet researchers stop inventing that which had already been invented. These and other tantalizing hints suggest that this may have been one of the most important and revealing speeches of Khrushchev's long career. But, judging by what followed, its chief result seems to have been to contribute to his removal.[57]

In the very first speeches of Brezhnev and Kosygin after they assumed Khrushchev's duties as First Secretary and Premier respectively, there were hints of disagreement on the issue of priorities for consumers. Brezhnev, for example, declared: "The party considers its chief tasks in the field of domestic policy to be the development of the productive forces of our society, the steady improvement on this basis of the welfare of the Soviet people. . . ." This sounded very much like the traditional line that heavy industry must be given priority in development since on its growth allegedly rested the state's ultimate ability to raise the output of goods for consumers. But a strikingly more pro-consumer note was sounded in Premier Kosygin's speech the same day: "Our party says: There is no loftier, more vital task than that of insuring a steady growth of the living standards, of the welfare of the Soviet people."[58]

Also suggestive for the future was a decision taken a few days after Khrushchev's ouster to expand an experiment begun with his approval on July 1, 1964. As noted earlier, two Soviet clothing firms—the *Bolshevichka* in Moscow and the *Mayak* in Gorky—were permitted to enter into direct relations with clothing stores, and to plan and carry out their production on the basis of the stores' orders, with prices settled by negotiation between the producers and their customers. The objective was to avoid adding to the accumulation of unsaleable and unwanted consumer goods that had piled up in past years when production was planned from above with little knowledge of what consumers actually wanted. Meeting on October 19 and 20, 1964, the Council of the National Economy of the USSR in effect pronounced the experiment a success and ordered the extension of these arrangements to some other enterprises producing consumer goods. One report published abroad said the affected enterprises composed one-third of the apparel and footwear plants of the Soviet Union.[59]

It was notable, too, that in the early post-Khrushchev statements of the Soviet press and of the new Soviet leaders there was a constant emphasis on the intention to continue strengthening the military capabilities of the Soviet Union. Khrushchev, of course, had never proposed weakening Soviet military strength, but in the speech discussed above—in which he proposed first priority for higher living standards—he used the weaker formulation: "It is necessary always to maintain the defense of the country at the necessary level." The difference between Khrushchev's implied policy of keeping military preparations stable and the Brezhnev-Kosygin advocacy of "strengthening" that military strength may be a clue to a major secret issue in the final Kremlin battle of the Khrushchev era. It is conceivable that the military leaders of the country pressed for new expensive programs, including a large scale effort to defend the country with anti-missile missiles, and that Khrushchev's preference for diverting resources to consumer needs helped swing military support to his opponents. But, in view of Soviet secrecy on military matters, we can only speculate on such possibilities.

The major *Pravda* editorial of November 1, 1964, shed additional light on the Soviet economy at the end of the Khrushchev era and implied some additional points regarding the indictment of the ousted leader's errors in economic management. While noting that the country had had some economic successes, *Pravda* complained of shortcomings in the field of capital construction and declared that the Soviet Union had not yet mastered the "great art" of using material resources rationally. Then, in an obvious attack on Khrushchev's fondness for changes in economic organization, the newspaper added:

> It should be pointed out that the idea still exists among us that it is possible to solve intricate economic problems through administrative measures; all one has to do is to reorganize the apparatus, to merge two administrations into one or, on the contrary, to divide one trust into two, and everything will be fine. This is a most fallacious approach.

Instead, *Pravda* argued, the necessary scope had to be allowed for independent economic activity by enterprises and it was important to learn how to make good use of economic levers in operating the economy, particularly cost accounting, prices, credit, and profits. Such words must have encouraged the reformers anxious to reduce bureaucratic control over the Soviet economy, and to introduce changes such as those discussed earlier in this chapter.

Developments during November 1964 made clear that the post-Khrushchev regime was moving quickly to introduce economic changes. Early that month, residents of Moscow were permitted to buy five pounds of flour per family for home baking purposes, the first time flour had been on sale in more than a year. Shortly thereafter, the reductions ordered in 1956 in the legal size of private gardens and in the allowable numbers of private livestock of collective farmers, rural specialists and urban workers were cancelled. The reductions were assailed as "unfounded" and collective farms were ordered to help provide pasture and feed for collective farmers' private livestock. In his speech on November 6, Communist party First Secretary Brezhnev complained that the limitations on private farming had been introduced "although economic conditions were still not ripe for such a step." This major reversal of policy—reminiscent of the Malenkov-Khrushchev line in 1953 —seemed both an effort to gain popularity for the new regime, and an admission of the inability of the country's state and collective farms fully to meet Soviet food needs.

An even more dramatic move was made at the Communist party Central Committee meeting on November 16. Khrushchev's November 1962 division of the Communist party organization at the provincial and lower levels into two separate groups, one industrial and the other agricultural, was cancelled. The *Pravda* editorial of November 18, explaining the reintegration of the party organization, spelled out the failure of Khrushchev's frantic efforts to solve Soviet economic problems through organizational changes:

> Life has not confirmed the timeliness and expediency of this [1962] reorganization, which was carried out without the necessary preparation, in an atmosphere of unjustified haste, without weighing all its consequences . . . The division of the party organization into industrial and agricultural divisions produced many difficulties and complications. The reorganization contradicted life. Life has shown that in practice it is impossible to make a demarcation of the spheres of activity of the industrial and agricultural party organizations . . . [The reorganization] led to the confusion of the rights, functions, and obligations of the party, administrative and economic organs, and pushed the party committees to substitute for the economic organs . . . Instead of the control apparatus becoming simpler and cheaper, in the past two years the apparatus of the provincial organs has grown considerably . . . The work conditions of the cadres have become more complicated, and the possibility of rendering aid to the rural areas from the industrial centers has become smaller . . . Moreover the reorganization led in many sectors of economic construction to a weakening of the influence of party organs on production activity.

After this move, Moscow buzzed with rumors that other Krushchev economic policies would soon be altered. One rumor held that the regional economic councils, or *sovnarkhozy*, introduced in 1957 would be abolished. Similar hints of change came in the Soviet press during this period. One article seemed to suggest that Khrushchev's 1963 chemical program would be cut back substantially. Another article, by a provincial party secretary, denounced the excessive area planted to corn in a region where other crops gave better results. The whole atmosphere suggested that a new era of Soviet economic history was beginning.

CHAPTER VI

Foreign Economic Relations

IN MAY 1964, the chairman of De Beers Consolidated Mines, Ltd., the primary force in the world diamond market, announced that his firm had ended its contract to act as the Soviet Union's diamond selling agent in the West. The chairman made plain that the action was a political move, one designed to punish the Soviet Union for its support of plans to organize a trade boycott against South Africa.[1]

The incident was revealing on at least two counts. The political motive for the De Beers move was typical of much that has happened in Soviet foreign economic relations. In this area political factors have often played key roles along with economic factors in determining what the Soviet Union and its economic partners would do. Moreover, the De Beers decision provided a reminder that in the field of diamonds the Soviet Union had chosen against engaging in price competition but had been cooperating with the chief Western price-setter for this commodity. This served to emphasize how oversimplified some earlier Western notions had been. Those earlier ideas, based on experience with Soviet price-depressing sales of aluminum, tin, and petroleum in some markets, had emphasized what some called the "Red Trade Menace." Alarmists had raised the nightmare of a broad Soviet drive to disorganize world markets and to drive world prices down to ruinous levels.

The history of Soviet foreign economic relations since Stalin's death has been profoundly influenced by both political and economic factors. On the one hand, this area has been an important sector of the cold war. Both sides have sought to advance their interests by using trade and aid as weapons. With the United States in the fore, the Western nations have sought, with varying

189

degrees of enthusiasm, to hamper the rise of Soviet economic and military strength by an embargo on strategic goods. This effort, however, had lost much of its force by the mid-1960's. By expanding its trade with the underdeveloped countries and extending economic aid to some of them, the Soviet Union has sought to draw them into its orbit and to impress upon their peoples the virtues of the Soviet economic system. When the United States tried in the early 1960's to destroy the Castro regime in Cuba by ending American sugar purchases from Cuba and prohibiting most American exports to that island, the Soviet Union came to Castro's rescue. Within a matter of months, it became Cuba's chief economic partner both as customer and as supplier. Yet even amidst all the political conflict reflected in the Soviet Union's economic relations, economic factors have always been at work influencing in varying degrees the decisions that have been made. And as the ferocity of the cold war eased in the years after Stalin, economic factors began to play a more significant role in affecting East-West economic relations. Ironically, in these same years the growing discord within the Communist world—particularly between the Soviet Union on the one hand and Albania and China on the other—increased the motivation on both sides to subordinate their economic relations to their political struggle.

In his last major theoretical pronouncement, published five months before his death, Stalin noted what he called the disintegration of the single, comprehensive world market. He declared that the international economy of 1952 was composed of "two parallel world markets . . . counterposed to one another." He hailed what he regarded as the successful cooperation and rapid economic growth of the socialist world market embracing the Soviet Union, Communist China, and the Eastern European nations, and he predicted confidently: "There can be no doubt that with such a high tempo of industrial development, these countries will soon reach the point where they will not only have no need to import goods from capitalist countries but will themselves feel the need to dispose of the surplus goods they produce."[2]

The background of Stalin's thinking is provided by the fact that in 1952 over 80 per cent of the total Soviet foreign trade volume, amounting then to $5,300,000,000, consisted of commerce with other Communist-ruled nations. The rest was trade carried on primarily with Western Europe, notably with Britain

and Finland. But subsequent events showed clearly how wide of
the mark he had been in predicting that "soon" the Communist-
ruled nations would "have no need to import goods from capitalist countries." By 1963, the value of Soviet foreign trade had
increased to about $14,300,000,000, of which only about 70 per
cent was with other Communist-ruled nations. The value of Soviet trade with "capitalist nations" in 1963 was almost equal to the
total value of Soviet foreign trade in 1952.[3] A more detailed picture of the development of Soviet commerce since World War II
is shown in Table 23.

Table 23. SOVIET FOREIGN TRADE SINCE WORLD WAR II

	1946	1953	1958	1963
		(billions of dollars)		
Total foreign trade	1.4	5.7	8.6	14.3
with socialist nations	.8	4.8	6.4	10.1
with other nations	.6	.9	2.2	4.2
Exports	.6	2.9	4.3	7.3
to socialist nations	.4	2.5	3.1	5.1
to other nations	.2	.4	1.2	2.2
Imports	.8	2.8	4.3	7.0
from socialist nations	.4	2.3	3.3	5.0
from other nations	.4	.5	1.0	2.0

SOURCE: *SSSR v Tsifrakh v 1963 godu*, p. 41.

The data of this table show clearly that since 1953 Soviet trade
with non-Communist nations has grown much more rapidly than
Soviet trade with Communist-ruled nations. Between 1953 and
1963, the Soviet Union's commerce with non-Communist countries increased almost five times in value; in that same period its
trade with Communist-ruled countries only little more than
doubled.

The value of Soviet foreign trade has increased substantially
since 1952, and the geographic dispersion of this commerce has
widened very considerably. But while the Soviet Union in the
mid-1960's is second only to the United States in volume of
national production, the value of Soviet foreign trade in 1963 was
not only less than that of the United States, but also less than
that of Britain, West Germany, and France.

The volume of Soviet economic aid to non-Communist under-developed countries has been substantial since the mid-1950's, but very far below that of the United States. During 1954–1963, the total volume of Soviet commitments in this area aggregated $3,377,000,000, almost all of it in the form of credits for purchases in the Soviet Union and for the payment of Soviet technicians sent to the recipient nations. Of this amount, only about $1,200,-000,000 had actually been received by the beneficiaries by the end of 1963. Four countries—India, Egypt, Afghanistan, and Indonesia—were scheduled to receive about two-thirds of the total Soviet commitments in this area. In the first half of 1964, the Soviet Union promised Algeria, Egypt, and India loans totalling over half a billion dollars. Though the value of Soviet development aid this past decade has been much less than that of the United States, it must be recognized that the relatively low interest rates charged (usually 2.5 per cent annually) and the relatively long periods of repayment provided in these credit agreements have often been very attractive to recipient nations. Moreover, Soviet spokesmen have emphasized that Soviet economic aid in an underdeveloped country does not confer upon the Soviet Union any property or other rights such as those received by private foreign investors. Thus the Soviet foreign aid program has also been used as propaganda against permitting private foreign investment in many nations, and to urge expropriation of existing foreign investments.

In mid-1964, a Soviet source put the total volume of Soviet loans and credits extended to other Communist countries at almost $9,000,000,000. Another Soviet source implied that Communist China had been the largest single recipient of this aid, stating that the Chinese had received 11 long term credits during 1950–1962 totalling over $2,000,000,000 (more precisely, 1,816,-000,000 rubles). But most of this, the Chinese have indicated, went to finance military aid during and after the Korean War, rather than being primarily a source of economic help.[4]

A further point may be made here for perspective. Total Soviet gross national product in the mid-1960's is conventionally estimated in the range of $250–300,000,000,000. If this estimate indicates a correct order of magnitude for total Soviet output—as seems likely—the annual Soviet exports of about $7,000,000,000 amount to less than 3 per cent of total Soviet output, not a very large percentage. Soviet foreign trade is important to the Moscow leadership because of its political impact, because of the access it provides to highly strategic goods—say, to new Western technology or to Western grain in a period following a bad harvest—or because it enables the Soviet Union to exchange goods it has in surplus for other goods which it needs badly. But the small quantity of foreign trade, relative to total Soviet production, normally—though not always—makes the Soviet Union less vulnerable to pressures arising in this area than are smaller countries heavily dependent upon foreign commerce.

In retrospect it may be difficult for some to understand the Western fears of the 1950's about a Soviet trade offensive that would disorganize world markets and cut prices to ruinous levels. Those apprehensions have clearly not been realized, but the rational kernel from which this concern springs should also be understood. The Soviet Union is the world's largest centrally directed economic organism, dwarfing by many times even the biggest American corporation. The Soviet government's monopoly of foreign trade permits it to increase or decrease commerce with a particular trading partner in response to non-economic as well as economic forces. Moreover, the Soviet government need not in any particular transaction have the same concern as a much smaller private trader with making a profit, or with selling at the highest price or buying at the lowest price. These features have sometimes been summarized by saying that the Soviet leaders do not have to worry about paying dividends to their stockholders. But what is now clear is that the maneuvering room the Soviet government enjoys in these respects is far from infinite. Its resources, too, are limited. It also must ultimately pay its bills, and therefore must balance its international payments somehow. Since 1950 the Soviet government has had to export probably more than $2,500,000,000 in gold to settle its international accounts. In 1963 alone Soviet gold exports amounted to about $500,000,000. The Central Intelligence Agency estimated in early 1964 that the Soviet Union had then only about $2,000,000,000 or less in its gold reserve. This is equivalent to only about a four year reserve at the 1963 gold export rate. Such a calculation ignores current gold production in the Soviet Union, which probably amounts to several hundred million dollars annually. But there is every reason to believe that the Soviet Union is a high cost gold producer. This seems to have been true both before and since the system of slave labor for mining gold was abandoned in the mid-1950's and replaced by the use of free workers. The latter have to be paid relatively high wages to induce them to work in the remote Siberian areas where most Soviet gold is mined. These considerations suggest some of the limitations on Moscow's ability to wage economic warfare.

The great concern aroused by Soviet price-depressing sales of petroleum, aluminum, and tin in the late 1950's now appears to have been exaggerated, for the most part. A Western analyst writing for the Joint Economic Committee of Congress has made the following important point about the markets for these commodities and Soviet motivation in these markets:

> These are administered markets where prices remain stable over long periods of time and where the quantities of the commodities handled are subject to fairly rigid direct or indirect controls administered by the sellers. In order to gain access to such markets, the USSR has often had to lower prices enough to attract marginal buyers. These bargain prices have caused considerable concern in the West that the USSR was attempting to disrupt the order of the market. Actually, however, a careful study of Soviet behavior in these cases indicates that after Soviet sales at bargain prices have attained the desired volume, the USSR has quietly raised its prices to the level of the market.

> It seems quite likely that no one was more surprised than Soviet exporters when in 1958 Soviet sales of tin were so large as to cause the temporary suspension of the International Tin Agreement. In contrast, Soviet market research in such fields as aluminum, gem diamonds, flax, and zinc seems to have been of much higher quality. Additional quantities of these and other materials have been successfully marketed in the West, either with no depressing effect on price or with only a temporary price reduction.[5]

None of this negates the fact that at times the Soviet Union has used foreign trade for political purposes. But in the main the Soviet Union normally acts like a commercial trader in Western markets, seeking to sell at the highest price and buy at the lowest. In Eastern Europe and China, at times, much has been made of the charge that the Soviet Union has used its political dominance there to sell at unreasonably high prices and to buy at unfairly low prices. In the broader world market the Soviet interest in price stabilization measures has been attested by its participation in the international agreements to stabilize the prices of wheat, sugar, and some other commodities. An outstanding case has been its cooperation with the dominant force in the world diamond market, the De Beers interests who have been in recent years the sole agents for Soviet diamond sales to the West. At the international trade conference held in Geneva in the spring of 1964, the Soviet Union argued for relatively high and stable prices for the raw material exports of the underdeveloped nations.

There has been much that is new in Soviet international economic policy since Stalin's death. In the 1930's the Soviet goal was self-sufficiency, autarky. The Soviet Union then exported primarily to obtain foreign currency to pay for essential imports. These imports were to make the Soviet Union more industrialized and more self-sufficient. Seeking to make itself independent of imported natural rubber, the Soviet Union pioneered in the 1930's in creating a national synthetic rubber industry. These were basically the tactics of a weak nation motivated by a defensive strategy. In the period immediately after World War II, Soviet political, military, and economic primacy over Eastern Europe permitted it to exploit that area in a variety of ways, notably by forming the "joint stock companies" which secured control over much of the economic life of Hungary, Rumania, and other of the Eastern European satellites. But *vis-à-vis* the West, the Soviet Union in Stalin's last years was still relatively weak and still pursued its strategy of the 1930's. The directors of Soviet foreign trade worked under a severe handicap in the late 1940's and early 1950's because of the then relatively tight Western embargo on sales of strategic goods to the Soviet Union. The embargo's supporters hoped to slow down the growth of Soviet power by denying it access to the West's advanced technology. But even those years did not see an air-tight embargo. This was evidenced by the sale of British jet engines to the Soviet Union in the early post World War II period. This sale presumably helped substantially to advance the state of Soviet technology in this militarily important area. In 1953, at the height of the embargo's stringency, the fifteen cooperating Western nations prohibited the export of 260 commodities to the Soviet bloc and limited sales of 90 other goods.

The sharp increase of Soviet activity in the world economy since Stalin's death has been made possible by the rapid growth of Soviet production. At least in limited areas and at specific times, the Soviet government has been able to go over from the defensive to the offensive, and use economic weapons to support its political policies. Soviet willingness to buy high priced Egyptian cotton in the mid-1950's as part of a campaign of splitting Egypt from the West was one early example. Another was the growing activity of Soviet envoys in offering economic and technical aid to underdeveloped non-Communist countries. In the 1950's, too, there began the push to open new markets for Soviet products, spearheaded by the highly successful effort to expand sales of Soviet oil. As Soviet economic power grew, the Kremlin used it several times as a means of exerting political pressure. The ending of Soviet trade with Israel as the result of the Suez crisis of 1956, the termination of all economic relations with Albania in the early 1960's, the cancellation of promised Soviet credits to Yugoslavia in the late 1950's, the threat of cancellation of Soviet orders in Finland on occasions when Moscow thought Helsinki needed a reminder that its government had to be acceptable to the Kremlin, and the Soviet withdrawal of its technicians from Communist China in mid-1960 are all examples of this new power and boldness. The peak use of this economic power, as noted above, was the Soviet rescue operation in the early 1960's which kept the Cuban economy functioning and made that country almost completely dependent on the Soviet Union after the United States initiated an embargo on American trade with Cuba. But it should be noted that Soviet economic warfare against China, Albania, and Yugoslavia has been as unsuccessful as United States economic warfare against Cuba in gaining political ends.

The story of Soviet participation in the world economy since Stalin is by no means one of growing strength alone. In Eastern Europe the past decade has seen the end of almost all the joint stock companies which were once such direct, effective expressions of Soviet economic hegemony over this area. After the Polish unrest and the Hungarian Revolution of 1956, major steps were taken to eliminate much of the old inequality between Eastern Europe and the Soviet Union. To help compensate for its past exploitation of the area, the Soviet Union cancelled many debts owed it by Eastern European countries. The Soviet Union poured substantial resources into Hungary to help repair the economic and political damage done by the revolution and the Soviet intervention. Eastern European negotiators were able to deal more nearly equally with Soviet trade representatives after 1956 and to insist upon prices more nearly reflecting world price levels—at least the nominal basis for trade among Communist-ruled nations. Nor should Rumania's successful defiance of Premier Khrushchev's 1962 demand that Bucharest accept his concept of international socialist economic integration and division of labor be overlooked.

Against this background we may now examine Soviet economic relations with three main areas of the world: the industrialized free world nations, the underdeveloped non-Communist countries, and the Communist-ruled nations.

TRADE WITH THE INDUSTRIALIZED WEST

Between 1952 and 1962, trade between the Soviet Union and the industrialized nations of the free world roughly tripled. In 1952 Soviet commerce with Western Europe, North America, and Japan reached a value of about $700,000,000; a decade later this total was almost $2,400,000,000. Between 1958 and 1963 alone, Soviet trade with the industrially developed capitalist countries doubled, and the total turnover reached almost $2,700,000,000 in the latter year. The rapidity of this growth may be seen by comparison of the 1955, 1962, and 1963 data on total trade turnover (exports plus imports) between the Soviet Union and its recent chief partners among these industrialized nations:[6]

| Country | Trade Turnover | | |
	1955	1962	1963
		(millions of dollars)	
Finland	234.0	395.4	426.8
United Kingdom	240.3	329.6	344.5
West Germany	53.1	338.8	279.8
France	95.8	238.4	174.3
Italy	33.8	230.0	272.5
Sweden	45.5	129.6	133.6
Japan	4.0	259.0	288.9

The forces operating to produce this rapid growth were not the same in all countries, of course, but two or three general factors were at work. The overall growth of Soviet production provided the Soviet regime with more commodities—mostly raw materials—that could be exchanged in Western Europe and Japan for goods those nations produced. No less important was the steady trend after 1953 toward weakening the Western world's strategic embargo on exports to the Soviet Union. This trend began after the Korean War and continued as successive Soviet "peace offensives" reduced tension between Moscow and Western Europe and Japan. By the early 1960's it was clear that there was very little of a non-military nature that the Soviet Union could not buy from one or another of these countries. Even the United States—which maintained the tightest embargo against strategic sales to the Soviet Union—eased its attitude somewhat in the late 1950's. A major Soviet exposition was permitted in New York City in mid-1959, while a similar large scale American exhibit took place in Moscow that year. By 1960 Soviet-American trade volume reached almost $85,000,000, a far cry from the $17,000,000 in trade done in 1952. But the shooting down of the United States U-2 plane near Sverdlovsk in May 1960 and then the Cuban crisis of October 1962 chilled Soviet-American relations and helped reduce the 1962 trade volume to $44,000,000. In 1963, of course, the American decision to permit large grain sales to the Soviet Union began what could possibly be a new phase in these trade relations. By March 1964, the United States Government, speaking through its Secretary of Commerce, seemed to have decided that it could not continue indefinitely to be far more restrictive in its attitude toward Soviet trade than were the nations of Western Europe. The United States Chamber of Commerce's April 1964 call for more Soviet-American trade also pointed in the same direction.[7] In 1963, Soviet-American trade turnover amounted to about $52,600,000, and in 1964 it soared far above that figure as large quantities of American grain were shipped to the USSR.

As might be expected, trade between the Soviet Union and these industrialized countries has been primarily an exchange of Soviet raw materials—oil, ores, metals, lumber, and textile fibers in the main—for Western machinery, ships of various kinds, and fabricated products such as pipe. Even by the mid-1960's the inferior quality of much Soviet machinery and the Soviet inability to merchandise such products in the West made industrial equipment and related complex products such as automobiles a minor factor in Soviet sales to Western Europe and Japan. The irony in this is apparent if we recall that the Soviet Union at this time produced ICBM's, sputniks, and hydrogen bombs. The Soviet Union in the mid-1960's still looked eagerly to the West for continued injections of the latter's advanced technology and equipment into the Soviet economy. The need was created, of course, by the backwardness of those many areas of the Soviet economy where technological advance had been ignored while all-out priority was being given research and development of increased military and space exploration capability. Thus the pattern of Soviet trade with the West in the 1960's resembled that of the 1920's.

Soviet trade with Italy in 1962 illustrates the pattern of Soviet trade with Western industrialized nations. In that year Soviet crude and refined petroleum accounted for over half of the value of all Soviet exports to Italy. Roughly 10 per cent each of these exports were provided by iron and steel and by lumber products. Most of the rest was accounted for by exports of coal, chemicals, textile fibers, and grain. On the import side, the Soviet Union that year received more than one-third of its Italian purchases in the form of machinery and equipment of various kinds, and almost a quarter in large diameter pipe needed for building oil and gas pipelines in the Soviet Union and Eastern Europe.[8] The vigorous 1962 and 1963 United States campaign against Western European sales of such large diameter pipe to the Soviet Union was defended on military grounds, but there can be little doubt that this campaign was primarily an act of economic warfare. The United States sought to impede the building of a pipeline from Soviet oil fields into Eastern Europe, apparently fearing this pipeline would be continued into Western Europe, greatly cutting the cost of delivering Soviet oil to Western Europe.

In basing its foreign trade with Western Europe and Japan so largely upon the sale of its raw materials, the Soviet Union has exposed itself to competition and political opposition from other suppliers of raw materials to these countries. The struggle between the international oil companies and the Soviet Union has been an epic story of commercial rivalry. When Soviet tin exports forced the price of tin down sharply in the late 1950's, such tin producers as Indonesia and Bolivia reacted very angrily. In addition, Soviet exports of raw materials have been limited by the needs of the Soviet economy. The Soviet Union has consequently not been able to pay with commodity exports for all the goods it would like to buy from the industrialized nations. It has had to export gold and has exerted considerable pressure for the extension of medium- and longer-term credits. In 1960 and 1961, Soviet drawings on medium term credits guaranteed by Western Europe governments are estimated to have been $200,000,000 annually.[9] In 1962 and 1963, another Western source has estimated, these credits to the Soviet Union had risen to about $300,000,000 annually. But in 1963, it is estimated, repayments of interest and principal on earlier Western credits came to about $240,000,000, leaving net credits of only $60,000,000. Total outstanding Soviet medium term credits at the end of 1963 were estimated at about $575,000,000. As the Russians looked forward to making large scale purchases for their chemical industry in the West, the tone of their comments suggested they hoped for long term credits which would increase their total indebtedness to Western nations to more than a billion dollars before 1970. In May 1964, during Anastas I. Mikoyan's visit to Japan, he indicated the magnitude of Soviet needs by suggesting that Japan alone extend the Soviet Union ten year credits amounting to $350,000,000 for the purchase of chemical factories and ships.

By the summer of 1964, it was clear that intensifying Western European competition for Soviet orders was creating great and successful pressure for the extension of large government-guaranteed credits to the Soviet Union. These credits appeared likely to be for periods of ten years or more, rather than for periods of up to five years, as earlier. Giant orders worth hundreds of millions of dollars were involved in this competition as Soviet buyers skillfully played off different would-be Western sellers against each other. The atmosphere of the period is best suggested by the fact that in August 1964 Lord Thomson, a leading British publisher, seriously discussed the possibility of floating a large long term Soviet bond issue in the London capital market with Premier Khrushchev. The latter, declaring his country had a "big appetite" for Western capital, suggested that the Soviet Union would be interested in borrowing as much as a billion pounds, almost three billion dollars. The amount mentioned was fantastic, of course, but the fact that the conversation occurred at all was vivid testimony to the drastic change in the atmosphere. Soviet leaders could hardly be blamed for believing they had bright prospects for getting vast Western aid in expanding their chemical industry and otherwise increasing and modernizing their industrial capabilities. But in the West some voices were already being raised to ask how the Soviet Union would repay these large credits when they fell due.[10] The debate waxed even hotter in the early fall of 1964 when the British government guaranteed a 15-year credit worth $67,000,000 to permit the Soviet Union to buy equipment for a polyester fiber plant. About the same time Japan granted the Soviet Union an eight-year credit to finance the purchase of a $10,000,000 fertilizer plant. Later, France promised seven-year credits totaling several hundred million dollars.

One additional point should be mentioned before this section of the discussion is concluded. This is the revaluation of the ruble at the beginning of 1961, a revaluation which amounted to a devaluation in terms of Western currencies. The official claim that the ruble was equal to 25 cents, maintained during the 1950's, was quite unrealistic. This was tacitly admitted by the Soviet Union during the later 1950's, when it permitted Western tourists to buy rubles at 10 cents each. The overvaluation of the ruble had no direct impact on Soviet trade with the West, which has generally been conducted in Western currencies. The ruble, of course, remains as it has been since the 1920's a purely domestic currency whose physical export or import—except for the very limited amounts needed by Soviet officials for cabfare or the like upon returning home—is prohibited. The discrepancy between the nominal value of the ruble and its real value in relation to Western currencies meant that in bookkeeping terms the Soviet Union appeared to lose money on its exports to the West and to make money on its imports. Presumably there was and is some mechanism by which the Soviet treasury balances off these seeming losses and gains. Nevertheless, it is clear that this must be a nuisance, complicating the problem of deciding what to export and what to import.

The action taken at the beginning of 1961 created a new "heavy" ruble which was much less overvalued than the old ruble. Internally the new ruble was set equal to 10 old rubles, with all other prices changed in proportion. But for external purposes the new ruble was declared equal to $1.11, that is equal only to 4.44 old rubles, rather than to 10 old rubles. This change was presented to the Soviet people as a "victory" for the ruble over the dollar. But of course it represented a sharp depreciation since on the basis of the old rate, the new "heavy" ruble should have been equal to $2.50, rather than $1.11. The depreciation, in short, was well over half of the previously claimed, but unrealistic, ruble value. At the same time the special favorable rate for Western tourists was eliminated.

TRADE WITH UNDERDEVELOPED NATIONS

In 1952, total Soviet trade (exports plus imports) with the underdeveloped non-Communist nations of the world, mainly those in Asia, Africa, and Latin America, was probably little more than $200,000,000. By 1963, it exceeded $1,500,000,000. The swift growth of Soviet commerce with a number of these nations is shown in the data below:[11]

Country	Trade Turnover		
	1955	1962	1963
		(millions of dollars)	
Egypt	26.4	176.3	258.5
India	11.7	196.4	316.4
Malaya	21.8	163.3	136.8
Afghanistan	24.5	64.8	64.4
Indonesia	3.8	97.2	79.6
Brazil	1.9	65.8	72.8
Ghana	8.2	26.5	38.2

On the other hand, Soviet trade with some of these nations, Argentina and Iran, for example, actually declined substantially between 1955 and 1962. Nevertheless, for this group of nations as a whole the role of the Soviet Union, as a customer or a supplier or both, was far greater in the early and mid-1960's than it had been a decade earlier. And a key aspect of this was the growth of the Soviet Union's role as a supplier of industrial goods and machinery to these nations.

The growth of Soviet economic activity in these areas was closely linked with growing Soviet interest in increasing its political influence among these nations, and the Soviet hope of winning converts for the Communist cause. Moreover, the scope of Soviet economic and political activity in the underdeveloped world has been greatly enlarged by the fact that so many former colonies have become independent since 1952.

By definition the underdeveloped countries participate in world trade primarily as exporters of raw materials and food products, buying manufactured products from the more developed nations. As a result, the Soviet Union has bought from these countries such products as natural rubber, cotton, cocoa beans, non-ferrous metals, and some foods. Machinery and equipment accounted for slightly over half of all Soviet exports to these countries in 1962. At various times, Soviet shipments of armaments have been important in trade with these countries, too. But normally the rest of Soviet sales to the underdeveloped nations consist of raw materials they lack—petroleum, lumber, metals—as well as miscellaneous manufactured products such as medicines, chemicals, and newsprint.

In the underdeveloped nations, the Soviet Union appears as a direct competitor of Western manufacturers, ready to deliver a wide variety of goods from complete plants to tractors, trucks, and automobiles. The Soviet Union appears in these countries, too, as a purveyor of technical services, offering technicians for geological prospecting, for designing new plants, and the like. The Soviet Union is at a competitive disadvantage because of the frequently poorer quality of its manufactured goods, because of its recent arrival as a supplier in areas accustomed to buying from the West, and because of the frequent difficulties purchasers of Soviet goods have in getting spare parts. The Soviet Union has sought to overcome its competitive disadvantages by a variety of techniques. It has concluded a large number of bilateral agreements which are essentially barter arrangements. It has offered long term agreements for purchase of some commodities if the seller would agree correspondingly to buy Soviet products. It has granted economic aid, usually in the form of loans carrying a very low interest rate and repayable over a period of 10 or 12 years or longer in local goods. Much Western comment has emphasized the political importance of Soviet loans to these countries. These have been viewed as a means of wooing nations away from the West, of impressing the recipients with Soviet economic and technical might, and of gaining admiration for communism. All these motives undoubtedly are important, but these loans often serve the economic purpose of giving the Soviet

Union entry into a new market, an entry which can later be expanded if relations go well.

The following table on the distribution of Soviet loans and grants for economic purposes to non-Communist underdeveloped nations during 1954–1963 shows the wide geographic dispersion of this program:

Table 24. TOTAL SOVIET LOANS TO NON-COMMUNIST UNDERDEVELOPED COUNTRIES, 1954–1963

Country	Amount (millions of dollars)	Country	Amount (millions of dollars)
Argentina	100	Somali Republic	57
Iran	39	Sudan	22
Iraq	184	Tunisia	28
Syria	150	Afghanistan	500
Turkey	10	Burma	14
Egypt	553	Cambodia	21
Yemen	26	Ceylon	30
Algeria	101	India	811
Ethiopia	102	Indonesia	369
Ghana	89	Nepal	10
Guinea	70	Pakistan	33
Mali	55	Iceland	3

SOURCE: *Annual Economic Indicators for the U.S.S.R.*, p. 115.

The table lists Soviet commitments to supply economic aid. The total figure of $3,377,000,000 is, however, more than three times the estimated actual receipt by these nations of $1,200,-000,000 on these commitments through 1963. There has been great variation in the projects financed through this aid. In Afghanistan, Soviet aid made possible the paving of Kabul's streets. It also financed a major road through and across the Hindu Kush, several food processing plants, and two hydroelectric projects. The Bhilai steel mill in India, equipped with Soviet machinery and built under Soviet technical direction, is the largest single project completed there to date, but other Soviet aid has covered a wide variety of plants and purposes, including aid in petroleum and gas exploration and development. In 1964 the Soviet Union agreed to help India build a second steel mill at Bokaro. Indonesia has received large amounts of arms from the Soviet Union, while other aid credits have gone for building a stadium and several plants, and financing Indonesian purchase of Soviet ships. The Aswan Dam in Egypt is the most publicized and most important Soviet aid project there, but a large variety of other projects has aimed at speeding the country's industrialization. They include the building of oil refineries and help in setting up an Egyptian steel industry. Other Soviet aid activities have extended from the building of the port of Hodeida in Yemen to reconstruction of the airport at Conakry in Guinea. The Soviet Union has usually, though not always, channeled its aid through the recipient government, thus facilitating increased expansion of state economic activity in the recipient nations.

In the first half of 1964, the pace of the extension of Soviet promises of additional economic aid to underdeveloped non-Communist countries quickened considerably. Besides the promised assistance to India in building the Bokaro steel plant, the Soviet government granted a $128,000,000 loan to Algeria, credits amounting to $277,000,000 to Egypt for its second five year plan beginning in 1965, and a loan totaling $2,800,000 to Kenya. Assuming that the Bokaro commitment will involve several hundred million dollars, these early 1964 aid promises add to well over half a billion dollars.[12]

The enthusiastic reception Premier Khrushchev received in Egypt in May 1964, when he visited there to participate in the ceremonies marking the completion of the first stage of the Aswan Dam, made clear the potentialities of the Soviet aid program for making friends and influencing people. But there is another side of the matter, too. Recipient countries have often been irritated by Soviet slowness in delivery of promised goods, by defects in Soviet equipment, and, at times, by Soviet attempts to use the aid as a means of exerting political pressure. It seems likely that the Russians have been disappointed more than once by the lack of spectacular results from their aid program and by the headaches it has brought them. On a popular level, it may be suspected that the average Russian has as little fondness for foreign aid as have isolationist, and much more affluent, Americans. The recipients of Soviet aid, moreover, have often shown themselves much more interested in playing off the Soviet Union against the United States, so as to get more help from both, than in becoming politically subservient to either.

RELATIONS WITH OTHER
COMMUNIST-RULED NATIONS

We noted earlier that the largest single share of Soviet foreign trade consists of commerce with other Communist-ruled nations as partners. But the proportion of this trade accounted for by these other Communist-ruled nations has declined—from about 80 per cent in 1952 to 70 per cent in 1963. Soviet trade with the non-Communist world rose roughly five times between 1952 and 1963; Soviet trade with other Communist nations increased less than 150 per cent in the same period. These sharply different trends reflected in part the natural expansion of Soviet trade into new areas as international tension declined after the Korean War and as many new sovereign nations appeared on the world political scene. But this experience also reflects the complex internal politics of the Communist world. Soviet-Albanian trade halted entirely in the early 1960's while Soviet-Chinese trade declined precipitously in these years following the rise of political differences between these countries. Soviet economic relations with Yugoslavia this past decade have also faithfully reflected the changing political climate between the two nations.

From an economic point of view, of course, the Communist-ruled nations are a very heterogeneous group. Czechoslovakia and East Germany are highly industrialized nations, relatively more industrialized than the Soviet Union, in fact. Poland, Hungary, and Rumania have made important strides toward industrialization, as have Bulgaria and Albania, to a lesser degree. In Asia, Communist China is one of the world's poorest and, relatively speaking, least industrialized nations. North Korea has begun to develop some significant industry and has recovered substantially from the terrible destruction of the Korean War, but North Vietnam and Mongolia have only the beginnings of industrialization. Yugoslavia, whose industrialization progress is perhaps in a category similar to that of Poland and Hungary, is so jealous of its political independence that only in the most formal terms can it be considered a member of any Communist group of states. Finally, Cuba presents the irony of a classic industrially under-

developed nation with a plantation agriculture, yet with a population many of whose members enjoyed something akin to the
American standard of living, complete with personal automobile
and television set, before Castro took power.

The result of this diversity of economic backgrounds is a corresponding diversity of trade patterns. At one extreme is East
Germany—the Soviet Union's largest trading partner—which has
to a large extent been converted into a huge industrial colony of
the Soviet Union. Almost 60 per cent of East Germany's 1962
exports to the Soviet Union consisted of machinery and equipment, while other significant exports included chemicals, clothing,
sewing machines and other durable consumer goods, and photo-
graphic materials. In return East Germany received primarily raw
materials and food: coal, oil, metals, cotton, flax, and large quantities of grain. Cuba on the other hand sold the Soviet Union
almost nothing but sugar in 1961 and 1962 while receiving a large
variety of machinery, raw materials, building materials, medicines, chemicals, and foods. In 1962, of course, Cuba also received
Soviet missiles and nuclear weapons, but these are not listed in the
published trade statistics.

As a general proposition, however, the Soviet Union has supplied most of the other Communist-ruled nations with machinery,
raw materials, and foodstuffs depending upon their needs, and has
received in return other machinery, raw materials, and foodstuffs,
depending upon each country's level of economic development
and natural resources. In the special case of China, the most important Soviet exports at the time of peak trade in the late 1950's
were machinery and equipment for China's industrialization and
essential supplies of petroleum. The Chinese shipped in return
mineral raw materials, textiles and clothing, and substantial quantities of food. But the rapidity with which Sino-Soviet trade
dropped in the 1960's showed that the close and basic economic
relationship which had been established earlier was not strong
enough to prevent the fissure born of political antagonisms. The
great dependence of Albania upon the Soviet economy similarly
did not prevent a political break. Albania survived the shock
because the Chinese moved quickly to replace the Soviet Union
after the latter broke off all trade relations and withdrew all its
technical experts from that country. But despite these examples
it seems clear that the heavy dependence of most of the Com-

munist-ruled nations upon the Soviet Union as a customer and as a supplier has often given Moscow an important leverage, when needed, to secure political conformity. Rumania, however, was able to reduce its economic dependence upon the Soviet Union in the 1961–1963 period by increasing its trade with Western Europe much more rapidly than it enlarged its commerce with the Soviet Union.

The changing pattern of Soviet trade (exports plus imports) with other Communist-ruled nations during the post-Stalin period may be seen from the data on the size of this commerce in four representative years, 1955, 1959, 1962, and 1963:

Table 25. SOVIET TRADE WITH OTHER COMMUNIST-RULED NATIONS, 1955, 1959, 1962, AND 1963

Country	1955	1959	1962	1963
		(million of dollars)		
China	1391.9	2054.9	749.8	599.6
East Germany	985.1	1919.6	2445.4	2614.9
Czechoslovakia	742.4	1184.9	1595.4	1797.8
Poland	718.4	803.0	1158.3	1275.9
Rumania	477.6	481.9	723.1	808.4
Hungary	261.8	466.3	799.9	865.7
Bulgaria	248.9	550.7	836.5	939.3
Yugoslavia	33.9	99.3	118.3	183.0
Albania	20.9	63.7	†	†
Mongolia	175.6	128.2	186.6	165.5
North Korea	84.9	125.7	168.9	170.1
North Vietnam	.3	35.4	84.9	91.9
Cuba	35.8*	7.0	604.8	564.2

* Before Castro took power.
† No trade reported.
SOURCE: *Vneshnyaya Torgovlya SSSR* for relevant years.

A closer look at Soviet trade data shows that in some years some of the Soviet Union's trading partners among the Communist bloc nations import much more from that country than they export to it. In 1962, for example, Mongolia received about $125,000,000 worth of Soviet goods, while sending only about $60,000,000 worth of its own commodities to the Soviet Union. In that same year East Germany received about $300,000,000 worth of goods—

or almost 30 per cent—more than it sent to the Soviet Union. Soviet exports to North Vietnam in 1962 were almost twice as great
in value as the imports received from that country, while that
same year Cuba received about $370,000,000 worth of Soviet
goods though exporting only about $235,000,000 worth of its own
production to that country. In 1963 Cuba's trade deficit with the
Soviet Union worsened as it imported about $400,000,000 worth
of Soviet goods while exporting to that country only $164,000,000
worth. These Soviet export balances reflected Soviet credits and/
or grants to these countries.

Complete data on Soviet economic aid to other Communist-
ruled countries are not available with any detailed breakdown by
country and year. Available information indicates that in Eastern
Europe, between 1945 and 1955, Albania received credits and
grants amounting to $106,000,000; Bulgaria received $198,000,-
000; Czechoslovakia, $48,000,000; East Germany, $363,000,000;
Hungary, $43,000,000; Poland, $614,000,000; and Rumania, $94,-
000,000. Data for 1956–1961 are shown in Table 26.

Table 26. SOVIET CREDITS AND GRANTS TO EASTERN
EUROPEAN COUNTRIES, 1956–1961

Country	1956	1957	1958	1959	1960	1961
			(millions of dollars)			
Albania	*	48	*	93	*	*
Bulgaria	92	72	44	*	162	*
Czechoslovakia	*	14	*	*	*	*
East Germany	20	260	235	*	*	475
Hungary	41	262	35	*	*	*
Poland	300	*	*	*	*	*
Rumania	95	*	*	*	*	*

* None given.
SOURCE: *Dimensions of Soviet Economic Power*, p. 427.

The listed Soviet credits for 1956 and 1957 amount to about $1.2
billion, or almost as much as the credits extended these countries
in the previous decade. The link with the Polish and Hungarian
disturbances of 1956 is clear.

In Asia, North Korea received Soviet loans and grants totalling
$690,000,000 between 1945 and 1962, North Vietnam, $368,900,-

000—of which $200,000,000 was pledged in 1960—and Mongolia
$658,000,000, of which over $320,000,000 was pledged in 1960
and 1961. Credits for economic aid to China—as measured by the
excess of Soviet exports to China over imports from that country
during 1950–1955—amounted to almost $1,000,000,000. But de-
spite these vast sums invested in Soviet aid to these countries, only
Mongolia was in the Soviet camp in the Sino-Soviet political
dispute of the mid-1960's. North Korea and North Vietnam stood
with the Chinese against the Russians.[13]

Theoretically, economic relations among Communist-ruled nations should be ruled by the principle of proletarian internationalism, by a spirit of brotherly cooperation and eagerness to be of
mutual aid. Communist writers like to contrast these "warm and
brotherly ties" with the purely commercial spirit normally prevailing in relations among capitalist nations. But experience since
World War II has shown that vague ideas about proletarian internationalism have been grossly inadequate to regulate or to explain
Communist bloc economic relations. Commercial and nationalistic
considerations have played very important roles, increasingly so
with the passage of time.

There can be little doubt that at the time Stalin died in 1953
many officials in other Communist-ruled countries had great
grievances against the Soviet Union on economic grounds. As
early as 1948–1949, these resentments had been voiced publicly
by the Yugoslavs after they were expelled at Stalin's order from
the Communist Information Bureau (Cominform). The Yugoslav complaints—which later experience showed were shared also
by many other Communist-ruled countries—centered about the
belief that the Soviet Union sought to exploit the weaker Communist-ruled nations by forcing them to accept unfair prices—to
pay high prices for Soviet goods and to get low prices for their
own—and by gaining control over much of their domestic economies through the so-called "joint" companies. The post-Stalin
rulers were sensitive to these complaints, as they demonstrated in
the mid-1950's when most of the "joint" companies were dissolved in the first years after Stalin's death. Nevertheless the issue
of Soviet exploitation played a role in the Polish near-revolt and
the Hungarian Revolution of 1956, leading the Soviet Union to
overhaul its economic relations with Eastern Europe drastically in
an effort to remove sources of hostility. A large volume of debts

owed the Soviet Union by the Eastern European countries was cancelled; new loans were extended to help improve those nations' economies; and promises were made that fairer prices would be used in subsequent trade.

The problem of prices in international trade among Communists has been and still is a thorny one. In theory, prices in a Communist-ruled state should reflect the different amounts of socially necessary labor needed to produce various commodities. But nobody has yet succeeded in turning this theoretical principle into a functioning structure of prices. In each Communist-ruled nation, the existing price system embodies many arbitrary elements and is usually quite different in many respects from the set of prices prevailing in other Communist-ruled nations. The differences in these national price structures are so great that it has been impossible to gain agreement to conduct trade among these nations on the basis of the domestic prices of any one country—say the Soviet Union. In general two types of solutions appear to have been favored. For commodities actively traded in world markets—raw materials, foodstuffs, chemicals, relatively simple standard machines—world prices have been taken as the basis for price negotiation, and then modified in response to many factors, not least the relative bargaining power and skill of the negotiators. During much of the 1950's, average world prices in 1950 were apparently often taken as the initial basis for discussion. Since the late 1950's, average world prices of 1957 or 1958 appear to have played a similar role. Presumably a more recent base will be adopted soon. But for commodities not traded on world markets—for example, complex special purpose machines or unique aggregates of equipment for particular plants—prices seem often to have been based on domestic costs of the producing nation plus some agreed percentage of profit.

The justification for using world prices—determined by trade among capitalist nations—has been put this way by a Soviet source:

> The price relations on the world market, taken for extended periods and cleansed of the elements of speculative rises and falls in them, may be taken as an approximate characterization of the relations of the magnitudes of socially necessary expenditure of labor on the production of goods on the scale of the world economy.

World market prices, taken as the basis for establishing prices in trade between socialist countries, have essential defects. For example, they are formed under the influence of capitalist monopolies, which try to guarantee themselves maximum profit on invested capital and to realize non-equivalent exchange in international trade. Certainly on the world market there exists along with non-equivalent exchange a tendency to realize exchange in correspondence with world labor expenditures. One of the distinguishing peculiarities of monopolistic capitalism is the intertwining of two contradictions—monopoly and competition . . . Competition on the world market gives rise to a tendency to equalization of foreign trade prices, to their approximation of the really essential objective basis—world value.[14]

This conception of world prices as values to be adjusted is sufficiently fuzzy to provide a great deal of room for maneuver and bargaining. The extent of deviation from world prices possible under this system is indicated by this statement by the Premier of Poland made in 1957 in an effort to counteract anti-Soviet feeling existing in that country over the very low price paid earlier by the Soviet Union for Polish coal:

If, under the method of firm prices applied in trade between our countries for periods of one or two years, coal prices in trade with the USSR were somewhat lower than coal prices on other markets, then correspondingly the prices of some goods delivered to Poland by the Soviet Union were lower than prices on the world market. This concerns, for example, iron ores, textiles, ships (the difference in the price of iron ore even amounted to several dollars [per ton] compared to the price of ores of the same quality on other markets). For equilibrating the price deviation on coal other Polish goods were sold to the Soviet Union at prices higher than the prices on world markets (the price of wool cloth, exported to the Soviet Union in the amount of approximately 5,000,000 meters, was higher by 5–6 rubles a meter in comparison with the prices at which we could sell this cloth on markets). This means that the basic agreement reached by the Ministries of Foreign Trade was based on the level of world prices. If both sides agreed to some deviations for particular goods, the principle in settling accounts was the following: The sum of the deviations above and below must be mutually equal so that neither side would suffer loss.[15]

Whether the final settlement achieved the equality asserted by the Polish Premier may, of course, be doubted.

Whatever the importance of world prices in these negotiations, the prices used in Soviet trade with the bloc appear to have been based on many considerations, not least of which has been the bargaining power of the negotiating nations. Since, as a general rule, Soviet bargaining power would be expected to be greater than that of any of the smaller Communist-ruled nations, there is at least a presumption that, over all, the Soviet Union may have been able to enjoy some advantages. Some economists in the Western world have gone further and argued that even since 1956 the Soviet Union has been able to make very substantial profits by enjoying advantageous prices in its trade with Eastern Europe. But the measurement problems here are complex and alternative interpretations are possible, so that caution seems advisable in reaching conclusions about the degree to which Soviet exploitation has actually taken place in recent years.[16]

One clear source of Soviet advantage in its trade with other Communist-ruled nations before 1961 arose from the overvaluation of the ruble in relation to the currencies of the partners. To the extent that trade took place in prices that were converted into rubles at the official rate, the ruble overvaluation helped the Soviet Union buy cheaply and sell dearly. This was implicitly recognized in 1957 when the existing exchange rates were supplemented by the creation of new rates applicable to non-commercial transactions such as tourism, services, diplomatic costs, and the like. These latter rates were obtained by a study of prices in different countries for some 75 consumer goods and services. The comparison of the foreign trade exchange rates with these non-commercial rates suggested that the former were overvalued for seven out of eight countries.

At the time of the 1961 ruble reform, the former great discrepancy between the foreign trade and non-commercial exchange rates was radically altered. The foreign trade ruble was devalued in terms of the other Communist currencies—as well as Western currencies—by setting one new ruble equal to only 4.44 old rubles. But the non-commercial rates were changed by setting one new ruble equal to 10 old rubles. Relative to the Eastern European currencies, the value of the foreign trade ruble became less than the value of the ruble for non-commercial payments. Be-

fore the reform, for example, one foreign trade ruble had been
worth 1.5 Rumanian lei, but less than one lei at the non-commercial rate. After the reform, one new foreign trade ruble was
worth 6.7 lei, while one new ruble was equal to almost 10 lei at
the non-commercial rate. Only in the case of the Chinese yuan
did the former overvaluation remain. Originally one foreign trade
ruble had been worth one-half yuan, while for non-commercial
payments one ruble equalled one-sixth of a yuan. After the reform, one new ruble was worth 2.2 yuan for foreign trade, but
only about 1.7 yuan for non-commercial payments. Even here,
however, the degree of overvaluation was sharply decreased.[17]

The most dramatic chapter in the history of Soviet economic
relations with other Communist-ruled countries has, of course,
been provided by China. In the 1950's, China was the largest
recipient of Soviet loans and credits, as well as, for a number of
years, the most important single trading partner of the Soviet
Union. In the public Peking-Moscow debate that has raged in
recent years, Soviet spokesmen have often accused the Chinese of
ingratitude. They have pointed to the enormous contribution the
Soviet Union made to Chinese industrialization during the 1950's
when thousands of Soviet experts worked in China, when many
new Chinese industries and plants were founded with the aid of
Soviet machinery and technical aid, and when large numbers of
Chinese skilled workers and scientists were trained in the Soviet
Union. The failure of these close economic ties to prevent the
outbreak of political hostility between these two countries in the
mid-1960's is vividly illustrated by the bitterness of the polemics
the two sides exchanged regarding their past economic relations.
Here is a typical Soviet statement:

> The Chinese propagandists make up lies from whole cloth in
> their effort to show that there was no Soviet aid to China at all,
> but only "usual trade operations." But why was it a "trade
> operation" when the USSR in 1950—at a time when the Soviet
> Union suffered many difficulties connected with the liquida-
> tion of the consequences of the war—gave China a $300,000,000
> credit? The total of the 11 long term credits extended to China
> on favorable conditions during 1950–1962 amounted to 1,816,-
> 000,000 rubles . . . The USSR transferred to China tens of
> thousands of sets of scientific and technical documents. If China
> had had to obtain these blueprints from the capitalists or to
> work them out with its own forces, it would have had to pay

many billions of rubles and long years of hard work. But China paid only the value of the expenditures required to make copies of these technical documents and to ship them, an amount totalling only 4,000,000 rubles by January 1, 1963. The USSR helped the Chinese Peoples Republic equip during a short time more than 200 large industrial enterprises, shops, and objects with the latest technology. It helped create many new branches of industry. All this was not a "usual trade operation," but an expression of the brotherly friendship and internationalism of the Communist party of the Soviet Union and of the Soviet people. The fact that the Chinese leaders pervert the essence of the relations of the Soviet Communist party, the Soviet Government, and the Chinese Peoples Republic speaks only of the latter's rotten intentions. Trying to extinguish the people's memory of Soviet aid, the factory markings are even being removed from Soviet machine tools and machinery in China.

The Chinese leaders treat the question of internationalism and of the relations among socialist countries in a spirit of national egoism. Not so long ago they said that the more economically developed countries must transfer to the backward countries all that part of the former nations' national income which exceeds the level of the backward nations.[18]

The last point sounded an extremely sensitive chord in Sino-Soviet relations because the Soviet Union now accuses China of demanding that the more prosperous Communist-ruled countries halt their economic advance and shift enormous amounts of capital to finance the economic advance of the more backward Communist-ruled nations. China would, of course, be the chief beneficiary of any such policy. But such a policy is politically impossible for the Soviet or Eastern European rulers.

Since the Chinese have made complaints about their treatment in economic relations by the Soviet Union a major point in their propaganda, it is worth reproducing here at some length the text of the Chinese indictment in this area as given in a letter to the Soviet Communist party Central Committee:

> We have always considered that the Soviet people's friendly aid has played a beneficial role in helping China to lay the preliminary foundations for her socialist industrialization . . .
>
> . . . but we must point out that, so far from being gratis, Soviet aid to China was rendered mainly in the form of trade and that it was certainly not a one-way affair. China has paid

and is paying the Soviet Union in goods, gold or convertible foreign exchange for all Soviet-supplied complete sets of equipment and other goods, including those made available on credit plus interest. It is necessary to add that the prices of many of the goods we imported from the Soviet Union were much higher than those on the world market . . .

As for the Soviet loans to China, it must be pointed out that China used them mostly for the purchase of materiel from the Soviet Union, the greater part of which was used up in the war to resist U.S. aggression and to aid Korea . . . For many years we have been paying the principal and interest on these Soviet loans, which account for a considerable part of our yearly exports to the Soviet Union. Thus even the war materiel supplied to China in the war to resist U.S. aggression and aid Korea has not been given gratis . . .

. . . in spite of our objections you turned your backs on the principles guiding international relations and unscrupulously withdrew the 1,390 Soviet experts working in China, tore up 343 contracts and supplementary contracts concerning experts, and scrapped 257 projects of scientific and technical co-operation, all within the short span of a month.

You were well aware that the Soviet experts were posted in over 250 enterprises and establishments in the economic field and the fields of national defense, culture, education and scientific research, and that they were undertaking important tasks involving technical design, the construction of projects, the installation of equipment, trial production and scientific research. As a result of your peremptory orders to the Soviet experts to discontinue their work and return to the Soviet Union, many of our country's important designing and scientific research projects had to stop halfway, some of the construction projects had to be suspended and some of the factories and mines which were conducting trial production could not go into production according to schedule. Your perfidious action disrupted China's original national economic plan and inflicted enormous losses upon China's socialist construction.

You were going completely against communist ethics when you took advantage of China's serious natural disasters to adopt these grave measures.

Your action fully demonstrates that you violate the principle of mutual assistance between socialist countries and use the sending of experts as an instrument for exerting political pressure on fraternal countries, butting into their internal affairs and impeding and sabotaging their socialist construction.[19]

The withdrawal of the Soviet experts referred to took place in August 1960. And it should be noted here that in the letter quoted above the Chinese demanded Soviet compensation for the damage caused China by this withdrawal. Only after payment of such compensation, the Chinese leaders declared, could China accept a new Soviet offer to send additional Soviet experts as part of an effort to settle the bitter dispute. And here is what the Chinese had to say on the question of Sino-Soviet trade:

> Nobody is in a better position than you to know the real cause for the curtailment of Sino-Soviet trade over the last few years. This curtailment was precisely the result of your extending the differences from the field of ideology to that of state relations. Your sudden withdrawal of all the Soviet experts working in China upset the schedules of construction and the production arrangements of many of our factories, mines and other enterprises and establishments, and had a direct impact on our need for the import of complete sets of equipment. Such being the case, did you expect us to keep on buying them just for display?

> Moreover, in pursuance of your policy of further imposing restrictions on and discriminating against China in the economic and commercial fields, since 1960 you have deliberately placed obstacles in the way of economic and trade negotiations between our two countries and held up or refused supplies of important goods which China needs. You have insisted on providing large amounts of goods which we do not really need or which we do not need at all, while holding back, or supplying very few of the goods which we need badly. For several years you have used trade between our two countries as an instrument for bringing political pressure to bear on China. How could this avoid cutting down the volume of Sino-Soviet trade?

> From 1959 to 1961, our country suffered extraordinary natural disasters for three years in succession and could not supply you with as large quantities of agricultural produce and processed products as before. This was the result of factors beyond human control. It is utterly unreasonable for you to attack

China on this account and blame her for this reduction in trade.[20]

The above comments illuminate the long hidden realities in Soviet-Chinese economic relations. We close this discussion by presenting the data on the two nations' trade since Mao Tse-tung conquered the Chinese mainland. Table 27 shows how radically the volume and pattern of that trade have changed over the years:

Table 27.   SINO-SOVIET TRADE, 1950–1963

Year	Soviet Exports to China	Soviet Imports from China
	(millions of dollars)	
1950	388.2	191.3
1951	476.3	331.9
1952	550.2	413.7
1953	705.5	474.7
1954	759.3	578.3
1955	748.3	643.5
1956	733.0	764.2
1957	544.1	738.1
1958	634.0	881.3
1959	954.6	1100.3
1960	816.3	847.3
1961	367.0	550.9
1962	233.2	515.8
1963	187.0	412.6

SOURCE: Harry Schwartz, *Tsars, Mandarins, and Commissars: A History of Chinese-Russian Relations*, p. 248; *Vneshnyaya Torgovlya SSSR za 1963 god*, p. 13.

THE U.S.S.R. AND COMECON

In the portion of the world dominated by market economies, international division of labor tends to be determined by basic economic factors, by the force of comparative advantage exerted through competition. Protectionist devices such as tariffs and quotas distort the smooth workings of this system, and so do considerations of military security. But even after all the necessary qualifications have been made, the existence of an intricately integrated economy in much of the world is clear, the product in large degree of economic forces working without central direction.

Such a spontaneous integration is impossible in the countries ruled by orthodox Communist parties that believe in central economic planning and reject the idea of primary reliance upon market forces. A major reason that all of these countries have state monopolies of foreign trade is precisely in order to try to insulate their domestic economies so far as possible from developments in world markets. For the same reason all of these centrally planned countries have purely domestic currencies and have not sought freely convertible currencies. Yet even these countries recognize, in principle at least, the virtues of the international division of labor and its potential advantages. How are those advantages to be gained in countries which emphasize national economic planning, and which have separate arbitrary price systems that make extraordinarily difficult even elementary comparisons of costs among them? This is the problem the Soviet Union has been seeking to solve in recent years through the Council of Mutual Economic Assistance, or Comecon.

Over much of the first decade after World War II, the Soviet Union sought coordination of its economy with that of Eastern Europe through what F. L. Pryor has called the "Russian Embassy System of Coordination." In effect during these years, Soviet personnel—some of them diplomats, others advisers—gave orders to local officials on major questions of economic policy.[21]

In addition, moreover, the Soviet Union controlled directly much of the non-agricultural economy of Eastern Europe through its participation in the "joint" companies mentioned earlier. But the evidence suggests that these sources of Soviet influence were not very effective in achieving a rational division of labor. In part this was because of poor coordination among different sections of the Soviet economic bureaucracy. In greater part, this resulted from the lack of economic sophistication of Soviet leaders and officials in the Stalin era. Certainly the energetic efforts that were made in the late 1940's and early 1950's to make each of the Eastern European countries a miniature replica of the Soviet economy, each with its own steel, machinery, chemical, farm machinery and other industries points in this direction. The result was a tendency toward needless duplication and parallel investment in the Soviet Union and many of the Eastern European countries, despite the fact that many of the latter did not have the raw material bases needed to support the heavy industrial complexes they began building in this period. Nor, in general, did these countries provide large enough domestic markets to justify many of the new industries they were building.

Comecon itself was founded in January 1949 with the Soviet Union, Bulgaria, Czechoslovakia, Hungary, Poland and Rumania as members. Albania—which has absented itself from Comecon meetings since Premier Khrushchev's open attack on the Albanian leadership at the 22nd Soviet Communist party Congress in late 1961—joined in February 1949, East Germany in September 1950, and the Mongolian Peoples Republic in June 1962. Other Asian Communist countries and Cuba have at various times sent observers to meetings of Comecon bodies but they do not belong to the organization. In September 1964 Yugoslavia agreed to participate in some of Comecon's activities and to work with some of the organization's 23 standing committees. But Yugoslavia did not become a full-fledged Comecon member.

Though viewed in the West originally as Russia's answer to the Marshall Plan, Comecon did little in its first years. A Soviet source has summed up its activities to the mid-1950's in these words: "Economic coordination between the members consisted mainly of coordination of foreign trade. The loans, credits, and scientific and technical assistance which the member countries (above all the Soviet Union) extended to each other largely went to promote Socialist industrialization . . . and lay the foundations of socialism."[22]

An effort to achieve greater specialization and economic integration of Comecon members began in 1954, including the creation of special committees to deal with different phases of industrial problems. Permanent standing commissions of experts in twelve different major economic areas were finally created in May 1956. These years saw some initial attempts to coordinate the different national economic plans for 1956–1960. The most important development in this area took place in February 1956 when Nikita Khrushchev publicly laid down the new Soviet line on economic integration in these words:

Close economic cooperation gives extraordinary possibilities for the best possible utilization of production capacity and raw material resources. Happily, it combines the interests of each country with those of the whole socialist camp. The growth of specialization and cooperation is of great importance. Today it is no longer necessary for each socialist country to develop all branches of heavy industry, as had to be done by the Soviet Union, which for a long time was the only socialist nation and lived under capitalist encirclement. Now the socialist states form a powerful community and their defense ability and security are based on the industrial power of the entire socialist camp. Each European peoples democracy can therefore specialize in developing those industries and producing those goods for which it has the most favorable natural and economic conditions. This, incidentally, provides the necessary prerequisites for freeing large resources to develop agriculture and light industry, and on this basis to satisfy more fully the material and cultural needs of the people.[23]

The bankruptcy of Stalin's policy of crude exploitation of and dictation to the satellites must have been impressed upon his successors as early as mid-1953 by the anti-Soviet disturbances in Czechoslovakia and East Germany. In Hungary the situation was so bad that a reliable source has quoted Khrushchev as fearing that without reforms "we would have been booted out summarily." It was with Soviet encouragement, therefore, that Imre Nagy took over as Premier of Hungary in mid-1953 and dropped much of the policy of trying to build a comprehensive Soviet-type heavy industry in that country. Nagy has quoted Mikoyan as telling the Hungarians in June 1953: "The matter of economic planning shows a certain adventurous spirit, particularly the excessive development of your own iron smelting industry. Hungary has no iron ore, nor coke. All this must be imported. No one in Hungary has yet figured out exactly the price of a ton of iron ore and steel in Hungary. Hungary is building foundries for which no one has yet promised to supply the ore." In the grim winter of 1954–1955, the Eastern European countries found themselves competing against each other more and more in capitalist markets because of the parallel manufacturing systems they had built up. At the same time the Soviet Union was being forced by its own needs and problems to cut its exports of raw materials and other essential products to them very sharply. These were the kinds of forces that led the post-Stalin leaders to re-examine radically their economic relations with Eastern Europe.[24] But the Hungarian Revolution of 1956 made clear that the concessions granted earlier had not been enough. Hoping to calm the passions that had exploded in Hungary, the Soviet leaders released during those dramatic days a statement that in effect admitted past Soviet dictation over the Eastern European economies and promised an end to it:

> . . . there have been many difficulties, unsolved problems and downright mistakes, including mistakes in the mutual relations among the socialist countries—violations and errors against the principle of equality in relations among the socialist states.
>
> The 20th Congress of the Communist party of the Soviet Union very firmly condemned these violations and mistakes, and set the task of the consistent application by the Soviet Union of Leninist principles of equality of peoples in its relations with the other socialist countries . . .
>
> The Soviet government is prepared to discuss together with the governments of other socialist states measures ensuring further development and strengthening of economic links among the socialist countries in order to remove any possibility of violation of the principles of national sovereignty, mutual benefit and equality in economic relations.
>
> This principle must also be extended to advisers.[25]

Four days after the publication of this statement, the Soviet government used troops to crush the Hungarian Revolution. But even after that dread show of force, the other nations of the Communist bloc had gained enormously. As subsequent experience was to show, the national sovereignty of Comecon's members became a real force and the principle of unanimity required within that organization was no longer a mere legal fiction. Henceforth the Soviet Union had to bargain and compromise with the members of Comecon, rather than simply imposing its will and orders upon them.

Since the dramatic revolutionary days of 1956 a great deal of evolution has taken place in Comecon. It has accomplished a great deal toward the partial economic integration of its member states, but it has clearly fallen far short of the hopes and desires of the Soviet government in this field.

The accomplishments of Comecon come under several head-ings. It has promoted international division of labor and national specialization among its members with respect to many individual products. Different countries have agreed to stop producing some goods and to expand their output of others in response to this effort to get lower cost production, longer production runs in individual factories and the like. By August 1964, specialization agreements in Comecon covered 1,200 types of machinery and 800 chemicals.[26]

A good deal has also been accomplished in the effort to integrate Comecon members' economic plans for 1966–1970 and longer range economic plans intended to direct development to 1980. Major studies have been and are being carried out to try to develop rational criteria for investment choice among Comecon countries, to work out a meaningful price system to govern trade among them, and to calculate comparable data on national income, production, and other macroeconomic indicators needed for comparisons among these nations. Substantial work has been accomplished looking toward greater standardization of output in these countries. Beginnings have been made toward coordination of research and development so as to minimize needless duplication in this area. By mid-1964, the Comecon "Friendship" oil pipeline system had already started to bring Soviet oil directly from the Volga-Urals producing area to East Germany, Poland, Hungary, and Czechoslovakia. And similar major progress has been made toward integrating the electrical networks of European Russia and the Eastern European nations into one "Peace" electric grid. Important beginnings have been made toward creating a pool of 100,000 freight cars at the disposal of the Comecon members' railroad systems. And on January 1, 1964 the new Comecon bank, the International Bank for Economic Cooperation, began operation. It seeks to increase trade among Comecon members by fostering multilateral trade and multilateral clearings in their mutual commerce. This, hopefully, will provide greater flexibility and greater opportunity for trade than was possible under the previous system which relied mainly on bilateral trade agreements. Beginnings have been made on some joint investment projects, and toward greater cooperation by some Comecon members in the planning of their capital investment programs.[27]

The adoption in June 1962 of the "Basic Principles of the International Socialist Division of Labor" has been hailed by Soviet sources as giving the socialist world an "economic constitution."

These are by no means inconsiderable accomplishments, yet it is quite clear that the Soviet Union is disappointed in Comecon because that organization has failed to provide the degree of economic integration Moscow had hoped for. The right to assert national sovereignty within Comecon, won by the Eastern European countries in the mid-1950's, has permitted national jealousies, national selfishness, and national suspicions to play major roles. The result has been the defeat of the wide-ranging plans for Communist economic integration that Premier Khrushchev made public in mid-1962. Moreover, the members of Comecon have learned from sad experience that they cannot count on their fellow members always to deliver goods of prescribed quality and on schedule.

Khrushchev's aim was the abandonment of the system under which Comecon countries first draw up their individual national economic plans, and then coordinate them through negotiations in which usually only marginal adjustments are made among these countries. Instead he wanted the creation of a supra-national planning body that would prepare one economic plan—fully integrated from the start—for the entire Comecon area. He justified this goal in these words:

> Lenin foresaw the future collaboration of socialist nations as taking place in a single worldwide cooperative in which the economy would be conducted according to a common plan. In his address to the Third Congress of Workers' Cooperatives in 1918 he pointed out that only one thing was needed at the moment—the unanimous desire to go ahead with an open mind in this single worldwide cooperative. . . .

> The socialist world system is now at a stage when it is no longer possible correctly to chart its development by merely adding up the national economies. The task now is to do everything to consolidate the national economy of each, broaden its relations and gradually advance towards that single world-wide organism embracing the system as a whole that Lenin's genius foresaw. . . .

> With the emergence of socialism beyond the boundaries of a single country, its economic laws found much greater room for action and their operation became more and more complex.

For example, the law of planned and proportional development operating on the scale of the system as a whole calls for planning and definite proportions both in each of the socialist countries taken separately and on the scale of the entire commonwealth. To utilize the economic laws of socialism fully we must take due cognizance of their operation not only at national levels, but also on the international plane.[28]

His concrete proposal was that the socialist countries "go in for planning at the level of the Council for Mutual Economic Aid, and afterwards at the level of the socialist world system as a whole." And his initial demand was for an over-all investment plan "which would take into account both the national and the common interests." And then he added:

Cooperation in the Council has now reached a point where it is necessary to decide the trend of specialization in each country, that is, decide exactly which branches, in what complex and on what raw material base, should be built in each of the countries so as to meet our common needs in the most economic way. The time has come to draw up a balance sheet of production and consumption of the main types of manufacture in our countries for a period extending at least up to 1970 and in this way prepare a general scheme for inter-state specialization and coordination. The intention for the immediate years is to produce the more important types of manufacture on the basis of international specialization and coordination.

To make this more palatable to the small countries whose possibility for extending the range of their industrial output diversification would be reduced, Premier Khrushchev went on to declare, "The Soviet Union is prepared even to cut down production of certain types of manufacture should it be found more expedient to manufacture them in the other member countries of the Council."[29]

As this is written, two years later, it is clear that the Khrushchev grand design has been defeated. Rumania, the Eastern European country with the most rapid rate of economic growth in the early 1960's, led the opposition, but other Comecon members joined in to lesser or greater degrees. Each country feared that this proposal for Comecon-wide planning would permit the Soviet Union once again to dominate its economic development. But the divisions in Comecon on these issues are more complex than simply those arising from the differences in interests between the smaller members and the Soviet Union. The more industrialized states such as East Germany and Czechoslovakia also have different interests from the less industrialized states; old national animosities also play roles in the calculations of the member countries. The degree to which insistence upon national sovereignty and national self-interest triumphed in this debate over Khrushchev's idea of socialist internationalism is evident from the statement of the Rumanian Workers Party released in April 1964:

> Cooperation within Comecon is achieved on the basis of the principles of fully equal rights, of observance of national sovereignty and interests, of mutual advantage and comradely assistance.

> As concerns the method of economic cooperation, the socialist countries . . . have established that the main means of achieving the international socialist division of labor, the main form of cooperation between their national economies is to coordinate plans on the basis of bilateral and multilateral agreements.

> During the development of the relations of cooperation between the socialist countries which are members of Comecon, forms and measures have been suggested, such as a joint plan and a single planning body for all member countries, interstate technical-productive branch unions, enterprises jointly owned by several countries, inter-state economic complexes, etc.

> Our Party has very clearly expressed its point of view, declaring that, since the essence of the suggested measures lies in shifting some functions of economic management from the competence of the respective state to the attribution of super-state bodies or organisms, these measures are not in keeping with the principles which underlie the relations between the socialist countries.

> The idea of a single planning body for all Comecon countries has the most serious economic and political implications. The planned management of the national economy is one of the fundamental, essential and inalienable attributes of the sovereignty of the socialist state—the state plan being the chief means through which the socialist state achieves its political and socio-economic objectives, establishes the directions and rates of development of the national economy, its fundamental propor-

tions, the accumulations, the measures for raising the people's living standard and cultural level.

The sovereignty of the socialist state requires that it effectively and fully avail itself of the means for the practical implementation of these attributions, holding in its hand all the levers of managing economic and social life. Transmitting such levers to the competence of super-state or extra-state bodies would turn sovereignty into a notion without any content.

All these are also fully valid as concerns inter-state technical-productive branch unions, as well as enterprises commonly owned by two or several states. The State Plan is one and indivisible. No parts or sections can be separated from it in order to be transferred outside the state. The management of the national economy as a whole is not possible if the questions of managing some branches or enterprises are taken away from the competence of the Party and government of the respective country and transferred to extra-state bodies.

Sometimes such forms of super-state economic management are presented as deriving from Lenin's words on "the tendency of creating a single world economy, regulated by the proletariat of all nations according to a general plan, a tendency that appears quite evidently already in capitalism and which undoubtedly will be developed and fully accomplished in socialism."

This presentation, however, ignores the fact that Lenin referred to a problem of the time when socialism will be victorious throughout the world, when "the general plan" of a "single world economy" will be carried out by the proletariat "of all nations."[30]

This kind of opposition, at least for the time being, sounded the death knell for Premier Khrushchev's original plans for Comecon. As a consequence, he turned to a new effort to get closer bilateral cooperation toward integration. By mid-1964 the Soviet government had reached agreements with Bulgaria, Czechoslovakia, Poland, and Hungary to set up inter-governmental committees at the cabinet level to foster moves for bilateral economic and technical cooperation among these countries. As for the Rumanians, the announcement in May 1964 that they would hold political and economic talks with the United States in Washington suggested that they intended to pursue their policy of national communism as they saw fit. At the conclusion of those negotiations, the United States Government's decision to guarantee credits extended to Rumania by American sellers of industrial equipment indicated that the Bucharest regime was no longer considered a satellite of the Soviet Union.

There is an ironic aspect to the Rumanian victory over the Soviet conception of Comecon. For many years Soviet and Communist propaganda has blamed the industrial underdevelopment of Asian, African, and Latin American countries upon Western "imperialism" and its "colonial policies." The impression has been spread that any country which does not have a major and comprehensive heavy industry is necessarily a second-class country. The Rumanians took this propaganda literally and applied it to themselves. Their position has been that they must be permitted to have an extensive heavy industry fully comparable to that of Czechoslovakia and East Germany. The Rumanians have indignantly rejected a socialist international division of labor through which, it has seemed to them, Premier Khrushchev planned to keep them in a colonial status, forcing them to remain primarily suppliers of raw materials and agricultural products. The same issues, of course, arose in Soviet relations with Cuba. The Castro regime at first viewed sugar production in Cuba as the mark of colonial slavery. It looked impatiently to the time when sugar production would be cut back heavily and Cuba would be a modern industrialized state, the most industrialized country in Latin America for its size and population. Only after heavy losses and high costs had been incurred in the effort to realize this dream did the Cubans, presumably with some Soviet prompting, come to accept a radically different view. In the mid-1960's the Castro regime understands that it must seek to maximize sugar production, undo the damage done to that crop by earlier policy, and postpone its industrialization dreams beyond 1970. The Soviet willingness in 1963 and 1964 to conclude a long term sugar purchase contract with Cuba at a stable price—less than the then existing world market price but well above the much lower quotations of the 1950's—clearly played a key role in the Castro regime's decision to reverse its original economic policy. That government now accepts the need for a sugar specialization it had once thought only the product of Cuba's exploitation by foreigners.

In the 1950's there had been speculation that Comecon might be expanded to include all the Communist-ruled states. At one point the Chinese even declared publicly that they would prepare their economic plans taking account of the Comecon plans, implying the possibility of future Chinese entrance into Comecon. But by the mid-1960's, the explosion of the Sino-Soviet dispute into a public quarrel had radically changed the perspectives. The entrance of Outer Mongolia into Comecon in 1962 was a logical consequence of the Mongolians' support for Moscow, though the economic position and problems of Mongolia are far different from those of the rest of Comecon. North Korea and North Vietnam, which support the Chinese for the most part in the dispute, are hardly likely to join Comecon unless and until their larger neighbor does. How unlikely it is that China will join the Soviet Union in Comecon may be seen from the following section of a letter sent by the Chinese leadership to the Soviet Communist party Central Committee on February 29, 1964:

> You constantly accuse us of "going it alone" and claim that you stand for extensive economic ties and division of labor among the socialist countries. But what is your actual record in this respect?
>
> You infringe the independence and sovereignty of fraternal countries and oppose their efforts to develop their economy on an independent basis in accordance with their own needs and potentialities.
>
> You bully those fraternal countries whose economies are less advanced and oppose their policy of industrialization and try to force them to remain agricultural countries and serve as your sources of raw materials and as outlets for your goods.
>
> You bully fraternal countries which are industrially more developed and insist that they stop manufacturing their traditional products and become accessory factories serving your industries.
>
> Moreover, you have introduced the jungle law of capitalism into relations between socialist countries. You openly follow the example of the Common Market which was organized by monopoly capitalist groups.
>
> All of these actions of yours are wrong.

In the economic, scientific, technical and cultural spheres, we stand for relations of cooperation of a new type, based on genuine equality and mutual benefit between China and the Soviet Union and among all the socialist countries.

We hold that it is necessary to transform the present Council of Mutual Economic Assistance of socialist countries to accord with the principle of proletarian internationalism and turn this organization, which is now solely controlled by the leaders of the Communist party of the Soviet Union, into one based on genuine equality and mutual benefit, which the fraternal countries of the socialist camp may join of their own free will. It is hoped that you will favorably respond to our suggestion.[31]

The close resemblance of this point of view to the more softly and cautiously stated Rumanian view quoted above is self-evident.

The Soviet government shows no disposition to scrap Comecon because of the limits on economic integration among that organization's members caused by disagreements among them, especially the disagreement by Rumania. In agreeing to the creation of the Comecon bank, the International Bank for Economic Cooperation (IBEC), the Soviet regime has helped create an instrumentality which could have great importance for the future. And it has agreed to the creation of a new unit of account—the transferable ruble. This is employed in the IBEC's transactions and for settlement of accounts among the IBEC's members. The transferable ruble could conceivably become a truly international currency in the future.

IBEC's activities during its first months of activity during 1964 have been of two kinds: it has sought to foster a multilateral clearings system among its members through the use of transferable rubles. This has required a new form of foreign trade negotiations among Comecon members. The first stage consists of bilateral talks in which preliminary agreements are reached between each pair of Comecon members on their annual trade and in which a balance of trade is not needed. The second stage consists of multilateral negotiations in which the effort is made by each country to reach a balance in its trade with all the other Comecon members. In addition to its role as a clearing house, the IBEC—which has a capital of 300,000,000 rubles subscribed by its members—makes short term loans to its members. These are authorized to permit systematic payment for goods, to cover seasonal needs, and to permit expansion of trade (presumably beyond original plans). The Soviet Union is the largest investor in the bank, having contributed 38 per cent of the capital. But all member states have one vote each, and in the highest directing body of the bank, the bank council, each member state has a veto power.

IBEC's sponsors apparently hope to develop it into a major international financial institution and to extend use of the transferable ruble—which for the time being is purely an accounting device—beyond the limits of Comecon's membership. The use of IBEC for financing its members' economic relations with underdeveloped countries and for coordinating and extending Communist economic aid to such countries has been discussed, but apparently not yet implemented at this writing. It remains to be seen what the future holds for both the transferable ruble and IBEC.[32]

When Leonid I. Brezhnev succeeded Nikita S. Khrushchev as Soviet Communist party First Secretary, he hastened to reassure other Communist countries. In his first speech after assuming office, made on October 19, 1964, he declared: "Our party will strive for the strengthening of the unity of the community of fraternal Socialist countries on a fully equal footing and on the basis of correct combination of the common interests of the Socialist community with the interests of the people of each country. . . ." How this vague formula would be applied in Comecon and elsewhere by the post-Khrushchev regime remained to be seen.[33]

After Khrushchev's removal, it was also revealed that the Soviet Union had joined "Intermetall." Originally formed by several of Comecon's Eastern European members, this organization seeks to coordinate the operations of the member states' rolling mills so that they may be utilized most efficiently.

CHAPTER VII

Communism by 1980?

As THE 1960's neared their mid-point, it was clear that the Soviet economy had lost much of its former capacity to impress and inspire awe in other nations. The alarm about the higher rate of Soviet economic growth that had marked the 1960 American presidential race was conspicuously absent in the 1964 contest. The leaders of Communist China, a country still recovering from its own economic debacle of 1959–1962, addressed the leaders of the Soviet Communist party with these mocking words in February 1964: "We would like to say in passing that . . . we are very much concerned about the present economic situation in the Soviet Union. If you should feel the need for the help of Chinese experts in certain fields, we would be glad to send them."[1]

Even Premier Khrushchev, the buoyant propagandist who had so often earlier predicted capitalism's economic defeat by superior Soviet performance, reflected the changed situation by warning, before his ouster: "If the socialist system gives a person fewer economic and spiritual goods than the capitalist system, certain people are going to think it over and say: 'Why the devil did we substitute one for the other?' "[2] His subsequent removal from power resulted in part, as we have seen, from the unsatisfactory results of his economic policy as compared with the extravagant predictions he had made.

For the moment at least there seemed to be tacit agreement on all sides that—despite *pro forma* objections by Soviet statisticians to the 1964 C.I.A. estimates—the celebrated Soviet-American economic race was going badly for the Soviet Union. The slowing down of Soviet economic growth during 1960–1963 and the improvement in American economic performance had proved Khrushchev a poor prophet.

There was much irony in this evaluation since it prevailed at the end of a period that had proved in many respects the most productive in Soviet and Russian economic history. Here is the way the positive aspects of the first full post-Stalin decade, 1954–1963, were summarized by an outstanding Soviet economist:

> About 60 per cent of the industrial production of the entire period of the Soviet state's existence was produced in these ten years; capital investments during that time accounted for more than two-thirds of the total invested during the 46 years. Both power plant capacity and the amount of electricity generated more than tripled during the decade. The metallurgical industry turned out more than 450,000,000 tons of pig iron and over 630,000,000 tons of steel, amounts considerably exceeding the output of these metals during the preceding century. Petroleum production was more than 1,000,000,000 tons, or more than was obtained in the entire period since the middle of the 19th century.[3]

Academician Arzumanyan, who wrote these words, might have made other claims as well. Between 1953 and 1964 a vast technological revolution took place in Soviet industry with resulting great increases in productivity. In these years the Soviet Union not only became a fully modern military power with all of the modern weapons created by science at its command, but it partially built and partially bought abroad a merchant fleet making it one of the world's great marine powers as well as acquiring a jet-powered civil aviation system fully comparable to that of any major nation. For the long run, the most important accomplishment of the first post-Stalin decade may have been its vast expansion of Soviet higher education and the rapid rise in trained personnel—particularly of scientists and technicians—which that expansion made possible.

Agriculture proved the Achilles heel of the Soviet economy in these years. The nearly disastrous 1963 grain harvest was merely the climax of a half decade during which the promise of rapid farm production advance seemingly offered by the gains of 1953–1958 proved illusory. All of Khrushchev's 1957 hopes for quickly providing his people with a Western diet abundant in meat and other protein foods were dashed. Instead, in early 1964 much of the average Soviet citizen's daily bread was made from grain bought at great cost from the United States, Canada, and elsewhere. There was poetic justice in this, of course, for in 1957 Khrushchev had sneered at the "moldy bread" of the United States and promised he would never pay gold for American meat. In 1964 he was paying gold for American wheat.

One clear thread runs through the entire complex economic record of the period we are considering. It is the consistency with which great plans have been announced with much publicity and boasting and then abandoned a few years later. This pattern began with the Malenkov program to raise the standard of living, a program announced in 1953 and already doomed to failure before its originator's "resignation" as Premier in 1955 signified its demise. The pattern continued with the Sixth Five Year Plan that was announced in early 1956, and essentially abandoned by the end of that year, though the formal announcement did not come until September 1957. Khrushchev's programs for equalling American meat production in 1960 and for abolishing the income tax by 1965 met a similar fate. And so too did the Seven Year Plan for 1959–1965. That document became essentially a dead letter in 1963 when the decision was taken to adopt a special two year plan for 1964 and 1965 whose final targets were in many cases quite different from the 1965 goals of the original Seven Year Plan. The record offers no support for any belief that Soviet economic planners enjoy omniscience. The reverse is more nearly true. It is relevant here, too, to recall that a few years ago Premier Khrushchev expressed the expectation that by 1965 the Communist-ruled nations of the world would produce more than half of all the world's industrial production. That forecast is being missed by a wide margin. Even according to Soviet calculations, in 1963 the Communist-ruled nations accounted for only 38 per cent of world industrial output.

This rather consistent inability of Soviet leaders to see ahead perfectly even for relatively short periods such as five or seven years inevitably must raise the most serious doubts about the 20 year program for economic development during 1961–1980 embodied in the Third Program of the Soviet Communist party. That Program, adopted in October 1961, claims to provide a blueprint for putting the Soviet Union on the very threshold of the ideal Communist society by 1980, declaring in its last words: "The Party solemnly proclaims: The present generation of Soviet people will live under Communism!" In the wake of Khrushchev's removal, it might have been supposed that his successors would scrap it as a prime example of the purged leader's "harebrained scheming." But in their first pronouncements, at least, the Brezhnev-Kosygin team indicated their continued adherence to this Program. This attitude was rather obviously open to change, however.

No comparably bright perspectives have ever previously been spelled out in detail to Soviet consumers. Per capita real income is to be more than 250 per cent higher in 1980 than in 1960. The average real income per employed worker is promised to be almost double the 1960 level by 1970. What these promises mean concretely is spelled out this way:

> The entire population will be able to satisfy amply its wants for high quality and varied food products. The role of live-stock products (meat, fats, eggs, dairy products) and of fruit and high grade vegetables in the people's diet will rise substantially in the near future. The demand of all parts of the population for high quality consumer goods . . . will be generously satisfied. The output of automobiles for the public will be considerably expanded.

But this is not all that is promised. By 1970 the housing shortage is to be ended and all families living in overcrowded and poor housing are promised new apartments. By 1980 "every family, including newlyweds, will have a well-appointed apartment satisfying the needs for healthy and cultured living." And by 1980 all rent is to be abolished as are to be payments for public transportation and for such public utilities as water, gas, and heating. By 1970 the standard work week will be 35–36 hours, while minimum vacations will be increased first to three weeks and then to a month annually. By 1980, the Program promises, "The Soviet state will present to the world a model of really full and all-embracing satisfaction of the growing material and cultural requirements of mankind."[4]

And the Program implies that all this can be accomplished even with a continuing heavy arms burden, for it declares that a reduction in military expenditures "would make it possible to exceed substantially the plans for raising the living standard of the working people."

The first point to be made about this ambitious set of plans is that the Soviet Union has stumbled badly in the first years following the adoption of this Program. The reduction in housing construction in the mid-1960's, the bad 1963 grain harvest, the 1962 increase in meat and butter prices, these are changes quite at variance with the expectations encouraged by the Program. Even by Soviet calculation, the country's national income increased an average of only somewhat more than 5 per cent annually during 1961–1963. But this is only about half the growth rate required to reach the 1970 goal of a national income 250 per cent that of 1960. Similarly the rate of industrial production growth during 1961–1964 has been less than that required to meet either the 1970 or 1980 goal, while agricultural output in 1963 was, as we have seen, actually less than that in 1960. That fact hardly augurs well for the goal of 150 per cent more farm production in 1970 than in 1960, despite the improved 1964 harvest.

In the light of the evidence now available, it is difficult to doubt that the relatively poor performance of the Soviet economy since 1960 has already caused the Moscow leaders quietly to abandon the Program's production goals, at least for 1970 and perhaps even for 1980. The reason for this emerges clearly from a study of Table 28 which compares 1960 actual production with the 1965 output goals announced in late 1963 and also with the 1970 and 1980 targets of the Program.

Table 28.   SOVIET OUTPUT IN 1960 AND GOALS
FOR 1965, 1970, AND 1980

Commodity	Unit	1960 Output	1965 Goal*	1970 Goal	1980 Goal
Steel	mil. metric tons	65	89.3	145	250
Oil	mil. metric tons	148	240	390	690–710
Electricity	billion kwh	292.3	508	900–1000	2700–3000
Shoes	million pair	419	470	825	900–1000
Fertilizers	mil. metric tons	13.9	35	77	125–135

* Set by Two Year Plan, not by Seven Year Plan.
Sources: Harry Schwartz, *Russia Enters the 1960's*, p. 241; *Pravda*, December 17, 1963.

The central point is made most simply if we assume that the 1965 goals are achieved on schedule. On that assumption we may calculate the average annual absolute increase in output for each commodity during 1960–1965, and the average annual absolute increase in output required for each commodity during 1965–1970 in order to reach the 1970 targets on schedule. In the case of steel, for example, we find that the 1960–1965 annual increase will be less than 5,000,000 tons, but that the required 1965–1970 average annual increase will be over 11,000,000 tons. In the case of electricity, correspondingly the 1960–1965 average annual increase of about 43,000,000,000 kilowatt-hours is far less than the roughly 80–100,000,000,000 kilowatt-hour annual increase required during 1965–1970. The situation is similar for oil and shoes. Only in the case of fertilizer does the 1965–1970 annual increase needed to reach the 1970 goal seem reasonable in terms of the planned 1960–1965 increase. But since there seems small likelihood of the 1965 fertilizer production goal being reached on schedule, the 1970 target seems of dubious realism. In any case, it is extremely difficult to believe that Soviet production of steel, oil, electricity, and shoes can increase so much more rapidly during the second half of the 1960's than during the first half of the 1960's. It seems much more reasonable to suppose that, in drawing up their special two year plan for 1964–1965, the Soviet leaders decided that the party Program's goals for 1970 were, in the main, impossible of fulfillment and quietly abandoned them. In short, the Soviet Communist party's 1970 industrial output targets already appear chimerical.

We cannot apply the same test to the Program's agricultural goals because farm production is a far more irregular phenomenon than industrial output, and also because no complete, revised set of such farm goals has been announced for 1965. Nevertheless, we may see the immense distance that must be covered if the 1970 and 1980 goals are to be reached on schedule. Table 29 compares farm output in 1960 and 1963 with those goals.

Here again the goals for 1970 and 1980 are so overblown and call for so much more rapid a growth of production than anything to be expected in the light of recent Soviet agricultural history that the temptation to label these targets, especially those for 1970, pure fantasy is very strong. At the least, a heavy burden of proof lies on those who believe these goals to be in any serious sense realistic and attainable on schedule.

The above discussion suggests that a highly skeptical attitude is

Table 29. FARM OUTPUT IN 1960 AND 1963,
AND GOALS FOR 1970 AND 1980

Commodity	Unit	1960 Output	1963 Output	1970 Goal	1980 Goal
Grain	mil. metric tons	134.4	134.0*	229	295–311
Meat	mil. metric tons	8.7	10.2	25	30–32
Milk	mil. metric tons	61.7	61.2	135	170–180
Eggs	billions	27.4	28.8	68	110–116
Wool	mil. metric tons	.36	.37	.8	1.04–1.15
Cotton	mil. metric tons	4.3	5.2	8	10–11
Sugar beets	mil. metric tons	57.7	44.0**	86	98–108

* Apparent official estimate.   ** Estimated.
SOURCES: Harry Schwartz, *Russia Enters the 1960's*, p. 249; *Pravda*, January 24, 1964; *New York Times*, November 7, 1963.

in order in viewing the grandiose claim that this generation of Soviet citizens will ever live in a state of Communist abundance resembling in any way the glittering perspectives sketched by Karl Marx a century ago. Almost certainly, the ambitious goals sketched in the party Program for 1970 are largely impossible of attainment by that date, primarily because of the poorer than anticipated performance of the Soviet economy during the first years of the 1960's. A byproduct of these conclusions is the rejection of the Soviet boasts that by 1970 the Soviet Union will have the world's highest standard of living and a greater industrial production than the United States. Those claims could only become reality if the United States in 1970 were in the throes of a major depression. The entire history of the years since World War II testifies eloquently to the determination of most influential political elements of the United States that such a catastrophe must be averted. As and when needed, the instruments available to assure continued economic growth and near full employment in the United States will be employed actively by the government to supplement the natural forces operating within the private economy. The Soviet Union is most unlikely to win that fervently desired economic victory over the United States during this decade.

But to state these conclusions is not to deny the likelihood that the Soviet Union will make substantial economic progress in the years ahead, including resumption of the rise in the standard of living of its people which was interrupted in the early 1960's. Even average weather conditions in the years after 1964, for example, could lift farm production well above the depressed levels of 1963. And while the ambitious expansion of fertilizer production scheduled for the rest of the 1960's may be less effective than Premier Khrushchev hoped, it and the accompanying programs for substantial investment in irrigation and for increasing insecticide and herbicide output should also contribute to raising future Soviet farm production. In industry the Soviet Union has already proved that it has the resources, the knowledge, and the will to obtain rapid production increases. There is no obvious reason, short of major war, to expect Soviet industrial stagnation or decline in the years ahead. Khrushchev's last years in power saw a significant slowdown in the pace of Soviet industrial advance. But even the 7 per cent gain indicated for 1964 is a far cry from the complete cessation of growth, and much higher than the rate normally achieved in such countries as the United States and Britain.

The great unknown, of course, is the pace of future Soviet economic expansion. But the key variables likely to determine that pace may be indicated briefly.

One is clearly the burden of arms expenditures the Soviet Union will have to bear in the years ahead. Any major reduction of these expenditures could permit the Soviet government to shift large quantities of resources and many of its finest managers and technicians to the task of meeting the needs of the civilian economy. Such a shift could do much to counteract the retarding influences noted earlier as operating upon the rate of Soviet growth. Here political developments, both in Soviet relations with the West and in Soviet relations with Communist China, will be decisive. From an economic point of view, the case for Soviet arms reduction is strong, but Soviet military pressure against this is probably felt strongly by the post-Khrushchev regime.

Partially reducing the pressures for curtailment of arms spending is the ability of the Soviet Union to gain long term loans from the West. The decision of British authorities in 1964 to underwrite long term 15 year credits for Soviet purchases of chemical machinery for production of synthetic fibers could mark a major turning point, since presumably other Western sellers will be under great pressure to extend similar long term credits.[5] The question must inevitably arise, how long will the United States deny itself a share of the large scheduled Soviet purchases of machinery for producing chemicals and consumer goods? But the continued failure to settle the problem of Lend-Lease debts remaining from World War II and the continued strong suspicion of the Soviet Union among the American people suggest that any reversal of recent American trade policy, if it takes place at all, will have to follow the 1964 Presidential election.

A third key variable is the success of the Brezhnev-Kosygin team and those who may follow it in providing greater incentive for farmers. Nothing is clearer than that the stagnation—and worse—of Soviet agricultural output since 1958 is intimately related to the disinclination of many Soviet farmers to work hard or conscientiously. The almost incredible facts revealed in late 1963 about the extent to which the then available supplies of fertilizers were misused or wasted suggests how central the task of providing greater farm incentive is if the recent radical turn toward a more intensive agriculture is to succeed.

Finally, there remains to be seen how powerfully the winds of change now blowing through the Soviet economy will affect the outmoded, clumsy and frequently irrational mechanism directing that economy. The vigorous press discussion of recent years has shown that Soviet economists understand that central planning as traditionally practiced in the Soviet Union must be radically modified if improved efficiency and greater satisfaction of consumer wants are to be obtained. Those who see in the mathematical techniques of input-output analysis, linear programming and the like the tools for more efficient planning have clearly gained strength. In May 1964 a special meeting convened by the Soviet Academy of Science heard the direct order that the most rapid and comprehensive introduction of mathematical techniques into Soviet economic planning must be obtained. But, as we have seen, other approaches too have gained strength. Voices are heard urging the introduction of an interest rate on capital in a manner similar perhaps to that used by the Hungarians in imposing their five per cent capital use tax at the beginning of 1964. The radical reorganization of the East German economy aimed at making the attainment of profits the central criterion in judging enterprises' success or failure has been widely publicized among Soviet economic executives. The political reconciliation between the Soviet Union and Yugoslavia has made the latter's effort to create a socialist market economy much more respectable than in earlier years. Before Premier Khrushchev's ouster, it was difficult to avoid the impression that the Soviet economy is on the verge of major changes aimed at securing more rational decision making and at taking advantage of techniques and practices once denounced as "capitalistic." But the conservative forces within the Soviet Union are still strong, and it remains to be seen how effective their opposition to any moves that might weaken the direct power of the Communist party over Soviet economic life will be.[6] These conservative forces could conceivably be more influential in the post-Khrushchev period, though this seems unlikely.

In the mid-1960's the Soviet leadership seems far more chastened than it had been earlier. Buffeted by economic setbacks and under intense pressure from the Soviet people, who want finally to reap the full benefits of their spectacular economic growth, many Soviet leaders know better than ever before that their future depends upon the degree to which they can satisfy their people's demands. The progress achieved by the Soviet Union since Stalin's death has somehow neither shaken the amazingly resilient and prosperous capitalism of the West nor brought about any rebirth of ideological fervor at home. Unimpressed by sputniks, hydrogen bombs, shiny jet airliners, or grandiose promises for the future, Soviet workers and farmers face their masters with the daily question stated by Alexander Solzhenitsyn—in his novel "For the Good of the Cause"—as "What's in it for me?" After decades of emphasis upon steel, machine tools, and weapons of intimidation and destruction, the men in the Kremlin must now face directly the question Stalin evaded so long and at such great cost: "If socialism is not production for the sake of consumption by the popular masses, what is the purpose of socialist production?"[7] Upon their success in answering these compelling questions to the satisfaction of the Soviet people will depend the future fate of the leaders of the Soviet Union and of the system to which that nation gave birth in 1917.

During his years as head of the Soviet Communist party and the Soviet state, Khrushchev never tired of boasting about the speed with which the Soviet Union would allegedly surpass the United

States economically and thus "prove" the superiority of the Soviet system. His ignominious removal from power represented, in part, his own closest colleagues' verdict that in this as in other matters his predictions had proved fantasies. He had counted on the Soviet economy to continue to move ahead very rapidly in the 1960's, while the American economy inched ahead slowly at best, or perhaps lapsed into stagnation or depression. Instead, the United States economy moved ahead more vigorously than earlier in the first half of the 1960's, while Soviet economic growth slowed sharply. To use a comparison much favored by Khrushchev himself, it was the Soviet economy that proved an ailing and limping nag, and the American economy that showed itself a swift, high spirited steed. Yet, ironically, it was partly because of the fears aroused by Soviet performance and Khrushchev's boasting in the late 1950's that forces were vitalized in the United States that helped turn his dreams into nightmares.

No doubt the Soviet economy is capable of doing better in the future than it has in the recent past, and Khrushchev's successors may prove more effective leaders than he was in his last years in power. If so, the economic race between the United States and the Soviet Union may again become a matter of widespread American concern. But, so long as the government and private decision makers who determine the fate of the United States economy see that this country maintains high production and high employment with rising living standards and with progress against stubborn pockets of poverty, that concern can be a measured one. The pragmatic American economy—with its complex mixture of private initiative and government planning—has done well enough in the recent past to justify quiet confidence about its prospects for the foreseeable future against any probable Soviet economic challenge. When Soviet Premier Kosygin told a group of American businessmen on November 19, 1964, that his country wanted large, long-term American credits, he was in effect conceding that the United States had won the latest round in the economic competition with the Soviet Union.

APPENDIX

The Soviet Economy in 1965

ON DECEMBER 9, 1964, the Supreme Soviet met in Moscow and heard Premier Aleksei N. Kosygin speak on the 1965 economic plan and Finance Minister V. F. Garbuzov report on the 1965 budget. Less than two months had passed since former Premier Khrushchev's ouster, so that it was doubtful that the new regime had had opportunity to make more than marginal adjustments in the preliminary drafts that must have been prepared before the coup d'etat of the previous October. Both men said comparatively little about what had happened in 1964—thus deviating sharply from earlier practice—and neither put much stress upon the two year plan adopted for 1964–1965 in December 1963. It was left for outsiders to speculate whether this reticence was caused by the unsatisfactory economic performance in 1964 or by other factors.

Premier Kosygin presented these basic data on the estimated growth of key economic indices in 1964 and their planned growth in 1965:

	1964 (estimate)	1965 (plan)
	per cent	
National income	5	8
Gross industrial output*	7.8	8.1
Means of production	8.2	8.2
Consumer goods	6.5	7.7
State budget revenues	4.8	6.1
Real per capita income	3.9	7.3

* Applies to a planned group of commodities.

His estimate that 1964 growth in national income would be only 5 per cent indicated that year had been cruelly disappointing.

243

Even assuming the planned 8 per cent growth in national income was achieved in 1965, the total 1964–1965 national income increase would be only 13.5 per cent over 1963, rather than the 16.5 per cent forecast in the two year plan adopted in December 1963. Similarly his data implied that neither gross industrial production nor the output of means of production would reach the original 1965 goal of the two year plan. Only the more modest consumer goods target had not been abandoned.

The reasons for the poor performance of the economy in 1964 were implied by Premier Kosygin's remarks. Industrial output had grown unusually slowly in part because of the reduced availability of agricultural raw materials from the very poor 1963 harvest. Crop production in 1964 apparently increased over 1963 in many cases, but the Premier implied that livestock product output was down very sharply during 1964. The reduction of herds in 1963 and the poor condition of the surviving animals, many of whom were poorly fed because of the feed grain shortage, explain the livestock difficulties. Construction activity also apparently was below expectations. New housing construction in 1964 fell to 73,600,000 square meters, or well under half the two year goal of 175,000,000 square meters. The Premier's data also implied that the capital investment program had not been fulfilled in 1964.

Premier Kosygin gave a broad survey of the economy's weaknesses as Mr. Khrushchev's successors had found them. He revealed the existence of a fuel shortage, caused, he said, by the fact that the major fuel-consuming industries—steel, electricity, and rail transport—had kept to their Seven Year Plan schedules, while the rise of coal and gas output had fallen behind target. He assailed the continued inferiority of some types of Soviet machinery to foreign makes in construction and performance characteristics. He attacked the failure to achieve production targets in agriculture during recent years and blamed the deficiency on "serious errors" such as excessive administrative interference, unceasing organizational changes, and the violation of the principle of material self-interest. He stressed that, despite improved 1964 performance, the food and farm raw material needs of the Soviet economy could not yet be fully satisfied because of the shortfall of livestock production. The Premier emphasized the great need for tractors and other farm machinery, and for fertilizers. He remarked that, "In recent years there have been given many irresponsible recommendations and instructions on questions of farm technology, the structure of sown areas, the care of livestock" and other farm matters.

Premier Kosygin expressed much concern also about problems in other areas. He declared that, "During past years we invested in capital construction more means than scheduled by the Seven Year Plan, but we introduced less new productive capacity into action than planned. . . . We have many inadequacies in drawing up new projects, in planning capital investment, and in organizing construction. . . . We still build slowly and expensively, from year to year do not fulfill the plan for introducing new capacity into operation, and continue still to have a high volume of unfinished construction." Criticizing excessive centralization of the process under which lists of construction projects had been hitherto approved, he revealed that a new system, placing more responsibility on republic and departmental authorities, had been introduced. The Premier announced a decision to mark down existing unsalable stocks of sewing machines, fabrics, shoes, and other goods by 1.3 billion rubles (the loss to be borne by the budget) to permit a vast national bargain sale that would clear warehouses. He assailed the great number of duplicating organs in economic administration, and the time losses caused by the need to get agreement among these organs. He called for simplification of this vast administrative apparatus. He attacked managers who hushed up criticism of their mistakes, or paid no attention to criticism, saying such managers must be replaced. He bewailed the existence of vast amounts of unutilized equipment in Soviet factories and on construction sites. These deficiencies had all been assailed by Khrushchev more than once, but Kosygin's speech made evident the former leader's inability to cope with these weaknesses and their causes.

The 1965 plans outlined at the Supreme Soviet continued to stress Khrushchevian themes. Thus a further reduction of 500,000,000 rubles in the 1965 arms budget was announced, while an increase of 4.5 per cent in average Soviet wages was projected for 1964, compared with an average annual wage increase of 2.4 per cent during the preceding six years. To speed up the rate of wage increases, the schedule for introducing specific steps in this program was advanced. All minimum wages for workers and clerical employees were to be raised to 40–45 rubles by January 1, 1965 rather than in the second half of 1965, and wage increases for workers in many service industries originally scheduled for the second half of 1965 were ordered to go into effect on May 1, 1965. Farmers were promised higher milk prices although retail milk prices were to remain unchanged. New housing construction in 1965, it was promised, would reach a record 84,000,000 square meters. In 1965 1,800,000 refrigerators were to be sold, 76 per cent more than in 1964. The resemblances to Malenkov's policy in the immediate post-Stalin era of 1953 are quite marked.

Among the chief industrial production targets announced for 1965 were: steel—90,000,000 metric tons; electricity—510,000,-000,000 kilowatt-hours; oil—242,000,000 metric tons; gas—128,-000,000,000 cubic meters; fertilizers—33,500,000 metric tons (a cut of 1,500,000 tons from the original goal, suggesting that a general cutback had been ordered in the Khrushchev chemical program); leather shoes—477,000,000 pair; and sugar—8,610,000 metric tons. A sharp increase in the volume of consumer services provided in 1965 was promised, as well as increases in pensions for invalids and for families left without a breadwinner.

But contrary to earlier rumors, the Supreme Soviet session made no change in the *sovnarkhoz* system, and at least one speaker rose to defend it. Many changes seemed still to be ahead in the post-Khrushchev era.

Notes

CHAPTER I

1. Isaac Deutscher, *Stalin A Political Biography*. New York: Vintage Books, 1960, p. 304.
2. J. Stalin, *Voprosy Leninizma*. Moscow: 1952, pp. 362–63.
3. *Pravda*, February 10, 1946.
4. A. Smirnov, *Ekonomicheskoye Soderzhaniye Naloga s Oborota*. Moscow: 1963, p. 227. The author wishes to thank Leon Herman for calling his attention to this reference.
5. *New York Times*, June 6, 1956.
6. Harry Schwartz, *Russia's Soviet Economy*, 2d ed. Englewood Cliffs, N.J.: Prentice-Hall, 1958, p. 535.
7. *Pravda* and *Izvestia*, December 1, 1963.
8. *Pravda*, June 29, 1963.
9. *Ibid.*, October 3, 1952.
10. *Ibid.*, March 7, 1964.
11. *Plenum Tsentralnogo Komiteta Kommunisticheskoy Partii Sovetskogo Soyuza 15–19 Dekabrya 1958 goda. Stenografichesky Otchet.* Moscow: 1958, p. 7.
12. *Ibid.*, p. 13.
13. *Narodnoye Khozyaistvo SSSR v 1961 godu.* Moscow: 1962, p. 300.
14. *Ibid.*, p. 381.
15. Gregory Grossman, "The Soviet Economy in the Post-Stalin Decade," in William Petersen, ed. *The Realities of World Communism.* Englewood Cliffs, N.J.: Prentice-Hall, 1963, p. 63.

CHAPTER II

1. Nicolas Spulber, *Soviet Strategy for Economic Growth*. Bloomington: Indiana University Press, 1964, p. 83.
2. Harry Schwartz, *Russia's Soviet Economy, op. cit.*, p. 638.
3. *Pravda*, February 16, 1964.
4. Albert Boiter, "When the Kettle Boils Over . . .," *Problems of Communism*, January–February, 1964, pp. 36–38.
5. *Pravda*, July 14, 1964.
6. *Vestnik Statistiki*, No. 11, 1963, p. 93; *Pravda*, July 23, 1964.
7. *SSSR v Tsifrakh v 1963 godu.* Moscow: 1964, p. 14; *Kazakhstanskaya Pravda*, July 25, 1964.
8. *National Economy of the USSR.* Moscow: 1957, p. 22; *SSSR v Tsifrakh v 1962 godu.* Moscow: 1963, pp. 13–14; *SSSR v Tsifrakh v 1963 godu, op. cit.*, pp. 16–17.
9. Data taken from the official Soviet statistical handbooks for 1958–1963.
10. *Pravda*, July 23, 1964.
11. This discussion is based primarily upon the report of the Joint Eco-

248 THE SOVIET ECONOMY SINCE STALIN

nomic Committee of Congress, *Annual Economic Indicators for the U.S.S.R.* Washington: Government Printing Office, 1964, pp. 91–95. (Hereafter cited as *Indicators.*) Additional valuable information on this topic is contained in the Joint Committee's earlier report, *Dimensions of Soviet Economic Power.* Washington: Government Printing Office, 1962. (Hereafter cited as *Dimensions.*) Also valuable is Abram Bergson, *The Real National Income of Soviet Russia Since 1928.* Cambridge: Harvard University Press, 1961.

12. "Soviet Economic Problems Multiply," Central Intelligence Agency press release dated January 9, 1964.

13. *Narodnoye Khozyaistvo SSSR v 1962 godu.* Moscow: 1963, p. 433.

14. *Indicators, op. cit.,* p. 49.

15. Morris Bornstein, "A Comparison of Soviet and United States National Product," in Franklyn D. Holzman, ed. *Readings on the Soviet Economy.* Chicago: Rand McNally, 1962, pp. 385, 392. Cf. also Harry Schwartz, "The Difficulties of Comparative Measurement," *Challenge,* June 1964, pp. 13–16.

16. *Dimensions, op. cit.,* Part II, p. 76; *Indicators, op. cit.,* p. 96.

17. *Indicators, op. cit.,* pp. 91–94. These conclusions are not contradicted seriously even by the computations of Professor G. W. Nutter, who has been perhaps the most bearish student of Soviet industrial growth. During 1953–1957, he concludes that industrial output grew between 8 and 12 per cent annually in the case of civilian goods, the rate dropping sharply only in 1958, for which he records a 4 per cent rise. Cf. his *The Growth of Industrial Production in the Soviet Union.* Princeton: Princeton University Press, 1962, p. 222.

18. Joseph W. Willett, "The Recent Record in Agricultural Production," in *Dimensions, op. cit.,* Part II, p. 99.

19. *Pravda,* May 24, 1957.

CHAPTER III

1. *Pravda,* April 1, 1953, contained the price cut decree. The Finance Minister's statement appeared in *Izvestia,* June 28, 1953.

2. *Pravda,* October 25, 1953.

3. *Ibid.,* August 9, 1953.

4. *Ibid.,* September 15, 1953.

5. S. Shvarts, "Protivorechiya Sovetskoi Selskokhozyaistvennoi Politiki," *Sotsialistichesky Vestnik,* April 1954, p. 21.

6. *Selskoye Khozyaistvo,* August 31, 1954.

7. *Pravda,* October 23, 1953.

8. N. S. Khrushchev, *Stroitelstvo Kommunizma v SSSR i Razvitiye Selskogo Khozyaistvo.* Moscow: 1962, *tom* 1, pp. 85–86.

9. *Pravda,* March 21, 1954.

10. Quoted in R. Conquest, *Power and Policy in the U.S.S.R.* New York: St. Martin's Press, 1961, p. 237.

11. For basic data on the virgin lands program see *Selskoye Khozyaistvo SSSR.* Moscow: 1960, p. 223.

12. Wolfgang Leonhard, *The Kremlin Since Stalin.* New York: Praeger, 1962, p. 88.

13. *Pravda,* March 13, 1954.

14. Harry Schwartz, *The Red Phoenix.* New York: Praeger, 1961, p. 140; *Indicators, op. cit.,* p. 66.

15. *Pravda,* December 28, 1954.

16. *Ibid.,* February 3, 1955.

17. *Direktivy KPSS i Sovetskogo Pravitelstva po Khozyaistvennym Voprosam.* Moscow: 1958, *tom* 4.

18. This summary of the Bergson findings is based on the current ruble factor cost data given in Abram Bergson, *The Real National Income of Soviet Russia Since 1928.* Cambridge: Harvard University Press, 1961, pp. 237, 245.

CHAPTER IV

1. Abram Bergson, *The Real National Income of Soviet Russia Since 1928, op. cit.,* p. 290, puts the average annual growth of net national product during 1950–1955 at 7.3 per cent and during 1955–1958 at 7 per cent.

2. *Narodnoye Khozyaistvo SSSR v 1961 godu, op. cit.,* p. 170.

3. Rush V. Greenslade and Phyllis Wallace, "Industrial Production in the U.S.S.R.," in *Dimensions, op. cit.,* p. 120.

4. *Narodnoye Khozyaistvo SSSR v 1961 godu, op. cit.,* p. 292.

5. Joseph W. Willett, "The Recent Record in Agricultural Production," in *Dimensions, op. cit.,* p. 98.

6. Alec Nove, "Social Welfare in the U.S.S.R.," in Abraham Brumberg, ed. *Russia Under Khrushchev.* New York: Praeger, 1961, pp. 571–90.

7. *New York Times,* June 5, 1956.

8. *Pravda,* February 15, 1956.

9. *Ibid.*

10. Edmund Nash, "Recent Trends in Labor Controls in the Soviet Union," in *Dimensions, op. cit.,* p. 394; Schwartz, *op. cit.,* pp. 152–53; Paul Barton, "An End to Concentration Camps?" *Problems of Communism,* March–April 1962, pp. 41–45.

11. Barton, *op. cit.,* p. 45.

12. *Pravda,* August 2, 1957.

13. *Narodnoye Khozyaistvo SSSR v 1960 godu, op. cit.,* p. 611.

14. Bulganin's speech appeared in *Pravda,* July 17, 1955.

15. *Pravda,* December 25, 1956.

16. Harry Schwartz, *The Red Phoenix, op. cit.,* pp. 150–51.

17. *Pravda,* February 16, 1957.

18. *Ibid.,* February 4, 1959.

19. *Ibid.,* December 19, 1958.

20. Alec Nove, "The Soviet Industrial Reorganization," *Problems of Communism,* November–December 1957, p. 20.

21. *Pravda,* May 8, 1957.

22. For the text of the law, cf. *Direktivy KPSS i Sovetskogo Pravitelstva po Khozyaistvennym Voprosam, op. cit., tom* 4, pp. 732–38.

23. *Pravda,* May 8, 1957.

24. *Vedomosti Verkhovnogo Soveta SSSR,* No. 9, 1958.

25. Central Committee decision of August 4, 1958 in *Spravochnik Sekretarya Pervichnoi Partiinoi Organizatsii.* Moscow: 1960, pp. 199–203.

26. *Direktivy KPSS i Sovetskogo Pravitelstva po Khozyaistvennym Voprosam, op. cit.,* pp. 781–83.

27. F. D. Holzman, "The Soviet Bond Hoax," *Problems of Communism,* September–October 1957, p. 47.

28. Gregory Grossman, "Communism in a Hurry: The 'Time Factor' in Soviet Economics," in A. Brumberg, ed. *Russia Under Khrushchev, op. cit.,* pp. 213–14.

29. *Pravda,* August 24, 1958.

30. *Ibid.,* May 10, 1958.

31. *Ibid.*, June 6, 1958.

32. *Ibid.*, October 5 and 8, 1958.

33. I. M. Levin, *Planirovaniye i Analiz Truda i Zarabotnoi Platy na Promyshlennom Predpriyatii.* Moscow: 1961, p. 159. Cf. also *Dimensions, op. cit.*, pp. 354–56.

34. *Indicators, op. cit.*, p. 66.

35. *Pravda,* June 12, 1957.

36. *Ibid.*, December 19, 1957.

37. The charter for the factory union committees is in *Pravda,* July 16, 1958.

38. *Ibid.*, July 18, 1958. S. Shvarts, "Rostki Khozyaistvennoi Demokrati," *Sotsialitichesky Vestnik,* September 1958, pp. 160–64.

39. *Pravda,* January 15, 1960.

40. Age-group size data taken or estimated from *Pravda,* February 4, 1960. A good discussion of the educational reform and its significance for the labor force is given in Nicholas DeWitt, "Upheaval in Education," *Problems of Communism,* January–February 1959, pp. 25–34.

40a. *Uchitelskaya Gazeta,* August 13, 1964.

41. *Pravda,* February 3, 1955.

42. *Dimensions, op. cit.*, p. 99.

43. *Selskoye Khozyaistvo SSSR, op. cit.*, p. 229.

44. *Pravda,* October 15, 1958.

45. *Selskoye Khozyaistvo SSSR, op. cit.*, p. 329.

46. Both quotations are from *Pravda,* December 19, 1958.

47. *Ibid.*, May 24, 1957.

48. *Ibid.*, June 21, 1958.

49. *Selskoye Khozyaistvo SSSR, op. cit., passim.*

50. Lazar Volin, "Reforms in Agriculture," *Problems of Communism,* January–February 1959, p. 39. (Old rubles in original converted to new rubles here.)

51. *Pravda,* March 11, 1955.

52. *Ibid.*, March 10, 1956.

53. *Ibid.*, July 4, 1957.

54. *Ibid.*, October 4, 1952.

55. *Ibid.*, January 25, 1958.

56. *Ibid.*, March 28, 1958.

57. *Ibid.*, June 21, 1958.

58. For an excellent and more detailed discussion of the changes in Soviet agricultural policy treated here cf. Frank A. Durgin, Jr., "Monetization and Policy in Soviet Agriculture Since 1952," *Soviet Studies,* April 1964.

CHAPTER V

1. *Pravda,* January 28 and February 5, 1959.

2. *Narodnoye Khozyaistvo SSSR v 1962 godu, op. cit.*, p. 543.

3. *Pravda,* January 25, 1961.

4. *New York Times,* May 21, 1961.

5. Harry Schwartz, *Russia Enters the 1960's.* Philadelphia: J. B. Lippincott, 1962, pp. 191–92.

6. *Ibid.* and *Pravda,* December 17, 1963.

7. *Pravda,* July 9, 1964.

8. *Narodnoye Khozyaistvo SSSR v 1962 godu, op. cit.*, p. 501; *Pravda,* January 8 and February 5, 1964.

9. The 1963 plan figure is from *Pravda,* December 11, 1962.

10. *Ibid.*, January 15, 1960.
11. *Ibid.*, July 2, 1959.
12. *Finansy i Kredit SSSR*. Moscow: 1962, ch. VIII.
13. *Ekonomicheskaya Zhizn SSSR*. Moscow: 1961, pp. 714–15.
14. Schwartz, *Russia Enters the 1960's, op. cit.*, p. 273.
15. *Ibid.*, p. 196.
16. *Pravda*, June 29, 1963.
17. *Ibid.*, July 2, 1959.
18. *Ibid.*
19. Nicolas Spulber, *The Soviet Economy*. New York: Norton, 1962, pp. 68–69.
20. Alfred Zauberman, "Liberman's Rules of the Game for Soviet Industry," *Slavic Review*, December 1963, pp. 734–35; *Pravda*, September 9, 1962.
21. *Pravda*, November 20, 1962.
22. Robert W. Campbell, "Marx, Kantorovich and Novozhilov: *Stoimost'* Versus Reality," *Slavic Review*, October 1961, pp. 408–09.
23. Quotations taken from *USSR*, September 1964, pp. 10–17.
24. Taken from *Kommunist*, No. 5, 1964.
25. *Ibid.*, and *Ekonomicheskaya Gazeta*, July 4, 1964, pp. 16–18.
26. *Sotsialisticbesky Trud*, May 1964, pp. 16–17. Cf. also Alec Nove, *Economic Rationality and Soviet Politics*. New York: Praeger, 1964, *passim.*
27. Gregory Grossman, "Structure and Organization of the Soviet Economy," *Slavic Review*, June 1962, p. 217.
28. This account is based on the full text of the speech in *Pravda*, November 20, 1962.
29. *Ibid.*, July 14, 1964.
30. V. Tolstikov in *Izvestia*, April 19, 1964.
31. *Pravda*, December 29, 1959.
32. N. S. Khrushchev, *Stroitelstvo Kommunizma v SSSR i Razvitiye Selskogo Khozyaistva, op. cit., tom.* 4, p. 181.
33. *Ibid., tom* 5, p. 319.
34. *Ibid., tom* 6, p. 284. Much of this volume is devoted to this campaign.
35. *Ibid.*, pp. 334–441, and *Pravda*, March 24, 1962.
36. *Pravda*, June 1, 1962.
37. *Ibid.*, June 30, 1962.
38. Albert Boiter, "When the Kettle Boils Over . . .," *Problems of Communism*, January–February 1964, p. 38.
39. *Pravda*, November 20, 1962.
40. *Ibid.*, November 13, 1962.
41. *Ibid.*, December 10, 1963.
41a. *Ibid.*, February 11, 1964.
42. *Ibid.*, March 7, 1964.
43. *Ibid.*, March 24, 1964.
44. *Ibid.*, April 24, 1964.
45. The Khrushchev speech is in *Pravda*, July 14, 1964. The Khrushchev data on collective farmers' earnings was contained in a *Tass* summary released February 14, 1964, but the data did not appear in the published version of his speech. Cf. the July 21, 1964 memorandum of the Radio Free Europe Research Department on "*Kolkhoz* Pensions."
46. *Selskaya Zhizn*, August 5, 1964.
47. *New York Times*, August 11, 1964.
48. *Narodnoye Khozyaistvo SSSR v 1961 godu, op. cit.*, p. 601 gives data for 1952–1961. The 1963 data are calculated from information in *Narodnoye*

Khozyaistvo SSSR v 1962 godu, op. cit., p. 487 and in *SSSR v Tsifrakh v 1963 godu, op. cit.,* p. 175.

49. *Pravda,* May 10, 1960.
50. *Ibid.,* July 14, 1964.
51. *Ibid.,* October 20, 1964.
52. *New York Times,* October 25, 1964; *Pravda,* November 6, 1964.
53. *Pravda,* October 21, 1964.
54. *Ibid.,* August 10, 1964.
55. *Ibid.,* August 17, 1964.
56. *Ibid.,* August 23 and September 1, 1964.
57. *Ibid.,* October 2, 1964.
58. Both quotations are from *Pravda,* October 20, 1964.
59. *Izvestia* and the *New York Times,* October 21, 1964.

CHAPTER VI

1. *New York Times,* May 17, 1964.
2. *Pravda,* October 3, 1952.
3. *Narodnoye Khozyaistvo SSSR v 1962 godu, op. cit.,* p. 548; *SSSR v Tsifrakh v 1963 godu, op. cit.,* p. 41.
4. *Indicators, op. cit.,* p. 115; *Mezhdunarodnaya Zhizn,* No. 4, 1964, p. 68; *Pravda,* May 7, 1964.
5. Penelope Hartlund Thunberg, "The Soviet Union in the World Economy," in *Dimensions, op. cit.,* pp. 431–32.
6. *Indicators, op. cit.,* p. 114; *Vneshnyaya Torgovlya SSSR za 1956 god* and *Vneshnyaya Torgovlya SSSR za 1963 god, passim.*
7. *New York Times,* March 17 and April 28, 1964.
8. *Vneshnyaya Torgovlya SSSR za 1962 god, op. cit.,* pp. 116–19.
9. *Dimensions, op. cit.,* p. 454.
10. *The Statist,* August 7, 1964, pp. 349–52; *New York Times,* August 16, 1964.
11. *Indicators, op. cit.,* p. 114; *Vneshnyaya Torgovlya SSSR za 1963 god, op. cit.,* pp. 10–15.
12. *New York Times,* May 5, 10, 24, and 25, 1964.
13. *Dimensions, op. cit.,* p. 474.
14. *Ekonomicheskoye Sotrudnichestvo i Vzaimopomoshch Sotsialisticheskikh Stran.* Moscow: 1962, pp. 56–57.
15. Quoted in *Ibid.,* pp. 62–63 from *Kommunist,* No. 1, 1957, p. 106.
16. A balanced discussion of these issues is contained in Chapter V of Frederick L. Pryor, *The Communist Foreign Trade System.* Cambridge: The M.I.T. Press, 1963. Cf. also Feng-hwa Mah, "The Terms of Sino-Soviet Trade," *The China Quarterly,* January–March 1964, pp. 174–91.
17. Pryor, *op. cit.,* pp. 151 and 241. Kang Chao and Feng-hwa Mah, "A Study of the Ruble-Yuan Exchange Rate," *The China Quarterly, loc. cit.,* pp. 198–99.
18. *Pravda,* May 7, 1964.
19. *Peking Review,* May 8, 1964, pp. 13–14.
20. *Ibid.,* pp. 14–15. For further background on this dispute, cf. Harry Schwartz, *Tsars, Mandarins, and Commissars.* Philadelphia: J. B. Lippincott, 1964, *passim.*
21. Pryor, *op. cit.,* p. 200.
22. *International Affairs* (Moscow), April 1964, p. 56.
23. *Pravda,* February 15, 1956.

24. Cf. Imre Nagy, *Imre Nagy on Communism*. New York: Praeger, 1957, pp. 80, 106, and 189.

25. *Pravda*, October 31, 1956.

26. *Ibid.*, August 4, 1964.

27. For Soviet views of the progress of Comecon see the articles by K. Nazarkin and by A. Alexeyev and L. Ivanova in *Mezhdunarodnaya Zhizn*, No. 4, 1964. Cf. also *Ekonomicheskaya Gazeta*, April 16, 1964, p. 37 and April 25, 1964, p. 19, and *Pravda*, August 4, 1964.

28. N. S. Khrushchev, "Vital Questions of the Development of the Socialist World System," *World Marxist Review*, September 1962, pp. 3, 5.

29. *Ibid.*, p. 13.

30. Quotation taken from the *Agerpress* translation of the "Statement on the Stand of the Rumanian Workers Party Concerning the Problems of the World Communist and Working Class Movement Endorsed by the Enlarged Plenum of the C.C. of the R.W.P. Held in April 1964."

31. *Peking Review*, May 8, 1964, p. 15.

32. The most detailed Soviet discussion of IBEC published to date is the article by the Bank's chairman: K. Nazarkin, "A New Form of Cooperation," *International Affairs* (Moscow), April 1964, pp. 59–63.

33. *New York Times*, October 20, 1964.

CHAPTER VII

1. *Peking Review*, May 8, 1964, p. 14.

2. *Pravda*, April 4, 1964.

3. *Ibid.*, February 24, 1964.

4. These and other references to the party Program are taken from *Pravda*, November 2, 1961.

5. *The Economist*, May 23, 1964, p. 825.

6. A good summary of the discussion within the Soviet Union is contained in Leon Herman, "The Limits of Forced Economic Growth in the USSR," *World Politics*, April 1964, pp. 407–18.

7. Academician Arzumanyan in *Pravda*, February 24, 1964.

Index

Afghanistan, 192, 202, 204
agricultural organization, 47, 58, 105, 159–166
agricultural output, 31, 41, 51, 71, 75, 106, 112, 122, 130, 236, 238, 240
Albania, 196, 206–209, 220
Algeria, 192, 204–205
American aid, 15; credits, 98–99, 242; trade, 198
Argentina, 202, 204
armed forces, 15, 104, 134
atomic power, 85, 97
automobiles, 17, 50

banking system, 24, 137
Bergson, A., 72
Beria, L. P., 56
biological yield, 29
Bolivia, 199
Bornstein, M., 48
Brazil, 202
bread, 36, 124, 169
Brezhnev, L. I., 180, 186, 231
budget, 246
Bulganin, N. A., 82–84, 88, 110
Bulgaria, 206, 208–209, 220, 227
butter, 38, 124, 166

capital construction, 86, 137, 153, 188
capital investment, 37, 45, 47, 86, 93, 112, 135–139, 166, 175, 233
Castro, F., 190
cement, 30, 49, 95, 125
C.I.A. (Central Intelligence Agency), 33, 43–45, 193
chemicals, 47, 97–98, 139, 170, 200
China, Communist, 190, 192, 194, 196, 206–208; Soviet rift with, 214–218, 229–230
cloth, 49, 128
coal, 30, 49, 93, 95

collective farms, 13, 20, 25, 27, 59, 112–119, 160, 162, 171, 174
COMECON (Council of Mutual Economic Assistance), 218–229
communication, 243–245
Congress of the Soviet Communist party, nineteenth, 29; twentieth, 75, 84, 222; twenty-first, 122; twenty-second, 137, 163
construction, 47
consumer goods, 47, 58, 61, 69–71, 74, 85, 124, 128
corn, 75, 106, 172, 175
cost accounting, 36, 188
cotton, 52, 119, 133, 172, 238
Councils for Coordination and Planning, 148
crop rotation, 163–164
Cuba, 35, 190, 206–209, 220, 228
Czechoslovakia, 206, 208–209, 220, 221, 223, 226–228

defense expenditures, 45, 46, 66, 126, 134, 239
Dulles, A., 33

East Germany, 57, 206–209, 220–228
economic race with U.S., 33, 48, 54, 95, 109–111, 122, 232, 238, 241–242
education, 80, 105, 183, 233
egg, 109, 120, 133, 172, 238
Egypt, 192, 196, 202, 204–205
electricity, 30, 49, 72, 93, 95, 125, 127, 223, 233, 236
Ethiopia, 204

fertilizers, 49, 93, 106, 139, 170, 201, 236, 240
Finland, 191, 196, 197
firms, 158
fishing industry, 128

254

Five Year Plans, Fifth, 61; First, 14; Sixth, 36, 79, 84–86, 93, 234
foreign aid, 35, 37, 190, 192, 204
foreign trade, 191, 197, 208
France, 191, 197, 201

garden plots, private, 20, 25, 59, 60, 114–115
gas, 40
Ghana, 202, 204
gold, 35, 111, 193, 200
Gosplan, 20, 89
grain, price of, 119, 172; Soviet purchases in West of, 11, 35, 51, 54, 111, 124, 169; state procurements of, 52, 63, 108–109, 120, 168–169, 181
grain harvest, 29, 31, 36, 51, 62, 107–108, 131, 168, 181. 233, 238
Great Britain, 15, 98, 136, 190–191, 195, 197, 201, 239
gross national product, 42, 48, 72, 192
gross social product, 41, 43, 48
Grossman, G., 32
growth, rate of, 37, 42, 49, 121, 124, 181, 232
Guinea, 204–205

heavy industry, 17, 58, 69, 74, 85, 124
housing, 36, 47, 81–82, 83, 99, 129
Hungary, 85, 122, 195, 206, 208–210, 220–223, 227
hydroelectric stations, 57, 96
hydrogen bomb, 16, 58, 65

IBEC (International Bank for Economic Cooperation), 223, 230–231
income tax, 19, 38, 59, 123, 176–178
India, 192, 202, 204
Indonesia, 192, 199, 202, 205
industrial organization, 22, 36, 56, 67, 89–92, 149
industrial production, 30, 41, 69, 74, 85, 122, 181, 233, 236
input-output analysis, 144
Iran, 202, 204
Iraq, 204
irrigation, 139, 161, 170, 175
Italy, 197, 199

Japan, 135, 197, 200–201
joint stock companies, 195, 196, 210, 219

Kaganovich, L. M., 88, 110
Kantorovich, L. V., 143
Kenya, 205
Khachaturov, T., 146
khozraschet, 20, 23
Khrushchev, N. S. on agriculture, 28, 53, 59, 63, 87, 105; capital construction, 137–139, 153; capital investment, 96–97; chemical industry, 98; consumer goods, 141, 158–159; dividing party, provincial government, 1962, 152; economic organization, 87, 149; planning, 114, 140, 153; profit, 143; relations among Communist countries, 221–225; reorganizing agriculture, 161, 182; Seven Year Plan, 122–124; standard of living, 185; state bonds, 94; war, 77; removal of, 121, 180–186; "secret" of, 75–76
Kosygin, A. N., 180, 186, 242
Kovalevsky, N. K., 34
Kozlov, F. R., 134
Kulev, I. A., 86

labor laws, 20, 36, 79
labor productivity, 46, 100, 181
labor turnover, 83
labor unions, 13, 20, 24, 78, 102–104
Lend-Lease debts, 240
Lenin, V. I., 12, 13
Liberman, Y. G., 142, 148–149
linear programming, 143
livestock, 31, 53, 54, 119, 130

machine tools, 30, 47, 49
MTS (Machine Tractor Stations), 20, 26, 36, 60, 113, 115–119
Malaya, 202
Malenkov, G. M., 29, 55–69, 88, 110
Mali, 204
Malyshev, I., 145
mathematical economics, 36
meat, 38, 53, 54, 109, 124, 133, 166, 172, 238
mestnichestvo, 91, 92
Mikoyan, A. I., 58, 62, 76, 134, 200

milk, 109, 120, 133, 172, 238
minerals, 40, 95
Molotov, V. M., 34, 88, 110
Mongolia, 206, 208, 220

Nagy, I., 221
Nemchinov, V., 146
NEP (New Economic Policy), 12
North Korea, 206, 208–209
North Vietnam, 206, 208–209
nuclear weapons, 12, 16
NVP (normative value of process-
    ing), 147

oil, 30, 40, 49, 72, 95, 125, 127, 196
    223, 233, 236
Ostrovityanov, A., 67

party control commissions, 140
pensions, old age, 38, 78, 80, 174
permanent production conference,
    102, 104
Pervukhin, M. G., 86, 88
pig iron, 93, 125, 127, 233
planning, economic, 20–22, 114, 240
Poland, 196, 206, 208–209, 210, 212,
    220, 227
population, 17, 31, 39–41, 52, 105
potatoes, 52, 119, 133, 172
prices, 17, 38, 57, 119, 172, 184, 211–
    213
Prombank (industrial bank), 137
Pryor, F. L., 219

recoupment period, 95–96
refrigerators, 128
ruble, "heavy," 19; 1961 revaluation
    of, 201–202, 213
Rumania, 195, 197, 206–209, 220,
    225–229, 230

science expenditures, 45, 46
secret police, 18, 72
Selkhozbank (agricultural bank),
    137
Seven Year Plan, 122–124, 126–134,
    138, 164, 176, 234
Shepilov, D., 68, 88
Shkatov, V., 184
shoes, 17, 49, 95, 129, 236
slave labor, 18, 36, 75, 79
Sobolev, S., 144
social security, 174
sovnarkhozy, 89, 148, 156

Soyuzselkhoztekhnika   (All-Union
    Farm Machinery Association),
    162
space achievements, 34, 37, 95
Stalin, J., 11–32
standard of living, 35, 61, 133–134,
    175
state bonds, 57, 94
state farms, 20, 27, 108, 160, 162
State Procurements Committee, 162
steel, 30, 49, 72, 93, 95, 125–127,
    233, 236
Stroibank, 137
sugar beets, 52, 119, 133, 172, 238
sulphuric acid, 30, 93
sunflower seeds, 52, 119, 172
Supreme Council of the National
    Economy, 156
Sweden, 197
Syria, 204

television sets, 49, 128
territorial production administra-
    tions, 165, 168
Third Program of the Soviet Com-
    munist party, 234–238
Torgbank (trade bank), 137
tractors, 30, 49
transportation, 84, 243–245
Trapeznikov, V. A., 183
Trotsky, L., 13
Tsekombank (communal bank), 137
Turkey, 204
turnover tax, 17, 18

Ustinov, D. F., 156

virgin lands program, 63–65, 75,
    106–108, 131–132, 164
Volin, L., 112
Volkov, O., 184
Volovchenko, I. P., 170
Voznesensky, N., 20

wages, 18, 19, 38, 78, 80, 83, 100–
    102, 123, 176, 178–180
war, 13, 77
West Germany, 191, 197
Wiles, P., 21
wool, 120, 133, 172, 238
work week, 46, 78, 80, 100, 123, 176

Yemen, 204–205
Yugoslavia, 196, 206, 208, 210, 220,
    241